VOLUME 581

MAY 2002

THE ANNALS

of The American Academy *of* Political
and Social Science

ALAN W. HESTON, *Editor*

GLOBALIZATION
AND DEMOCRACY

Special Editors of this Volume

RONALDO MUNCK
University of Liverpool
BARRY K. GILLS
University of Newcastle

 SAGE Publications   *THOUSAND OAKS   LONDON   NEW DELHI*

#49641591

The American Academy of Political and Social Science
c/o Fels Center of Government, University of Pennsylvania, 3814 Walnut Street,
Philadelphia, PA 19104; (215) 746-6500; (215) 898-1202 (fax); www.1891.org

Origin and Purpose. The Academy was organized December 14, 1889, to promote the progress of political and social science, especially through publications and meetings. The Academy does not take sides in controverted questions, but seeks to gather and present reliable information to assist the public in forming an intelligent and accurate judgment.

Meetings. The Academy occasionally holds a meeting in the spring extending over two days.

Publications. THE ANNALS of the American Academy of Political and Social Science is the bimonthly publication of The Academy. Each issue contains articles on some prominent social or political problem, written at the invitation of the editors. Also, monographs are published from time to time, numbers of which are distributed to pertinent professional organizations. These volumes constitute important reference works on the topics with which they deal, and they are extensively cited by authorities throughout the United States and abroad. The papers presented at the meetings of The Academy are included in THE ANNALS.

Membership. Each member of The Academy receives THE ANNALS and may attend the meetings of The Academy. Membership is open only to individuals. Annual dues: $65.00 for the regular paperbound edition (clothbound, $100.00). For members outside the U.S.A., add $24.00 for shipping of your subscription. Members may also purchase single issues of THE ANNALS for $20.00 each (clothbound, $28.00).

Subscriptions. THE ANNALS of the American Academy of Political and Social Science (ISSN 0002-7162) is published six times annually—in January, March, May, July, September, and November—by Sage Publications, 2455 Teller Road, Thousand Oaks, CA 91320. Telephone: (800) 818-SAGE (7243) and (805) 499-9774; FAX/Order line: (805) 375-1700. Copyright © 2002 by the American Academy of Political and Social Science. Institutions may subscribe to THE ANNALS at the annual rate: $420.00 (clothbound, $475.00). Add $24.00 per year for subscriptions outside the U.S.A. Institutional rates for single issues: $81.00 each (clothbound, $91.00).

Periodicals postage paid at Thousand Oaks, California, and at additional mailing offices.

Single issues of THE ANNALS may be obtained by individuals who are not members of The Academy for $32.00 each (clothbound, $42.00). Single issues of THE ANNALS have proven to be excellent supplementary texts for classroom use. Direct inquiries regarding adoptions to THE ANNALS c/o Sage Publications (address below).

All correspondence concerning membership in The Academy, dues renewals, inquiries about membership status, and/or purchase of single issues of THE ANNALS should be sent to THE ANNALS c/o Sage Publications, 2455 Teller Road, Thousand Oaks, CA 91320. Telephone: (800) 818-SAGE (7243) and (805) 499-9774; FAX/Order line: (805) 375-1700. *Please note that orders under $30 must be prepaid.* Sage affiliates in London and India will assist institutional subscribers abroad with regard to orders, claims, and inquiries for both subscriptions and single issues.

Printed on recycled, acid-free paper

THE ANNALS

© 2002 *by* The American Academy *of* Political *and* Social Science

Editorial Office: Fels Center of Government, University of Pennsylvania, 3814 Walnut Street, Philadelphia, PA 19104-6197.

For information about membership* (individuals only) and subscriptions (institutions), address:

SAGE PUBLICATIONS
2455 Teller Road
Thousand Oaks, CA 91320

Sage Production Staff: BARBARA CORRIGAN, SCOTT SPRINGER, and ROSE TYLAK

From India and South Asia, write to:
SAGE PUBLICATIONS INDIA Pvt. Ltd
P.O. Box 4215
New Delhi 110 048
INDIA

From Europe, the Middle East, and Africa, write to:
SAGE PUBLICATIONS LTD
6 Bonhill Street
London EC2A 4PU
UNITED KINGDOM

*Please note that members of The Academy receive THE ANNALS with their membership.
International Standard Serial Number ISSN 0002-7162
International Standard Book Number ISBN 0-7619-2701-8 (Vol. 581, 2002 paper)
International Standard Book Number ISBN 0-7619-2700-X (Vol. 581, 2002 cloth)
Manufactured in the United States of America. First printing, January 2002.

The articles appearing in THE ANNALS are abstracted or indexed in *Academic Abstracts, Academic Search, America: History and Life, Asia Pacific Database, Book Review Index, CAB Abstracts Database, Central Asia: Abstracts & Index, Communication Abstracts, Corporate ResourceNET, Criminal Justice Abstracts, Current Citations Express, Current Contents: Social & Behavioral Sciences, e-JEL, EconLit, Expanded Academic Index, Guide to Social Science & Religion in Periodical Literature, Health Business FullTEXT, HealthSTAR FullTEXT, Historical Abstracts, International Bibliography of the Social Sciences, International Political Science Abstracts, ISI Basic Social Sciences Index, Journal of Economic Literature on CD, LEXIS-NEXIS, MasterFILE FullTEXT, Middle East: Abstracts & Index, North Africa: Abstracts & Index, PAIS International, Periodical Abstracts, Political Science Abstracts, Sage Public Administration Abstracts, Social Science Source, Social Sciences Citation Index, Social Sciences Index Full Text, Social Services Abstracts, Social Work Abstracts, Sociological Abstracts, Southeast Asia: Abstracts & Index, Standard Periodical Directory (SPD), TOPICsearch, Wilson OmniFile V,* and *Wilson Social Sciences Index/Abstracts,* and are available on microfilm from University Microfilms, Ann Arbor, Michigan.

Information about membership rates, institutional subscriptions, and back issue prices may be found on the facing page.

Advertising. Current rates and specifications may be obtained by writing to THE ANNALS Advertising and Promotion Manager at the Thousand Oaks office (address above).

Claims. Claims for undelivered copies must be made no later than six months following month of publication. The publisher will supply missing copies when losses have been sustained in transit and when the reserve stock will permit.

Change of Address. Six weeks' advance notice must be given when notifying of change of address to ensure proper identification. Please specify name of journal. **POSTMASTER:** Send address changes to: THE ANNALS of the American Academy of Political and Social Science, c/o Sage Publications, 2455 Teller Road, Thousand Oaks, CA 91320.

THE ANNALS

of The American Academy of Political
and Social Science

ALAN W. HESTON, *Editor*

See page 2 for information on Academy membership and
purchase of single volumes of **The Annals.**

CONTENTS

GLOBALIZATION: WHAT IT IS
AND WHAT TO DO ABOUT IT

Globalization and free trade have been our foreign economic policies since the end of the last world war, and it has been on the whole a positive thing. Globalization has been a pacifying influence in international order and in global industrial development, for instance, in the West's relations with Japan, in Europe, and now in China. Thus, globalization is preferable to the alternative. Nevertheless, whatever globalization may be, it should not come at the expense of the social gains of the past century. In recent years, government elites have tended to talk too much about free trade and not enough about social justice and stability. However, modern global development is not a function of the development of capitalism but rather of the managerial corporation. The evolution of the nature of capitalism under the influence of the modern corporation and its management structure is one in which the owner (and much of the reward) has gone to the background, giving rise to the modern managerial corporation. The managerial corporation in turn has wanted influence in or over government—thus the shape of the present Bush administration in the United States.

When you hear it being said that we have entered a new era of permanent prosperity, you should take cover. Let us not assume that the age of slump, recession, and depression is past. Crisis is part of the system and its history, as so well expressed by Schumpter. In relation to the recent Asian and global crises of the past few years, I would begin with a warning—it is the greatest desire of those in finance that they be regarded as important and that those who are associated with them should think they are intelligent. However, financial crises are the result of stupidity and mismanagement, not of exploitation. So if stupidity is inevitable, then so are financial crises, and we should not confuse evil intentions or institutions with this. I recently criticized the International Monetary Fund (IMF) in one of its own publications. The IMF sees its objective as support of the banking and finance systems. Thus, it will be open to criticism until it sees its role as also sustaining the livelihood of ordinary people, that is, of the working classes. In factories such as those located in southeast Asian countries, the problem is to have standards that are not so much to the advantage of the corporations. The only possibility is to have an increasingly international standard of employment. In regard to globalization and global inequality, the very large number of the very poor, even within the richest of countries, is part of the unfinished business of the century and the millennium that must have high visibility and urgency. There is now a stirring discussion of inequality; I would like to see it intensified.

In terms of global governance, I am in favor of policy in greater harmony, another step away from the great disaster of unleashed sovereignty of the past century. Nothing so ensures hardship, poverty, and suffering as the absence of a responsible, effective, honest polity. In a humane world order, we must have a mechanism to suspend sovereignty, when this is necessary, to protect against human suffering and disaster. Let there be government in place of national disaster by the United Nations to bring about an effective and humane independence. The United Nations has now settled into a stable structure, has a certain immobility, and encounters "natural opposition," including those in the United States who identify themselves with the greatest possible stupidity.

But the countercoalition will be dominant—Democrats, intellectuals, unions, and journalists will support this oppositional coalition. The agenda and the goal are to reduce global inequality and global poverty. We must question the benign character of sovereignty. It is the responsibility of the fortunate countries and their peoples and governments to consider people as people, wherever they are, and to consider a strong responsibility for helping people.

There are three possible policies:

1.   Recognize the great misfortune of the past colonial era—of substituting for colonial government an ineffective government or no government. Realize the importance of stable honest government.

2.   Develop the responsibility of the fortunate peoples for the unfortunate.

3.   Provide the money and technical assistance that economic sufficiency requires. There is no novelty here.

JOHN KENNETH GALBRAITH

Reference

Schumpter, J. 1943. *Capitalism, socialism, and democracy.* London: Unwin University Books.

PREFACE

The current world situation makes it particularly opportune, we believe, to be discussing the interaction between the process known as "globalization" and the prospects for democracy across the world. The various contributors to this special issue of *The Annals* bring to bear a range of social and political science perspectives on the issue. They are, on the whole, critical perspectives in the sense that they take nothing for granted and seek to delve beneath the surface of media-related events. Most of the chapters were written before the events of 11 September and their sequels across the world, yet all take on a certain urgency after that date. We hope they make a contribution collectively to a better understanding of key aspects of globalization and help us understand better the challenges for democratization worldwide.

Ronaldo Munck opens with a wide-ranging consideration of the main theoretical issues at stake when we seek to relate democracy to globalization. Finding inspiration in the classic work of Karl Polanyi, he points toward the "double movement" of free-market expansion matched by a social mobilization seeking to temper it. His review article also pursues this theme through a critical gaze over a dozen recent influential texts on globalization. For Henry Teune, the main issue confronting us today is the construction of democracy on a global scale. Global democracy is a necessity insofar as national institutions and processes have been superseded by internationalizing forces. Teune outlines various approaches to global democracy but posits that it must include connecting with those excluded by the massive dynamics of globalization over the past two decades.

Fred Riggs, for his part, explores the interaction between globalization, ethnic diversity, and nationalisms from the point of view of the challenges they pose for democracies. He concludes that the prevailing models for organizing democracy were shaped too long ago to be adequate to the problems posed in the era of globalization. New, more effective ways to organize democracies are explored to move things on.

Christopher Chase-Dunn moves toward a future-oriented analysis, considering how "globalization from below" might move us toward a rational and democratic "global commonwealth." He remains optimistic about the prospects for semiperipheral socialist governments but argues that they will have to join with the transnational movements for globalization from below.

Myron Frankman also addresses the issue of global democracy, but from the perspective of a global currency. In a lucid overview of the Tobin Tax debates, Frankman carries out a critique of the political economy of globalization. He sees world-scale democratic institutions as the only way out of a strife-prone global "race for the bottom."

A number of contributors then address issues related to the prospects for the world's workers in the era of globalization. Henk Overbeek shows how neoliberal globalization has affected the regulation of global labor mobility.

He argues that we need to urgently find ways to prevent the regulation of global migration privileging deeper commodification over emancipation. Dimitris Stevis turns to labor and the environment in terms of social regulation and global democracy. He proposes a conceptual scheme designed to evaluate global social policy schemes in a way that evaluates their democratic potential. Dong-Sook S. Gills also addresses labor issues in a sweeping review of how the globalization of production has affected women workers in Asia. Gills argues that the analysis of women's labor in globalization should not be simply a description of women's suffering. Rather, as do Overbeek and Stevis, she stresses that workers have agency in the globalization process and can become a social force acting in their own interest.

Mustapha Kamal Pasha takes us into the troubled waters of democracy in the Islamic world in the era of predatory globalization. Refusing the Orientalist construction of Islam as basically an antimodern phenomenon, Pasha develops a persuasive and nuanced alternative view. He shows how the current phase of Islamisms is both due to complex internal dynamics in the Islamic cultural areas and is a constitutive element of neoliberal globalization and not a simple reaction to its predatory instincts.

G. Honor Fagan turns our attention to Ireland, often seen as a success story for the economic and especially cultural side of globalization. Fagan explores the problems in "placing" Ireland in the world between its American and its Third World identities. The recent "Celtic Tiger" economic/cultural boom is placed in its historical context, and a more nuanced view emerges, neither apologia nor unthinking critique.

Leslie Sklair directs our attention away from the subaltern classes to the new transnational capitalist class he sees as central to the globalization process. He shows how this new class engages in a variety of activities, from community and urban through national and global politics. Two interesting case studies, of the global tobacco industry and Codex Alimentarius, provide empirical underpinning to his arguments.

Barry Gills closes this collection with a broad sweep (re)consideration of how globalization may be democratized on one hand and democracy globalized on the other hand. He concludes that we are, indeed, living through the demise of the old order. After 11 September and its sequels, his call for a genuine multicivilizational dialogue may find a receptive audience.

RONALDO MUNCK
BARRY K. GILLS

ANNALS, *AAPSS*, **581**, May 2002

Globalization and Democracy: A New "Great Transformation"?

By RONALDO MUNCK

ABSTRACT: The relationship between democracy and development is (re)considered to set the scene for the pressing contemporary issue of how globalization might affect democracy and vice versa. To move beyond simplistic binary oppositions, we turn to the work of Karl Polanyi who famously posited a dual movement of market expansion on one hand matched by increasing social control over it on the other hand. We see how globalization, at one and the same time, creates a growing process of social exclusion within and between nations but also the social movements that will contest it and seek to democratize it.

Ronaldo Munck is a professor of political sociology and director of the Globalization and Social Exclusion Unit (www.gseu.org.uk) at the University of Liverpool. He is a founding executive member of the Global Studies Association (www.mmu.ac.uk / gsa), which is committed to pursuing relevant research on globalization and its discontents. He has written widely on labor, development, and Latin American issues, including most recently the collections Labour Worldwide in the Era of Globalization *(Palgrave),* Critical Development Theory: Contributions to a New Paradigm *(Zed Books), and* Cultural Politics in Latin America *(coedited with Anny Brooksbank-Jones) (Palgrave). He has recently published* Marx @ 2000 *(Zed Books) and is now working on a study of how globalization has affected social exclusion both within and between countries.*

THE extent to which globalization has hindered or assisted democratization is a major issue of the day, whether for social and political thinkers, policy makers, or concerned citizens. The various articles in this issue of *The Annals* address diverse aspects of theory and practice, range from the general to the specific, and add up, I hope, to a serious contribution to the debates. My own contribution here aims to provide an overall theoretical context and raises some pertinent questions. In the first instance, I relate the globalization and democracy debate to an earlier one on capitalism and democracy (addressed in Munck 1994) that I believe is still relevant today. In the second place, I introduce the main arguments around globalization as a negative and as a positive factor in relation to democratization. Finally, I turn to an old, yet increasingly influential, argument by Karl Polanyi who, in his postwar classic *The Great Transformation* (Polanyi 1957) argued that there was a "double movement" at work globally, of market expansion on one hand and of social control of it on the other hand.

DEVELOPMENT AND DEMOCRACY

Development and *democracy* are clearly two very slippery (labile) terms that are crying out to be unpacked (deconstructed). They are words that take on different meanings in conflicting political discourses. These are words but also clearly sites of a discursive ambiguity. Precisely because of their centrality in political discourse, their meaning and belonging are so contested.

They are floating signifiers waiting to be appropriated by different social and political forces that will give them this meaning. Arjun Appadurai, in his influential analysis of the various "scapes" at play in the process(es) of globalization, referred to how the "globally variable synaesthesia" (the stimulation of a mental sense impression relating to one sense by the stimulation of another) of the political and ideological "ideoscope" of democracy "has clearly become a master term" (Appadurai 1996, 37). Thus, democracy can be seen to be at the center of a whole variety of ideoscopes; for example, we could argue the process now known as globalization. What Appadurai directed us to is the complexity and fluidity of the globalization/democracy interrelationships, the profusion of meanings, and what Appadurai referred to as "ever new terminological kaleidoscopes" (Appadurai 1996, 37). Having established that the theoretical terrain is not simple and unilinear, we now need to move toward some clarification.

If we turn to the empirical level, the relationship between democracy and development seems relatively straightforward. In a recent major empirical survey of these relationships, Adam Przeworski and colleagues did not find "a shred of evidence that democracy need be sacrificed on the altar of development" (Przeworski et al. 2000, 271). That is to say, the once fashionable notion that dictatorships, or at least authoritarian regimes, were necessary to force development now seems definitively disproven. Przeworski et al. went on to argue for "indeterminacy" with regard to the political context of development: "Political regimes have no impact on the growth of total income when countries are observed across the entire spectrum of conditions" (Przeworski et al. 2000, 270). Democracies do not receive any less investment than nondemocracies even in poor countries. Yet this study does not argue either that democracy is good for development. The prognosis is a fairly pessimistic one, finding that there is little any government can do to produce development in poor countries.

However, at a conceptual level, the relationship between democracy and development is anything but straightforward. While there seems to be a certain elective affinity between democracy and development, we must beware of what Guillermo O'Donnell (1973) called the "universalistic fallacy," which sees this positive correlation operating in all places at all times. The relationship between these two elements, democracy and development, remains effectively a "black box" (Rueschemeyer, Stephens, and Stephens 1992, 32) where the precise causal relationship remains unclear. While the relationship is indeed a contingent one, we could argue, as Francesco Weffort (1990) did, that "democracy is the only path to modernity" (p. 39), at least if the latter is taken to mean something more than simple economic growth. So from earlier debates about whether development led to democracy, we have moved onto the terrain of democracy as a prerequisite for modernization. While there

are no necessary or absolute correlations between democracy and development, we can argue on a normative basis that democracy and development can constitute a virtuous circle and should go hand and hand.

This brief excursus back to the democracy and development debates serves as an introduction to the theme of democracy and globalization. We can posit that globalization represents, if nothing else, a significant worldwide development of capitalism. The development project, which dominated post–World War II history of the "West and the rest," at some stage of the 1980s gave way to what we can call the globalization project. As Leslie Sklair (2000) put it, "a transnational capitalist class based on the transnational corporations is emerging that is more or less in control of the processes of globalization" (p. 5). So if globalization is a sociopolitical project, what are its sociopolitical effects in terms of democratization? We should probably first have to accept that there is no simple one-to-one relationship; rather it should be seen as contingent and, probably, contradictory. There are, however, two main sets of arguments that we can consider separately for the purposes of presentation. On one hand, we have the arguments around globalization's deleterious effect on democracy worldwide. On the other hand, we develop the argument that globalization may open doors as well as close them and, at least potentially, creates new prospects for democracy.

GLOBALIZATION
VERSUS DEMOCRACY

There now seems to be fairly widespread consensus that globalization (read economic internationalization) undermines, subverts, or sets limits on democracy (read liberal democracy). For Scholte (2000b), summing up a rather more nuanced argument, the bottom line is that "globalization has undermined conventional liberal democracy, with its focus on national self-determination through a territorial state" (p. 261). We are referring here to a particular, historical, and Western conception of liberal democracy, national territory and sovereignty. For Anthony McGrew (1997b), thinking along similar "transformationalist" lines about globalization, "accelerating global and regional interconnectedness poses distinct challenges to liberal democratic forms of governance" (p. 12). So here also the challenges of globalization to democracy are seen as specific; in other words, what is being placed in question by globalization is the traditional form of national territorial sovereignty. The new flows of globalization, be they those of the financial markets or those of transnational crime syndicates, can easily bypass the traditional national modes of regulation. In essence then, what globalization problematizes is the elective affinity between liberal democracy and the sovereign nation state of the Westphalian order.

It is not hard to show, against the prophets of globalization as an irreversible and positive advance for humankind, that the international extension of market principles will not automatically foster democracy. Markets = democracy only in the simplest of neoliberal economics textbooks, and even their representatives on Earth, such as the World Bank, now recognize the limitations for capitalism of global free market liberalism (see World Bank 2000). Growing consumer choice (in the North) simply cannot be equated with democratic citizenship. It is now increasingly recognized that globalization has not affected all equally and has, rather, led to an increase in social exclusion both within and between nations (see Woods 2000). The notion that the new mass shareholders in the privatized public utilities or the part-time amateur investors in the stock market represent an extension of democracy is even more off the mark. Global financial markets, as key participant observer George Soros (1998) belatedly recognized, "are inherently unstable and there are social needs that cannot be met by giving market forces free rein . . . the current state of affairs is unsound and unsustainable" (p. xx). It is clear that it is what Soros called "market fundamentalism" that has rendered global capitalism unsustainable. The move beyond the so-called Washington consensus that has underpinned neoliberal globalization has already begun—albeit hesitantly and to a large extent behind closed doors—in the corridors of power.

Another area where globalization could be seen to further democracy is in relation to the new electronic communications. On the back cover of a recent book, *Communities in Cyberspace*, we read, "In cyberspace, communication and co-ordination are cheap, fast and global. With powerful new tools for interacting and organising in the hands of millions of people world-wide, what kinds of social spaces and groups, are people creating?" (Smith and Kollock 1999, back cover). In brief, will the Internet lead to self-governance, and does it represent a durable democratic revolution worldwide? Even enthusiasts for the Net find they must temper their arguments after the first flush of enthusiasm in the 1980s. Whatever their origins (often shrouded in myth), electronic communications do not today represent a simple democratic project (notwithstanding its contestatory potential) but, rather, a capitalist one. The very uneven worldwide spread of the so-called World Wide Web might make us hesitant to embrace enthusiastic Northern-centered arguments for it as vanguard of democracy. Essentially, if global communications (and the new, if already faltering, e-commerce) are part of a global "free" market, their democratic potential will necessarily be constrained.

We may also consider a particular social group, namely, the world's workers, to consider whether globalization hinders or facilitates democracy. Charles Tilly (1995) was nothing if not forthright in his article on the topic, titled "Globalization Threatens Labour's Rights" (p. 1). Tilly traces back the origins of labor rights to the mid–nineteenth century in western Europe. These rights were seen by Tilly to have been established through struggles with sovereign states and came to be guaranteed by the modern nation-state

through labor legislation and so on. Both citizenship and democracy came to depend on these rights, and in a real sense we can say that democracy was in essence a labor democracy, so central was the worker question. Now, from the mid–twentieth century onward, economic internationalization has, for Tilly, undermined nation-states and hence "their capacity to pursue effective social policies, including the enforcement of workers' rights" (p. 16). If democratic rights are embedded in states, their decline inevitably undermines democracy. In brief, Tilly argued that "globalization threatens established rights of labour through its undermining of state capacity to guarantee these rights" (p. 4). The case is powerful but, I believe, one sided and therefore not a basis on which to build a strategy for social transformation.

As a way of moving into the next section, I would like to argue against Tilly (1995) while accepting the gist of much of what he said and, certainly, the spirit in which he argued. What I see in Tilly is a seamless argument that does not allow any space for contradiction. I wonder whether we can really state categorically that "as states decline, so do workers rights" or "almost everywhere, organised labour is in retreat" (p. 21). In contrast to this view, however, it is now widely recognized (see, e.g., Moody 1997) that the impact of globalization on workers worldwide has brought about a profound process of rethinking and reorganizing within labor on a global scale, with even the once remote and conservative International Congress of Free Trade Unions advocating such radical measures as a global social movement unionism to counter capitalist globalization. Labor is not everywhere in retreat, and workers' rights, though undercut by neo-liberalism, are continuously and vigorously fought for across the world. While on one hand it does not allow for contradictory tendencies, Tilly's analysis is also itself ultimately contradictory as, for example, when he argued that "if workers are to enjoy collective rights in the new world order, they will have to invent new strategies at the scale of international capital" (p. 21), because the argument remains an abstract one insofar as Tilly can see no openings for democracy under globalization. It is also, in my view, ultimately contradictory because the obvious strategic response in terms of his negative and inherently nation-statist analysis would be to argue that the various national labor movements should simply be seeking to strengthen their respective nation-states so as to thus strengthen labor rights. My argument is simply that we should accept that globalization may open doors for contestation as well as close off certain more traditional avenues. Nor should we forget that we cannot move back to a traditional terrain of struggle when history has moved on.

GLOBALIZATION FACILITATES DEMOCRACY

Today, outside of the more fervent antiglobalization ranks, few analysts would deny that globalization may have positive effects for democratization as well as negative ones. Scholte (2000a) noted cautiously in this regard that while "the new geography has to date made governance less democratic," on the other hand, "contemporary globalization *has* [emphasis added] encouraged some innovations in democratic practices" (p. 263, order of argument reversed). What we again see here is that it is the particular form of globalization that has led to a democratic deficit. Thus, alternative or stronger modes of regulation could conceivably make globalization more democracy friendly. Anthony McGrew (1997a) also argued the positive case for globalization: "contrary to these developments [the negative features of globalization discussed in the previous section] globalization is also associated with processes of political empowerment and democratization" (p. 238). This means that we cannot really posit a unilateral or simple meaning to the globalization-democracy relationships. All we can be certain of is that the new concepts of a global politics and a global democracy draw into question received notions of the economy, politics, society, culture, and international relations.

In Argentina, the human rights campaigners against the military dictatorship had a slogan stating that "the defense of human dignity knows no boundaries" (cf. Beetham 1998). General Pinochet found that national sovereignty was no defense when the British law lords decided that he should answer abroad for abuses of human rights committed in Chile. What is important to note, as Anthony McGrew (1995) argued in relation to this topic, is that "the extent to which the traditional notions of sovereign political space and political community are being reconstituted by the nature of the international human rights regime and the activities of transnational social movements in the human rights domain" (p. 46). The key word here is "reconstituted" because nation-states are being reconfigured and not eliminated in the new global democracy. There is now a transnational democratic terrain infinitely more developed than when the United Nations was formed (cf. Archibugi, Balduni, and Donati 2000). Certainly this global democracy is uneven in its extension across the world, and it would be naïve to argue for the immediate coming of a new cosmopolitan democracy (cf. arguments in Archibugi and Held 1995 and the more critical piece by Zolo 2000). The democratic terrain is simply more complex in the era of globalization.

One of the most interesting debates to flow out of this new terrain is around the nature, or even existence, of global civil society. It seems easier to define what civil society is not—it is neither the state nor the market—than what it is, given the proliferations of meanings and political intentions behind them. For Scholte (2000a), "civil society exists when people make concerted efforts through voluntary associations to mould rules—both official, formal, legal arrangements and informal social contracts" (p. 175). Within this diversity we find old bodies such as the International Red Cross, truly uncivil elements such as transnational criminal syndicates, and the

various nongovernmental organizations, community movements, and pressure groups that go under the label of "new social movements." That these have acquired a greater transnational prominence in recent decades seems incontrovertible—we need only think of the international environmental movement(s). However, while not denying that global civil society can lead to empowerment, we should not confuse wishes with reality and should recognize that it is a fairly recent phenomenon and one not immune to the democratic deficit critique itself.

In relation to labor as transnational social agent, we can certainly note changes in the past decade or so, which point in more optimistic directions than Tilly's (1995) somber scenario. At every level from the suprastate International Congress of Free Trade Unions to the local union, passing through various regional and subregional levels, labor is responding to the new transnational capitalism (see Munck 2002 for details). Albeit with a delay of around a decade, labor is reconstituting as a social movement and seeking more adequate strategies for the new dispensation as set by capitalist globalization. While some strategists still seek to prioritize the national level against the global level of action (surely the two are not incompatible?), the transnational arena is becoming increasingly important for this particular old/new social actor. What is of great significance is a recent move toward understanding global as transnational but also as universal following Amartya Sen's

(2000) clear defense of global labor rights: "A truly *global* approach need not see human beings only as (or even primarily as) citizens of particular countries. . . . The increasingly globalised world economy calls for a similarly globalised approach to basic ethics and political and social procedures" (p. 127).

Even if we cannot say that globalization is good for democracy (to the extent that we can say it is bad for democracy), we can argue that it has transformed the democratic terrain. While the realist school of international relations may deride global democracy as impractical, they cannot fail to address the growing issues around global governance. The growing buzzword, even in the corridors of power, is the need for life "after competition" (see Group of Lisbon 1995). Global governance is based on national states but accepts a terrain beyond them, the transnational space. This is a space dominated by the giant transnational corporations but also populated by the growing transnational social movements. Democracy in the era of globalization must now include a transnational element. At this level, there is now a clearly perceived need to achieve a greater degree of social (and political) control over the forces of economic internationalization. Democratizing global governance will, arguably, be one of the major tasks in the century now opening up, and its impact will be felt at the global, national, regional, and local levels because globalization impacts everywhere.

THE DOUBLE MOVEMENT

Karl Polanyi (1957) wrote at the midpoint of the past century about the great transformation that led to England's industrial revolution in the nineteenth century. Yet it can also be argued (see Goldfrank 1990) that the great transformation in fact referred to the cataclysmic institutional transformation after the 1930s. In their different ways, the New Deal in the United States, Nazism in Germany, and Stalinism in the Soviet Union were examples of the double movement that Polanyi saw as the means whereby social control could be established over unregulated market mechanisms. In terms of our object of analysis here—the conflictual and multidirectional relationship between globalization and democratization—Polanyi's problematic of the 1950s may well inspire and provide direction (and historical context) to our inquiries in the first decade of the new century. To begin with, we may start with Polanyi's definition of the "double movement":

It can be personified as the action of two organising principles in society. . . . The one was the principle of economic liberalism, aiming at the establishment of a self-regulating market . . . using largely *laissez-faire* and free trade as its methods; the other was the principle of social protection aiming at the conservation of man and nature . . . using protective legislation, restrictive associations, and other instruments of intervention as its methods. (P. 132)

In translating Polanyi from mid–twentieth century to early twenty-first century, we could begin with the notion of globalization, which if nothing else represents the worldwide application of laissez-faire principles. Polanyi wrote for the nineteenth century that "markets spread all over the face of the globe and the amount of goods involved grew to unbelievable proportions" (p. 76); this is doubly true today, even for those who believe that globalization is only a tendency and that what we are witnessing is mainly internationalization. Yet—and this is why Polanyi is so contemporary—the counter-movement(s) through which society protects itself are equally inevitable in the long term. Wherever there was, as with the industrial revolution or now with the globalization revolution, "an unparalleled momentum to the mechanism of markets," there was also "a deep-seated movement [that] sprang into being to resist the pernicious effects of a market-controlled economy" (p. 76). As distinct from both liberalism and orthodox Marxism, Polanyi argued that this double movement was "the one comprehensive feature in the history of the age" (p. 76) and thus opens up a new research agenda for the era of globalization and its discontents we are living through now.

For Polanyi (1957), a major characteristic of the market society was that it had become "disembedded" socially; that is to say it was uprooted or divorced from its social and political institutions. What a disembedded and self-regulating market economy produces in people is insecurity and social anxiety. Protective counter-movements by society and the state must also seek to block the total

disembedding of the market through re-embedding it through state intervention and social legislation. Of course, in the era of globalization, that re-embedding will also occur at an international level to be effective, even more than was the case in the 1930s. As well as re-embedding, what occurs, or should occur, is decommodification of the factors of production and in particular that peculiar commodity, labor. Polanyi revealed in his seemingly naïve assumption that "labour is only another name for a human activity which goes with life itself. . . .The commodity description of labour . . . is entirely fictitious" (p. 72), which he followed with the argument that to see social legislation or trade unions as not having interfered with the mobility of labor is "to imply that those institutions have entirely failed in their purpose, which was exactly that of interfering with the laws of supply and demand in respect to human labour and removing it from the orbit of the market" (p. 1771).

What this argument is leading up to is a well-grounded understanding of globalization and democracy in terms of a double movement akin to that described and analyzed by Polanyi (1957). Stephen Gill (1995) has argued persuasively that Polanyi's double movement can be seen as a metaphor for the "socio-political forces which wish to assert more democratic control over political life" (p. 67). In this way, Polanyi can be seen as a theorist of counterhegemonic movements, a tradition given its founding statements by Antonio Gramsci and renewed today in the critical globalization studies. Of course, this can take various forms, from those who work mainly within the parameters of globalization to achieve some degree of regulation (with many critical globalizers now joining this camp), to the antiglobalizers in the streets by Seattle, through the various permutations in between, where most of the contributors to this volume are indeed situated.

The double movement at the heart of the great transformation(s) points us toward the issue of agency. Both orthodox Marxists and the globalists tend to collapse tendencies—toward self-regulating markets and globalization—into essences. The necessary countermovements of regulation, decommodification, and re-embedding provide us with a less necessitarian view of the world. Contemporary countermovements will, in all likelihood, not lead to a revival of the post–World War II settlement and social contract, because the world has indeed gone through a great transformation since the collapse of socialism and the acceleration of capitalist globalization. Undoubtedly, new global social modes of regulation will emerge. What is certain is that Polanyi, as a precursor of the theory of radical democracy, would be looking to ordinary people for democratic alternatives to current forms of globalization. Polanyi, judging from his anthropological work (see Dalton 1971), would also be attuned to the new politics of postdevelopment and its stress on indigenous cultures and on the overriding need for sustainability as a necessary criteria for any plausible development model,

which an unrestricted globalization project is clearly unable to meet.

In conclusion, I believe that Polanyi (1957) helps us get back to basics. We need to examine coolly whether a global democracy is possible (see Gorg and Hirsch 1998) and then whether it is desirable. In spite of sporadic enthusiasm for the United Nations as potential world government, in the era of globalization, very little indicates that this is a realistic option. We do, however, need to recognize that the dynamics of globalization seem to be outstripping the ability of its political shell to achieve stable governance. New forms of governance at a global level are emerging and are likely to be extended both horizontally and vertically. Nor should we ignore the very real potential that globalization—as a social and cultural process as much as an economic one—has to generate new relations and new forms of community at a transnational level. This is likely to be a more complex and messy process than a simple extension of liberal Western democratic norms as seems implicit in the various calls for a cosmopolitan democracy. The world is speeding up, but the political process is now beginning to catch up.

References

Appadurai, A. 1996. *Modernity at large: Cultural dimensions of globalization*. Minneapolis: University of Minnesota Press.

Archibugi, D., S. Balduni, and M. Donati. 2000. The United Nations as an agency of global democracy. In *Global democracy: Key debates*, edited by B. Holden. London: Routledge.

Archibugi, D., and D. Held, eds. 1995. *Cosmopolitan democracy*. Cambridge, UK: Polity.

Beetham, D. 1998. Human rights as a model for cosmopolitan democracy. In *Re-Imagining political community: Studies in cosmopolitan democracy*, edited by D. Archibugi, D. Held, and M. Köhler. Cambridge, UK: Polity.

Dalton, G., ed. 1971. *Primitive, archaic and modern economies: Essays of Karl Polanyi*. Boston: Beacon.

Gill, S. 1995. Theorising the interregnum: The double movement and global politics in the 1990s. In *International political economy: Understanding global disorder*, edited by B. Heltne. London: Zed Books.

Goldfrank, W. 1990. Fascism and the great transformation. In *The life and work of Karl Polanyi*, edited by K. Polanyi-Levitt. Montreal, Canada: Black Rose Books.

Gorg, C., and J. Hirsch. 1998. Is international democracy possible? *Review of International Political Economy* 5 (4): 585-615.

Group of Lisbon. 1995. *Limits to competition*. London: MIT Press.

McGrew, A. 1995. World order and political space. In *A global world?* edited by J. Anderson, C. Brook, and A. Cochrane. Oxford, UK: Oxford University Press.

———. 1997a. Democracy beyond borders? Globalization and the reconstruction of democratic theory and practice. In *The transformation of democracy? Globalization and territorial democracy*, edited by A. McGrew. Cambridge, UK: Polity Press in association with The Open University.

———. 1997b. Globalization and territorial democracy: An introduction. In *The transformation of democracy? Globalization and territorial democracy*, edited by A. McGrew. Cambridge, UK: Polity Press in association with The Open University.

Moody, K. 1997. *Workers in a lean world: Unions in an international economy*. London: Verso.

Munck, R. 1994. Democracy and development: Deconstruction and debates. In *Capitalism and development*, edited by L. Sklair. London: Routledge.

———. 2002. *Globalization and labour: The new great transformation?* London: Zed Books.

O'Donnell, G. 1973. *Modernisation and bureaucratic authoritarianism: Studies in South American politics*. Berkeley: University of California Press.

Polanyi, K. 1957. *The great transformation*. Boston: Beacon.

Przeworski, A., M. Alvarez, J. A. Cheibub, and F. Limongi. 2000. *Democracy and development: Political institutions and well-being in the world 1950-1990*. Cambridge, UK: Cambridge University Press.

Rueschemeyer, D., E. H. Stephens, and J. Stephens. 1992. *Capitalist development and democracy*. Cambridge, UK: Polity.

Scholte, J. A. 2000a. Global civil society. In *The political economy of globalization*, edited by N. Woods. London: Macmillan.

———. 2000b. *Globalization: A critical introduction*. London: Macmillan.

Sen, A. 2000. Work and rights. *International Labour Review* 139 (2): 119-28.

Sklair, L. 2000. *The transnational capitalist class*. Oxford, UK: Blackwell.

Smith, M., and P. Kollock, eds. 1999. *Communities in cyberspace*. London: Macmillan.

Soros, G. 1998. *The crisis of global capitalism*. London: Little, Brown.

Tilly, C. 1995. Globalisation threatens labor's rights. *International Labor and Working Class History* 47 (spring): 1-23.

Weffort, F. 1990. A América errada. *Lua Nova* 21:5-50.

Woods, N., ed. 2000. *The political economy of globalization*. London: Palgrave.

World Bank. 2000. *World development report, 1999-2000: Entering the 21st century*. Washington, DC: World Bank.

Zolo, D. 2000. The lords of peace: From the holy alliance to the new international criminal tribunals. In *Global democracy: Key debates*, edited by B. Holden. London: Routledge.

Global Democracy

By HENRY TEUNE

ABSTRACT: Globalization and democracy are brought together in the general theoretical concept of development. Globalization is the process of integration of social and economic systems into more encompassing ones, and democratization brings individuals into common systems of collective action on the principles of equality and accountability. Although the globalization processes since the middle of the 1970s pushed countries toward openness and democracy, today democratic political environments have become necessary for peaceful and orderly processes of globalization to continue. Democratic development is now proceeding beyond the local and national to the global. The conclusions present the problems that are being and must be addressed to make global political processes and institutions more responsive and accountable.

Henry Teune has been a member of the Political Science Department at the University of Pennsylvania since 1961. He has coauthored The Logic of Social Inquiry, Values and the Active Community, *and* The Developmental Logic of Social Systems. *He wrote* Growth. *A former president of the International Studies Association, he is currently project director of the international research program Democracy and Local Governance and principal investigator of the global project of Universities as Sites of Democratic Education. Professor Teune has been doing research and writing on the general topic of globalization since 1990.*

GLOBALIZATION exploded in the 1990s following the second democratic revolution. That era of globalization began in the middle of the 1970s. It was signaled by the oil crisis of 1973, a massive increase in the debt of developing countries from loans processed by the oil importing countries, and the promise and then the reality of the opening of China. It took another decade before the collapse of the Soviet Union, the home of the last great secular communalisms of the twentieth century, and the embrace of democracy by its successor states. By that time, nearly all the political barriers to the encapsulation of the world into a single economic system were gone. Only then, at the beginning of the 1990s, did globalization receive general notice. But democratization and globalization, even though tied together in a cascade of visible changes, were treated more or less independently. They both, however, were part of broader developmental processes, locked in a dynamic relationship still to be understood fully.

The main question of today is democracy on a global scale. The issues concerning global institutions and processes accountable to people everywhere have superseded those of national and local democracy of only a few years ago. It has long been believed that world development required including poor countries and populations into a global economy of growth, either to avoid the threat of angry disruptions or to sustain the moral underpinnings of capitalism. Today, an additional matter has been piled on top of this one: inclusion of the world's populations into global democratic institutions and political processes on a foundation of an expanded normative system of human rights.

The outlines of a global democracy can be seen now only through visionary lenses. During the past three decades, social scientists and professional observers described an emerging global political economy, but without democracy.[1] It took most of the 1990s to grasp that without democracy, globalization could not continue in a peaceful, orderly fashion. Democracy began to become the bedrock of the prosperity promised by globalization. It may well turn out to be the best invention for human survival and the betterment of everyday living. Indeed, in time, democracy in large-scale societies may be judged the most important discovery of the twentieth century since vaccines. Governments systematically killing their own peoples and nearly nonstop international wars of scale marked the first half of the twentieth century (Rummel 1996). By that century's end, the beginning of the institutionalization of a second democratic revolution, not only had major international wars ceased, but almost all governments openly subscribed to the principle that they should improve people's lives and should not kill, incarcerate, or expel them. As important was the muting of any credible national political challenges to rudimentary human rights. The killing of masses of people by legitimate authorities may be the most important international fact of the first half of the twentieth century. But the most important fact of this era of globalization is that almost all governments, save one or two, stopped doing that around the century's end, following the spread of democracy.

THE DEVELOPMENTAL PROCESSES OF GLOBALIZATION AND DEMOCRATIZATION

The relationships between democracy and globalization can be welded together in the concept of development, yielding greater theoretical power than either separately. As part of the developmental processes, both globalization and democratization are manifestations of the integration of diversity into systems of greater scale—higher interdependence, more extensive inclusion, greater equality among components—and at the same time, subsystem autonomy, creating smaller units and ending with autonomy and freedom of individuals. This fusion of globalization and democracy into the concept of global development must be done with dialectical logics. Development is the integration of diversity, the very process of generating variety. The world zigzags in different sectors and places between being more integrated through the bringing together of items and ideas into a flow and then seeming to fall apart because technology and innovations are changing everything. The world of entertainment seems more coordinated just as different distribution technologies challenge the position of artists and producers. The European Union comes together on human rights, and then the prospect of adding more countries adds to internal conflicts. Tribal voices in Africa and other areas of the world appear to be breaking down a region into a clatter of differences, while at the same time more individuals there acquire education, providing them with distinctive rather than group identities.

The development of local societies is the historical mainspring of globalization, involving processes of including and incorporating them into systems of greater scale. Development pushes local systems to open up. Globalization both projects a system outward and brings variety back into that system. It drives the export and import of variety and know-how: the technologies about how to integrate that variety and make something new. Globalization also stimulates local systems to acquire more connections with higher levels of human aggregation. Integrating villages into a city, a city into a metropolis, a metropolis into a nation, nations into an international system, and now an international system into a global one all can be described as processes of development. They are developmental in that they integrate diversity into systems of greater scale. They are globalizing in that they continue to reach out until all that is out there has been brought together into a single system. They are democratic in that each component becomes more autonomous with alternative direct linkages to the global system rather than through exclusive and competing intermediate hierarchies of control and subordination.

Development breaks down human groups and aggregations into distinctive individuals. This process of individualization is dramatically associated with the depravations of modernization, individual alienation, and the loss of community. Democratization is also a process of individualization but, from another perspective, is associated with an accumulation of individual rights in a community with a political system (Teune 2000). As systems develop, they provide more options for individuals. Without options, individuals must be loyal to the group to survive. Individuals can express their preferences and beliefs, but if the group has no choice in what it can do to survive, then there is no purpose to express views different from those of the group. Individuals acquire freedom only when the option to leave the group—to exit—emerges from the process of development (see Hirschman 1970). In addition to the presence of choices, the option of exit becomes available to individuals only if they have knowledge and capacity to make choices. There, of course, also must be a variety of groups and political systems known to be available and receptive to those choosing to migrate.

Most recent theorizing about the consequences of globalization is done with the logic of globalization, democracy, labor, education, and so forth, asserting that globalization is the driving force affecting and changing something else. Globalization is seen primarily as economics supporting a relentless spread of a single world market and a decentralized but integrated system of production. Democratization, in contrast, is taken to be a political process subject to the everyday political interests of specific countries and their dominant groups, influenced by powerful

democratic countries. Even though democracy spread globally, democratization was cast in national/country terms. Poland obtained democracy in one way, Hungary in another, Lithuania in still another. Yet it was a major global break of events in the Soviet Union and the withdrawal of its military presence that led to the spread of democracy after 1989, not only in Europe. This second democratic revolution was unlike the regional democratization across Latin America and southern Europe a few years earlier. Indeed, the last democratizations of countries toward the end of the 1990s came about in a rough way, with actual and threatened violence, as occurred in Indonesia and might soon be witnessed in the countries of the Middle East.

It is easy today to conclude that the primary force for the recent globalization was economic. It is also now possible to understand that the only way that kind of economic integration could have expanded so rapidly in a world of fragmented political communities was within a framework of a singular ideology necessary for the stabilization of expectations. That ideology was dual: the advantages of free trade among open economies and the promises of democracy. The alternatives to democracy at the end of the twentieth century had faded. The last of the great world empires had disappeared. The United States again displayed isolationist tendencies. Potential pretenders to empire in east Asia and the Middle East were not credible.

It is difficult today to specify theoretically the relationships between globalization and democracy. One initial connection was between globalization, a rapid decline in the central control of national governments and the opening up of choices to local communities to introduce or reestablish local democratic institutions (Teune 1995; see also Jacob, Ostrowski, and Teune 1993; see www.ssc.upenn.edu/dlg for papers including data elaborating the relationships between local globalization and democratization). That relationship has now changed, if only because local politics, once either weakened by assertions of national control over the economy or vigorously suppressed because of national communal ideologies of state socialism, have reemerged. Local governments are now supporting rather than leading democratic voices in the world, protecting their interests rather than promoting democratic inclusion of others. Another connection between globalization and democracy derives from their common values of openness and inclusion. Democracy must accommodate differences, and its institutions and processes are directed toward negotiation and compromise. Globalization must search for differences or else it cannot generate variety necessary for its continued outreach. Whatever the particular relationships between the two greatest processes of change at the end of the twentieth century, the fact is that they came together in radical changes of political systems toward democracy, sometimes rooted in real democratic institutions and practices but also often adopted as an international facade. The conclusion of all of that at the end of the century

was simple: We are all democrats now.

The softening of states and the opening up to democratic institutions and practices must be explained in part by the substantial external pressures from European countries and the United States. International agencies did aid the various transitions to democracy, including the design of new constitutions, the building of political parties, and the policing of early elections. There was at the very least a convergence rather than conflicts in the directions of those pressures. Most initial elections in the new democracies were declared successful by appropriate international bodies. In the early 1990s, whatever changes were occurring, they were peaceful even if threatened by the old nationalisms in Europe or the return of force in Asia. Most of the votes for the old nationalists, however, faded, and the prospects of the military did not improve.

Soon, the equation linking globalization and democracy began to change. Rather than globalization's being a force for openness and the consequent establishing of democracy, it began to become the environment necessary to sustain, indeed perhaps to nurture, globalization. Even the negative consequences of globalization that were impacting many economic strata, regions, and groups seemed to require a democratic response, as efforts at physical containment appeared inconclusive. But globalization also took on a symbolic presence sufficient to become the unseen force that could be targeted for all bad things happening.

By the middle of the 1990s, global development had moved to a point where the last steps toward the encapsulation of the world into a total economic system are largely minor matters, mostly adjusting the terms of membership into the encompassing World Trade Organization. This fact, of course, does not preclude strong reactions of violent local resistance and withdrawal from the global through retribalization. Indeed, there may be long periods of pause in visible measures toward global integration. The dynamics of globalization-democratization are unstable, and destabilization is an ever-present possibility, especially in the new democracies. But over time, the global system should stabilize with learning and the construction of global and regional institutions that address problems of the threats emanating from globalization perceived by individuals, groups, organizations, and even states. It is very likely that shocks to the global system manifest in the economic crises of southeast Asian countries in 1998 and the terrorist attacks on New York and Washington in the fall of 2001 will have stimulated the establishment of new and stronger global institutions in the arenas of global finance and policing, reinforcing other patterns of global cooperation.

DEMOCRACY AND
GLOBALIZATION (1995–)

After two decades of accelerating globalization in finance, markets, and decentralized manufacture, democracy became the prevailing, dominant political ideology worldwide. Democracy at the national level became the political environment most open and receptive to processes of globalization. Local governments acted to participate in expanding economic opportunities in the global arena. China, in anticipation of the consequences of membership in the World Trade Organization, took steps to encourage elections of effective village-level political leaders. Other countries allocated resources for their vision of a future globalization.

Toward the end of the past century, three worlds of democracy supplanted the previous First, Second, and Third Worlds of development that had become part of the conceptual lenses and vocabulary of social science analysis of a world of competition and conflict. In the First World are the established democracies with political parties, elections, and civil liberties protected by a strong judiciary; in the Second are the new democracies with political parties just taking hold but unstable after a few iterations of new elections; and in the Third are the virtual democratic "constitutional democratic" states, which have been or are being hijacked by a single political party or group. In the First World, there is evidence of a democratic transition moving democratic politics away from the traditional, mainstay nineteenth-century democratic institutions of political parties and elections. Political parties are weakening, and electoral participation is declining. In the Second, political parties and elections are stabilizing around a political center with diminishing direct political challenges on the fundamental issue of whether the country should continue to have a democratic political system. In the Third World of virtual democracies, there is limited acceptance of democratic institutions and a defensive posture that the conditions for more democratization in terms of a free media, political parties, and open associations are not yet ripe.

Outside of these communities of democracies, a small group of countries continues along an aggressively antidemocratic course. Most of the political groups in control of these countries resisted the modernization reflected in the cultural and economic modalities of the West. They also reject modern democracy based on the separation of the individual from the community and state. Islamic countries today constitute the main group of democratically underdeveloped countries. But globalization has substantially penetrated most of them, and there are local democratic pressures.

A few groups disaffected by this global political economy and its demands are engaged in planned violent attacks to destroy the global centers. This global war is not groups against groups or states against states or groups against states but a war between two worlds of development, one global and democratic and the other based on communalisms of exclusion and authoritarian control. Unlike the conventional modes of terrorism where one group intimidates, threatens, and uses violence to ensure credibility of intent and capacity to harm to achieve a political objective, the new global wars are between two loosely affiliated sets of

allied networks, one embedded in the global democratic political economies and the other outside of it. The balance of power between the two is clearly against the traditional, nondemocratic groupings. The faster the processes of development, the more hopeless is their cause. The logic of both democracy and globalization is that of reaching out, accommodating, and integrating diversity. And as the global system continues to develop, it is easier to accommodate yet new items and populations of diversity, including different values, even those previously believed to be damaging. As the global becomes more open and inclusive, the response of the old order is one of intensification of exclusion and defense against change.

As expected, the processes of economic globalization hit snags during the past few years because of monetary and political crises. The financial failures of Mexico and southeast Asia and the aftermath of terrorist attacks against the symbols of the global political order in 2001 brought together the First World of democracies to act to address these as well as future problems of globalization. The Second World of new democracies has a positive political interest in sustaining not only economic globalization but also the movement of peoples and ideas. It is likely that most of the surge in global productivity measures in the late 1990s was the consequence of better globally integrated communications and transportation systems, including the creation of manufacturing processes of flows and integration of components (just in time). Because the legitimacy of democratic polities is founded on the principles of individual freedom and human betterment, they must both be pursued in a stable global political system. That means that the global economic order must be based on democratic governance. It is likely that democratic values and practices of the new democracies are now more firmly embedded in their national and local politics than those of a free market economy. Several democratic elections in the new democracies have given power to "democratic" socialists; none have yet rejected or significantly curtailed democratic politics.

DEMOCRATIC DEVELOPMENT IN A GLOBAL POLITICAL ECONOMY

Democracy must be conceptualized developmentally. Although the general democratic principles of accountability to the people, responsiveness to interests, and individual human development must be addressed, particular democratic practices will reflect the complexities of the social systems and the traditions of societies as well as changing standards of democracy. Surely, the democratic beliefs and institutions of ancient Greek democracy with its exclusion of certain groups and early democracy in the United States with its limited participation in political parties and electoral politics would not meet minimal standards of democracy today.

Four general stages of democratic development can be identified. Each depends on the preceding one. Each takes place unevenly within and across national and local political systems. They are explained by increases in the complexity of societies and the capacities of economies to yield increasing output per head. Although continued economic growth may not be necessary for stable democratic political development, at this point in time, democracies must produce tangible manifestations of human betterment by access to material things and, in a very few places, in improvements in the quality of life.

The first step in democratic development is inclusionary democracy, bringing individuals, sometimes as members of groups, into democratic political systems on a minimal basis of political equality. This is a critical step. The challenge to inclusion is that citizenship today in the global communities of democracies is still primarily exclusively through the channel of a single state. Individuals who are not full participants in a democratic state have two avenues of linkages to global political decision making. Refugees have some voice in the United Nations High Commission on Refugees and other international bodies. People residing in countries where they do not have citizenship are being accorded citizenship with voting rights in a local political unit. The main solution to the democratic imperative of having a minimal linkage of people to the global political system is to provide organizations that bypass the state. There are several today, all with defective mechanisms but surely much better than before. As mentioned, one channel for political voice is through international governmental organizations. Another, potentially more effective, is strategically placed nongovernmental organizations, scientific associations being examples of organizations with capacity for sustained lobbying for the interests and well-being of their members. Still another is courts, in the United Nations and regionally, with jurisdiction to hear claims regardless of national citizenship. In addition, a few national judicial systems are beginning to recognize human rights independent of claims to national civil rights.

The second stage is participatory democracy, wherein rights to join organizations and vote are ubiquitous but expand to a variety of other formal means for individuals to express political views. That comes about through the proliferation of political interest groups, the linkages of those groups transnationally, and the improved prospects for political movements to gain organizational footholds in several places globally, in much the manner that environmental movements have. The spread of national requirements for public hearings before decisions are made, and the potential use of the referenda along lines well established in Switzerland are directions for participatory political development. At the very minimum is the political inclusion of nearly all people living in defined residential areas, neighborhoods, or condominiums. These new localities that are growing nearly everywhere are a new forum for political participation, albeit primary for a middle class. To support this democratic development, however, the principle of transparency has to be promoted. Here, as with the value of openness, democracy shares the value of transparency with that of a properly functioning market.

The third stage is distributive democracy, where the material means for human and social development are secured in systems of public welfare. At the minimum, this requires a diet adequate for physical and mental growth. At an intermediate level, this involves education and learning so that individuals have a chance to take control of their lives. At still a higher level, individuals can acquire resources so that their particular talents and preferences can be realized. It is obvious that there are vast differences around the world in this kind of democratic development. It is generally assumed that individuals who have their preferred level of material consumption will aspire to be in political systems that allow them to develop as individuals. It is at this particular stage that the relationships between economic development, democracy, and democratic stability begin to work.

A fourth stage of democratic development is substantive democracy—being a part of a good and just democratic polity. This can happen only in a decentralized world of many polities, operating under the principle of openness. It is also a world of open information and access, allowing individuals a full range of choices to pursue not only their own well-being but also the political communities that meet their definition of virtue. Today, only scattered population traces have freely chosen a political system that reflects their concept of a just society.

The distribution of democratic opportunities for individuals today is more unequal than perhaps the distribution of income and wealth. It is more likely that individuals living in relative poverty will acquire some wealth in the immediate future than that they will live in a stable democracy to which they are committed. The question of whether only those individuals with some wealth are capable of being involved in democratic governance remains. But it appears very likely that even poor democratic systems will become more global and wealthy than those that remain closed with authoritarian governance.

MAKING GLOBAL
ÉLITES MORE DEMOCRATIC

Global developments have given rise to global sectors of values, norms, and activities controlled by international elites. They are a necessary part of governing an emerging political economy. They are relatively recent at the global level in their capacity to act independently of countries. They make decisions that impact the global system, but without any clear institutions and norms for global democratic accountability. Part of the problem is that much of what is done in these sectors is hidden. They are nonterritorial in their operations and impact. Four such global normative structures have emerged and are acquiring political organizational resources in a global political system. They influence national and local political authorities but do not have formal legitimate powers to reward and punish independently from territorial authorities.

First are the norms of general global rights and obligations, human rights. Among the many groups and organizations striving to gain influence in defining and espousing human rights are lawyers and their associations, partisan minority groups, international bureaucrats, academic institutions, and of course, religious bodies. They all speak on behalf of all of the people and yet cannot be fully responsive to all of the concerns about human rights experienced in specific complexities of everyday living. Nonetheless, great progress has been made in elaborating human rights during the last decades of the twentieth century, and steps have been taken to codify gross violations of human rights as crimes against humanity. But most human rights groups themselves have a democratic deficit while promoting the values of democracy on which human rights are founded.

Second are the norms of trade and exchange. These are primarily now governed by a single international body, the World Trade Organization. It is organized to become more inclusive of not only countries but also of additional ranges of economic activities. Many of its actions have led to perceived and real losses to localities. The consequence has been substantial protest, of course, with the organizational support of nonlocal political interests. The global impact of decisions on trade on the fortunes of localities must be offset with some kind of local political involvement. This will probably require strengthening local democratic institutions that are likely initially to resist change but can also become part of the developmental processes of a globalization that is accountable to the people they most affect.

Third are scientific and engineering norms that involve standards about the accessibility, credibility, and proper use of knowledge in manufacture, medicine, and professional practices. Most of these groups are international/global societies that influence the behavior of their members. The global political economy is knowledge driven. Research priorities, distribution of information, and the standards of knowledge for proper use are under national regulations, which are also influenced by a few private foundations but ultimately controlled by the heavy hands of those actually producing the knowledge. Making science more visible will help to make it more democratically accountable. The challenge was democratizing national science and engineering, but that now has been replaced by doing so globally.

Fourth are the norms of good taste in the arts and entertainment. All art is politically responsive and carries a political impact. Most societies use art and entertainment for political purposes. Consumers everywhere drive the production of world art and entertainment in the great urban centers. Without rapid acceptance by consumers, particular forms of art have little chance. Yet the quest of global democracy is that it will nurture new forms of diversity in societies and polities. That will require diversification of art and entertainment and, at least in the short run,

some kinds of global subsidies. That is only beginning to happen after two decades of centralized, commercial production.

Making elites more responsive and accountable must be the task of international organizations and institutions. There are few compelling reasons for keeping these global institutions closed. The first step has been the growth in easy access through the Internet. Another has been the development of global media with multiple cultural and competitive perspectives. The decentralization and reduced costs of information are foundational for making the decision processes in these four global sectors more accountable.

THE PROSPECTS OF GLOBAL
DEMOCRACY: WHAT CAN BE DONE?

In considering the outlines and prospects of the development of global democracy, three different approaches are being taken. The first is a straightforward research agenda for potential action. This is the general modality of policy analysis, but for global democracy, it must proceed without the support and resources of national governments. Several such projects have been undertaken, including simple ones of taking inventories of the ways global enterprises or institutions affect particular localities and how they can be influenced in ways locally preferred. The second is to find out what is being done by groups and organizations interested in promoting or sabotaging particular global activities. There are several democratic success stories in political movements, especially in environmentalism, in health promotion, or in education. Here it is possible to learn lessons and provide knowledge to groups that might want to influence what is going on globally. The third is to begin to create blueprints for a global democratic order. This is a large challenge, but one that is necessary to begin. It must have a design for a great founding and a justification for making the global economic system accountable to as many people as possible. It would require a new kind of constitutional thinking, dealing with multiple and often conflicting forms of both individual and group representation in national political systems and at the same time in local, regional, and global organizations. A global constitutional convention as a trial run for what could evolve into a series of constitutional conventions is a concrete step to begin the process of designing the framework of a global democratic order.

A major obstacle to global political development is the alienation of so many who are not part of the global system or believe that their very identity is threatened by it. One of the great opportunities of a global economy is that a variety of mini-states have become viable. Today, several states that resulted from the collapse of the Soviet Union are prospering despite predictions of only a few years ago that such small states had no place in an international system. With integration into regional bodies and the European Union and good relations with neighbors, several of them—Estonia, Slovenia,

indeed the once perceived hopeless Slovakia—are stable and providing better lives for their peoples. A second opportunity of the global political economy is the diminution in the importance of territory for states. Territorial lines can be redrawn without threatening the survival or prosperity of any country. Indeed, the established practices of referenda to redefine boundaries can be used under visible and credible supervision of global institutions.

Helping democracy develop globally, however, is more than connecting with those excluded from the massive dynamics of globalization that changed the world during the past few decades. It will also require involvement of innovative institutions in the established democracies. The opportunities are in an engaged set of universities and other educational institutions that are global in aspiration, that have linkages to local societies around the world, and that are receptive to students from everywhere. The immediate future of global democracy depends on these institutions for leadership to develop global democratic institutions and processes and, especially, to articulate the values on which they must stand.

Note

1. Many understood that fundamental changes were under way but did not anticipate the rapid, last great changes sparked by the dissolution of the Soviet Union. At the end of the uncertain, turbulent decade of the 1970s, I commented, "First, in the 1970s (some would argue a bit earlier), the international system entered a state of transformation that is just beginning. 'Transformation' means that there

are new components and new actors and that relations among them as well as among the older components are changing rapidly. There are many consequences of this, but one is instability and unpredictability. . . . What must be done now is to define a global system and how it does and should behave" (Teune 1981, 527).

References

Hirschman, A. O. 1970. *Exit, voice and loyalty: Response to decline in firms, organisations and states.* Cambridge, MA: Harvard University Press.

Jacob, B. M., K. Ostrowski, and H. Teune, eds. 1993. *Democracy and local governance: Ten empirical studies.* Honolulu: Matsunaga Institute for Peace and University of Hawaii.

Rummel, R. J. 1996. *Power kills: Democracy as a method of non-violence.* New Brunswick, NJ: Transaction.

Teune, H. 1981. Human development in a global political economy. *International Studies Quarterly* 25:523-39.

Teune, H. 1995. Local government and democratic political development. *The Annals of the American Academy of Political and Social Science* 540:11-23.

Teune, H. 2000. Development, modernisation, democratisation and conflict. In *Of fears and foes: Security and insecurity in an evolving global political economy,* edited by J. Ciprut. Westport, CT: Praeger.

ANNALS, *AAPSS*, **581**, May 2002

Globalization, Ethnic Diversity, and Nationalism: The Challenge for Democracies

By FRED W. RIGGS

ABSTRACT: Globalization involves escalating human mobility—more and more people are able to move from place to place, not just as migrants seeking new homes but as sojourners visiting different countries where they may stay for longer or shorter periods of time. The result for any state is a growing diversity of its resident population and increasing pressure to support and represent the interests of its citizens living abroad. The prevailing models for organizing a democracy were shaped generations ago and may well be inadequate for coping with the new problems generated by modernity and globalization. Perhaps we need to think about new ways to organize democracies to be more effective.

Fred W. Riggs is a professor emeritus; he earned his Ph.D. from Columbia in 1948. Trained in international relations and Chinese philosophy, he subsequently specialized in comparative and development administration and became interested in the conceptual and terminological problems involved in writing about phenomena not recognized in conventional Western social science vocabularies. Most recently, he has been studying globalization as a contemporary process with far-reaching causes and consequences, especially in relation to the problems of democratization as it evolves when military authoritarianism or one-party dictatorships collapse.

ETHNIC HETEROGENEITY: DIVERSITY AND ETHNONATIONALISM

We often think of ethnic conflict and nationalism as a historical residue based on conflicts between communities whose members have long lived in tension with each other. Although it is true that all civilizations have, by definition, included cities and hinterlands in which culturally different peoples coexisted, the fact is that their ethnic differences were not, normally, a focus of conflict, although no doubt there were tensions between them. The contemporary problems generated by ethnic diversity are a complex result of modernity and globalization. To see why this is true, we need to distinguish between the generic fact of cultural heterogeneity that has existed ever since civilizations arose an urban basis and modern forms of ethnic pluralism. Modernity brought about qualitative changes based on the source of legitimation for governance, and globalization has extended these changes around the world.

Traditionally, in all civilizations, members of different communities coexisted symbiotically. Major conflicts erupted between ruling elites who normally depended on their subordinates, as clients or retainers, regardless of cultural differences, to support them in their interelite struggles. Ancient tensions between rival tribes and kingdoms have been transformed and reinterpreted in our times to provide primordial or historical rationalizations as justification for contemporary ethnic conflicts. However, to see why these conflicts have now exploded, we need to learn more about their modern origins and globalized importance. In this context, we can see that democratic values and institutions have both contributed to ethnic conflict and offer possible solutions.

In traditional societies, interethnic relations were based on caste rather than on class. In any caste-oriented social system—India provides the extreme case—the paradigm was universal legitimacy based on sacred premises: all social differences were institutionalized as hereditary and inviolate. The right to govern was vested in kings (by whatever title), who were seen as having a divine right to rule. Loyal service was viewed as a necessary exchange for benefits to be received from sacred sovereigns by virtue of their supernatural mandate. Cultural differences between castes and subcastes were not only viewed as unavoidable but could be seen as assets since each community could monopolize occupations and privileges that were protected and reciprocally exchanged with members of other communities.

Modernity eroded these relationships, replacing them with class-based notions rooted in the principles of equality and individualism. These new norms have eroded and replaced inequality and communalism as fundamental grounds of being. In this context, cultural differences became politically contentious. Members of each group began to expect equal opportunities in life and came to see other groups as rivals and potential enemies. The underlying basis for legitimation shifted from the sovereignty of rulers to the sovereignty of individuals. The divine right of kings was replaced by the human rights of individuals.

Precedents for this transformation can be found in several historical civilizations, but in the West it triumphed, providing a necessary context for industrialization, democratization, and global imperialism. However, as a result of the rise and collapse of industrial empires and the explosion of modern communications and transportation technologies, the whole world is now exposed to the utterly wrenching experience of trying to replace traditional caste-like social structures with modern class-based practices. Such a transformation cannot take place overnight. Instead, it is a violent and devastating process, producing many antagonisms: the more advantaged citizens seek to protect their threatened privileges while activists from marginalized communities strive to obtain the advantages promised to all by the new ethos. Moreover, although this transformative process was launched in the West, contemporary globalization has accelerated its spread throughout the planet. It has generated fundamental problems involving sovereignty, nationalism, conflict management, and constitutional design. Each of these will be discussed in turn in the following sections.

SOVEREIGNTY: STATES AND CITIZENSHIP

The shift from divine to popular sovereignty raised fundamental questions about the status of states and the rights of citizenship. If people were to be sovereign, they had to organize themselves to exercise this authority, and that involved creating forms of representative governance and establishing boundaries between the states in which governments could govern. The notion of sovereignty became attached both to these states and to the citizens who populated them. The results are perplexing and need to be understood to explain and deal with the ethnic problems that emerged in their wake.

At the state level, sovereignty involves exclusive jurisdiction by regimes over their own citizens and immunity from intervention by other states. No doubt, historically, there were many regimes that can in retrospect be thought of as states. However, they lacked both the exclusiveness and the immunity, from the seventeenth century to all post-Westphalian states. To understand this relatively modern phenomenon, we need to unpack the notion of a sovereign state and see how it is linked to the notion of popular sovereignty.

Sovereignty

In the post-Westphalian world, royal sovereignty was extended, generally, from kings to their kingdoms at the expense of the sacred and secular authority of popes and emperors at the imperial level and of feudal lords, dukes, and counts at lower levels. Subsequently, during the nineteenth century, when the right to govern was transferred from kings to peoples, the notion of state sovereignty was claimed by republics as well as kingdoms. Today, the word *sovereignty* is often attributed to states as though they had some intrinsic authority to govern within the arbitrarily constructed boundaries that have emerged from the violence of interstate conflicts, including the many new states that have arisen on the ashes of collapsed empires.

More realistically, the sovereignty of states is an artifact created by nonstates. States acquire their legitimacy from some source of sovereignty outside themselves. Traditionally, because sovereigns were seen as incarnating supernatural powers, they were able to invest the domains they ruled with an aura of sanctity. By contrast, modern states are essentially secular constructions. At an expedient level, they benefit from mutual nonaggression pacts whereby states agree to respect the rights claimed by their neighbors in exchange for the self-serving rights they claim for themselves.

More fundamentally, however, the legitimacy of states with representative government derives from their citizens who exercise sovereignty by delegating authority to their political representatives. State sovereignty, therefore, is derivative; it exists because it has been recognized by some nonstate source. No state is sovereign just because it is a state. Sovereignty based on the divinity of kings has been replaced by sovereignty based on the right of individuals to govern themselves. Of course, many states, in fact, have no real sovereignty because their rulers have seized power by violence or conspiracy. Much of the violence associated with the transfer of sovereignty from kings to citizens, therefore, hinges on

the rise of dictatorships attributable to the ambitions of their bosses and/or power vacuums created by lost legitimacy. Ultimately, however, the sovereignty of any state hinges on the powers delegated to it by those who exercise their authority by virtue of popular sovereignty.

Citizenship

Popular sovereignty, however, remains intangible until the rights of citizenship can be legitimized and sustained. As noted above, all traditional civilizations were ethnically heterogeneous under the aegis of kings and nobles to whom subordinates owed service and fealty. Ranks rooted in caste-like social systems privileged superiors and obligated inferiors. By contrast, the revolutionary principle expressed in the American Declaration of Independence, that all men are created equal, unsettled all these hierarchies and implied the right of all individuals not only to govern themselves but also to participate in some form of representative government. This implied, somehow, a universal right of citizenship: everyone ought to be able to exercise sovereignty by participating directly in making public choices or delegating the authority to their elected representatives.

In practice, of course, more powerful groups were reluctant to surrender their privileges, and marginalized groups were handicapped in their efforts to secure equal rights. The quest for equality of rights among citizens has been a long and painful struggle. It is difficult even to talk about it, however, because we lack a term for all the people who are linked to a state. Ordinarily, we think of them as the citizens of a state, but on closer scrutiny, it is clear that many people living in or associated with a state lack the legal status of citizens. These include resident aliens, conquered peoples, and others who may be disenfranchised for various reasons, including slavery, serfdom, age, gender, sexual preference, and criminal conduct. For present purposes, I shall use *members* to refer to all persons who are linked to a state in any status. Among the members of a state, those with constitutive rights to share in its exercise of sovereignty are called citizens. The problems involving ethnic minorities and nationalist protest movements typically involve members of a state who lack or reject the status of citizenship. We need, therefore, to understand the reasons some state members are not citizens.

Some of the reasons are fairly obvious. Criminals and social deviants plus children under a legal age limit are routinely denied voting rights. Aliens, especially when they have entered a country illegally, are also denied citizenship status. Because elections are typically organized by districts for local residents, wanderers who lack residency, including citizens in diaspora, often face obstacles to their exercise of voting rights and de facto citizenship. More important, conquered peoples living in dependencies or enclaves such as those reserved for indigenous populations are often denied citizenship. Slaves, serfs, and their descendants are typically denied equal rights.

Traditionally, language and religion often served as markers that distinguished members of dominant communities from others. Such distinctions were easily maintained under the caste-like conditions that prevailed where royal sovereignty was seen as supernaturally grounded. The secularization inherent in the move from sacred to popular sovereignty undermined these distinctions and made them seem increasingly irrational. A factitious rationality for racial distinctions was created by notions of social evolution that gained widespread acceptance during the nineteenth century. In the wake of Darwin's theory of evolution and Herbert Spencer's ideas about social evolution, it became widely accepted that the human race was itself divisible into separate races among whom some were more fit than others (see Darwin and evolution overview at http://landow.stg. brown.edu/victorian/darwin/ darwinov.html).

This fallacy appeared to legitimize racial discrimination as a substitute for traditional social distinctions that could no longer be accepted as a justifiable basis for granting citizenship to some members of a state while denying it to others.

Racist ideas have become so widespread that to this day they play an important role in the development of ethnic diversity and nationalism. The phrase *race and ethnicity* is widely used without any clear explanation of the distinction. Historically, however, one may well argue that culturally different communities were classed as ethnic when they were treated as eligible for citizenship but classed as racially distinct when they were permanently barred from citizenship. In many countries, this distinction has now eroded to such a degree that minority communities are universally viewed as ethnic. Racism persists as irrational prejudice, but few would argue, today, that racial differences provide a legitimate ground for excluding any community from citizenship in a state.

However, even when barriers to citizenship are no longer imposed by a state on some of its members, there are many communities whose members reject citizenship in the state where they live either because they prefer to remain citizens of another state in which they are already citizens or because they would like to create a new state for themselves. As the norms and hopes of democracy spread, an increasing number of members in all states are affected by citizenship problems. Membership of a state as mere subjects is no longer acceptable; everyone wants to be a citizen with the right to be represented in governance, whether in an existing state or in one that is only imagined. The choice of a state, however, raises questions of identity that are usually thought of as involving membership in a nation. The question of nationality is complex and problematic, however. We need to say more about it here.

NATIONS: STATES AND ETHNICITY

It seems plausible to argue that sovereignty cannot be exercised by any random collection of humans;

people become capable of exercising sovereignty only when they enjoy some sense of solidarity based on shared values and customs. This solidarity is reified into the concept of a nation. States are then thought to exercise sovereignty on behalf of a nation rather than just a motley collection of individuals who happen to be there. In contemporary usage, *nation* and *state* are confusingly linked, as in the word *nation-state*. In the name *United Nations, nation* has become a synonym for *state*. Our contemporary problems of ethnicity and nationalism can be understood only when we unpack this linkage. We need to see how nations are related both to states and to ethnic communities.

I shall think of a nation as a community whose members claim the right to govern themselves. Members of such a nation may be referred to as *nationals*, even though this word has some other confusingly different meanings. If ambiguity seems likely, we might put the word in quotation marks: a "national" is defined as a member of a nation—not, for example, as a noncitizen recognized as a member of a state, a perverse usage that prevails in the United States. In general, nationals or their leaders, nationalists, transfer the notion of personal sovereignty to a higher level that mediates between individuals and the state. Rejecting the idea that citizenship by itself is enough to support the right of a government to govern, nationalists claim that this right belongs more properly to a collectivity that can be called a nation. This notion provides a new criterion for citizenship: the privilege of being a citizen should be granted only to members of the nation that dominates a state. In principle, every state should represent a nation, and every nation should have its own state. All citizens would be nationals of the state's nation. If this ideal could be actualized, it would result in the creation of national states, an ideal type that surely does not yet exist anywhere in the world. The familiar term *nation-state* misleadingly implies the existence of a national state. At best, one can say that all nation-states are independent polities as determined by international norms. Membership of the United Nations is a widely accepted test for this status.

The utopian ideal of becoming a national state has, paradoxically, led to two contradictory strategies. Existing states have used their claims of sovereignty to create nations by assimilating or destroying their members who are not seen as nationals. In reverse, communities that want to gain recognition as nations but do not have a state of their own use the claim of sovereignty in their struggle to achieve statehood. We may refer to the outcome of the former process as state nations and the latter as ethnic nations. They represent different and competing projects in time as well as in space.

This distinction enables us to identify two different brands of nationalism. We can say that state nations promote state nationalism whereas ethnic nations encourage ethnic nationalism. State nationalism is older and well established in many states where ruling elites have assimilated or eliminated ethnic minorities. Ethnic nationalism is a more recent phenomenon. New nations born in the wake of collapsed empires mobilize and demand independence for their communities, as do indigenous peoples inhabiting enclaves in the older industrial democracies. Globalization has accelerated the emergence of these ethnic nations.

To the degree that state nations have assimilated cultural minorities, their confident exercise of the rights of citizenship permits ethnic heterogeneity to persist in a purely symbolic form. However, two categories of members of contemporary states have emerged as profoundly dissatisfied communities. One category consists of communities whose members are widely dispersed and unassimilated; they typically would welcome citizenship and its political opportunities but feel that for various reasons, and especially because of persisting racism, they remain economically and socially marginalized. The problems posed by continuing injustices based on discrimination and discontent among members of these communities are conveniently considered under the heading of ethnic diversity.

By contrast, the problems generated by nationalists who reject the status of citizens in the states where they are members and demand statehood or its equivalent for themselves provide the basis for ethnic nationalism. The distinction between ethnic diversity and nationalism is not only conceptually important; it requires different responses by concerned democracies. Policies that can solve the problems of ethnic diversity will not work for problems of ethnic nationalism. No sharp line can be drawn between the problems of diversity and nationalism, however, and in some contexts it is useful to be able to refer to both as modern forms of ethnic conflict.

Demands for justice by the aggrieved and marginalized members of any state often provoke resistance by members of the more privileged communities who fear that their privileges will be curtailed if these demands are met. Rationalizations offered in defense of the status quo sometimes take the form of a historical myth that views all demands for ethnic justice as a residual heritage based on ancient rivalries and conflicts. The fact that ethnic communities, even though socially constructed in response to modern problems, often use historical records and myths to rationalize their demands lends credence to this argument. Because of globalization, minorities in many countries are mobilizing to demand justice and respect, and established communities often resist these demands. I believe it is easier for a democracy to cope with the problems generated by ethnic diversity than it is for them to handle the issues raised by ethnic nationalism. However, I also think that democracies are more likely to handle both kinds of issues more successfully than despotic regimes, although admittedly, in the short run, totalitarian states dominated by a ruling party are able to suppress both kinds of ethnic conflict. When and if such regimes collapse, as seems inescapable, these conflicts still need

to be handled by the world's democracies.

CONSTITUTIONAL
CHOICES

Even in a democracy, however, it is by no means easy to empower ethnic minorities wishing to participate in the established decision-making processes of a state, and it is even more difficult to satisfy the demands of ethnonationalists who reject citizenship and demand independence. However, when comparisons are made between parliamentary regimes and those organized on the basis of the separation of powers principle (presidentialism), it seems clear that the former is more likely to be able to manage the problem of granting effective citizenship to minority communities. In ethnically diverse societies, perhaps they can also handle grants of autonomy (or independence) to ethnonations, but this is not so clear.

Diversity and proportional representation (PR)

A democracy can cope with ethnic diversity by means of multimember electoral districts and one of several available schemes for PR. Such schemes enable minority political parties to obtain a political voice, primarily through seats in parliament but also, quite often, by participation in coalition cabinets. Unfortunately, this solution seems to produce quite negative results when applied in a presidentialist (separation of powers) regime, even though it works quite well in parliamentary systems. Arguments for this conclusion are based on both empirical and theoretical considerations.

At the empirical level, we can look at the historical record of countries that have used PR. I have discussed this record elsewhere. I concluded that in presidentialist systems, by contrast with parliamentary regimes, PR produces "centrifugalized" party systems that are "always dysfunctional for the maintenance of presidentialism. Moreover, neither president nor congress seems to have any systemic means to counteract these party dynamisms" (http://www2.hawaii.edu/~fredr/pres.htm#ele; Linz and Valenzuela 1994).[2]

At the theoretical level, similar conclusions arise. In the election of presidents, it is important to mobilize a broad consensus in support of a leader who has to be head of state as well as head of government. Under PR, it is almost impossible to do that. Even with a runoff election, it is apparent that the candidate with a final majority was only the second or third choice for many voters. As for the congress, PR produces a multiplicity of parties and increases the difficulty of securing majorities in support of legislation. Moreover, representatives of small parties find themselves always outvoted and marginalized, leading to alienation and negativism. They do not have the possibility of participating in coalition cabinets as they would in parliamentary regimes.

For a presidentialist regime to survive without catastrophic breakdowns, it seems to be necessary to rely on an electoral system that produces a centripetal (middle-way, two-party system) in which party discipline compromises with constituency (district) loyalties and the special interests represented in legislative committees. Thus, the requisites for survival of democracy in a presidentialist regime include rules that generate oligarchic power and favor sedentary majorities in voting districts, a recipe that marginalizes minority communities.

Ethnic nationalism

In almost all the world's democracies, there are enclaves where ethnic communities find themselves marginalized and profoundly discontented. Their leaders demand self-government, either with full independence or with constitutional autonomy. All the countries that created industrial empires have by the end of the twentieth century surrendered authority over their conquered exclaves, that is, the possessions that were clearly separated normally by oceans from their homelands. However, in some of them, enclaves exist in which conquered indigenous peoples struggle to perpetuate their own ancient traditions despite pressures for assimilation by the country in which they find themselves. Although it is difficult for any state to grant full independence to the peoples inhabiting enclaves, I believe it may well be easier for those with parliamentary constitutional systems to offer autonomy than it is for countries with presidentialist regimes. Again, the argument can be made on both empirical and theoretical grounds.

Empirically

A quick look at existing cases seems to confirm this impression. We can think of many parliamentary systems in which autonomies have been established: the Aaland Islands in Finland, Greenland in Denmark, Catalonia and the Basque autonomies in Spain, Tyrol in Italy, Quebec and Nunavut in Canada, and Scotland and Wales in the United Kingdom. Northern Ireland is exceptional because it is torn internally between Unionists and Separatists, but the regime in London has been willing to devolve authority for self-government as soon as these factions agree.

By contrast, in presidentialist countries, there are few such autonomies, and struggles to establish them are often violent: consider the Chechnya case in Russia and Kosovo in Serbia. The ability of the United States to recognize autonomy in Puerto Rico, the Northern Marianas, and many American Indian reservations is exceptional and reflects some special circumstances in the U.S. situation. This suggests that it is also possible for a presidentialist regime to devolve authority to an enclave, but it may well be more difficult. To find the reasons, we need to look more deeply into the constitutional considerations.

Theoretically

Consider that granting autonomy is not just a matter of making a law that applies to everyone within a country's jurisdiction; it involves exempting those living within an enclave from these laws and authorizing them to create their own laws.

In a presidentialist regime, this means gaining support for such an exception not only from the president but also from the congress and the supreme court and perhaps also from the population at large by means of a referendum. These are high hurdles; the establishment of autonomies (reservations) for indigenous communities in the United States was possible, I believe, only because such decisions could bypass normal political procedures due to the special constitutional status accorded to treaties made by the United States with existing states, including tribal regimes.

In parliamentary regimes, by contrast, parliaments have the ultimate authority to make decisions, including fundamental laws that have constitutional significance. Procedurally, therefore, it is simpler in parliamentary than in presidentialist systems to make the decisions that involve surrendering authority over a minority community. That does not necessarily make it easy for a government to surrender power. However, when we take into account the dynamics of decision making in a congress as compared with a parliament, we can see how it may well be more difficult for the former to make such decisions.

Moreover, consider that in presidentialist regimes, the separation of powers requires congress to micromanage public policy making. There are two reasons. First, its committees second-guess in detail all presidential policy initiatives, and second, members of congress are responsive to local constituents who are likely to resist the delegation of authority to unrepresented enclaves even though they may welcome more authority for the local jurisdictions in which they enjoy power. Moreover, with an elected president as head of government, power is concentrated in one person, and even though a cabinet may comprise minority members, it is not a ruling body, and its members are primarily accountable to one person, the president, not to representatives of their own parties or communities.

By contrast, under parliamentary rule, the fusion of powers enables the cabinet, subject to parliamentary approval, to make fundamental policy decisions. Because the central government's interests override the particularistic interests of locally elected legislators, they may more easily surrender authority over enclaves, especially when cost/benefit analysis shows that they will gain as a result. Moreover, cabinet government means that it is possible to process a large number of decisions in a coordinated way, linking powerful senior career officials with politically responsible cabinet members. I believe they are likely to see that it is advantageous for a state to allow nonnationals to govern themselves. In exchange for the surrender of direct authority over an enclave, the regime avoids the political costs of perpetual conflict with its people and reduces the administrative expenses involved in efforts to enforce unacceptable laws on a rebellious minority. Moreover, the surrender of direct rule does not necessarily mean the loss of influence. The people living in any enclave will surely want to engage in external relations in-

volving trade, travel, and communication, and they will need help in many ways from their host country. Because of increased mobility, citizens of any autonomy must live and work in growing numbers outside their boundaries, under the control of their host states. In exchange for whatever external support or assistance a host state can provide, it may legitimately make reciprocal demands that promote harmony between the two jurisdictions.

No doubt, any such broad generalizations are subject to exceptions. Although the considerations mentioned above may apply to most cases, it is quite possible that exceptionally, a presidentialist system (like that of the United States) can work better than one might expect, and a parliamentary regime can fail. However, it is important to remember that exceptions are, indeed, exceptional. This is particularly important when thinking about the American case because superficial analysis often leads observers to conclude, illogically, that because it has succeeded pretty well, its constitutional system must therefore be well suited to the tasks facing all democracies. To make generalizations about any kind of system, we need to think about the normal cases and suspend judgment about the exceptions. To understand why the American case is so exceptional, we need to make close comparisons between it and other presidentialist systems. Comparisons with parliamentary regimes cannot show why this case differs so significantly from all other countries following the same constitutional principles.[3]

CONCLUSION

Returning to the context of globalization, it is important to recognize that the rapid escalation of all the different processes that are so rapidly linking everyone living on our planet today is a result of modernizing forces rooted in the industrial revolution, democratization, and the rise of ethnic nationalism. All of these changes entail the abandonment of traditional caste-like social differences rooted in hierarchic principles of inequality and sacred authority. They must be replaced by class-based social systems that presuppose human equality and justify differences based on individual effort and secular rationality. The state system that emerged since the Peace of Westphalia in the mid-seventeenth century facilitated these transitions, but it now needs to be reshaped in the context of globalization, not just because of the powerful market-based economic, banking, and monetary system that has emerged but also because old notions of state sovereignty rooted in national identities have become obsolete as human mobility has accelerated. All populations have become increasingly diverse, and the citizens of all states are more diasporized, living or visiting outside their own countries. Moreover, dispersed ethnic diasporic communities with distinctive interests of their own need to be accommodated politically both within the evolving global network of international organizations and in the design of democratic states. Notions of royal and state sovereignty need to give way to the principles of personal sovereignty. The fictitious ideal of a national state needs to be replaced by acceptance of the reality of multinational states, and the sovereignty of states needs to be seen as a fiction that requires reinterpretation in a global order. No doubt, states will survive but their functions will change. They need to accept superstructures based on confederalism and global organization in a complex network of autonomous systems dedicated to solving a host of complex and interdependent issues. These systems need to focus on preserving the environment, handling population growth, protecting workers, overcoming poverty, promoting health, and securing cultural values.

In this context, democratic states are more likely to succeed and survive if they follow parliamentary constitutional principles as do all the industrialized democracies except the United States. The continued adherence of some of them to the presidentialist design in part because of the U.S. example is likely to jeopardize their viability. However, all democracies also need to make some fundamental constitutional innovations that enable dispersed minorities, both at home and abroad, to be better represented, perhaps in separate legislative chambers (I have discussed these possibilities elsewhere; see *Mobility and the Internet: Problems of Global Democratization* at http://www2.hawaii.edu/~fredr/mobidem.htm).

The general conclusion offered here is that democracies are better able than are nondemocratic regimes to handle the problems of ethnic and diasporan identity posed by globalization. Among democracies, those with a parliamentary constitutional system can handle these problems more easily than can those following the separation of powers (presidentialist) model. However, all existing constitutional democracies are handicapped by their lack of separate legislative chambers able to represent geographically dispersed minorities, both within the country as ethnic communities and autonomous regions, and also to speak for citizens living abroad in diaspora. Finding ways to overcome this handicap is a major challenge for political design in a globalizing world.

Notes

1. Some of them have banded together to create an international alliance with their own Web site, Unrepresented Nations and Peoples (http://www.unpo.org/). Reports by scholarly outsiders about these nations can be found in the Minorities at Risk project (http://www.bsos.umd.edu/cidcm/mar) under the direction of Ted Gurr at the University of Maryland.

2. The analysis was based on data in Linz and Valenzuela (1994). Although this book contains only case studies of selected countries, I believe a comprehensive analysis of all Latin American regimes would confirm my conclusion.

3. For a detailed analysis based on comparisons with separation of powers constitutional systems, see my *Problems of Presidentialism and the American Exception* (http://www2.hawaii.edu/~fredr/pres.htm). Some further reflections on the relation of parliamentarism to the solution of problems of ethnic diversity can be found in my paper titled *Ethnic Diversity, Nationalism and Constitutional Democracy* (http://www2.hawaii.edu/~fredr/formost.htm).

Reference

Linz, Juan, and Arturo Valenzuela, eds. 1994. *The failure of presidential democracy.* Baltimore: Johns Hopkins University Press.

ANNALS, *AAPSS*, **581**, May 2002

Globalization from Below:
Toward a Collectively Rational
and Democratic Global Commonwealth

By CHRISTOPHER CHASE-DUNN

ABSTRACT: This article presents a model of the structures and processes of the modern world-system and proposes a project to transform the system into a democratic and collectively rational global commonwealth. Popular transnational social movements are challenging the ideological hegemony of corporate capitalism. The global women's movement, the labor movement, environmentalist movements, and indigenous movements are attempting to form strong alliances that can challenge the domination of an emerging transnational capitalist class. This article argues that new democratic socialist states in the semiperiphery will be crucial allies and sources of support for the antisystemic movements.

Christopher Chase-Dunn is Distinguished Professor of Sociology and director of the Institute for Research on World-Systems at the University of California, Riverside. His recent books are Rise and Demise: Comparing World-Systems *(with Tom Hall) and* The Spiral of Capitalism and Socialism: Toward Global Democracy *(with Terry Boswell). In 1993, he was elected to the Sociological Research Association, and in 2001, he was elected to the rank of fellow of the American Association for the Advancement of Science.*

THE world-systems perspective is a historical and structural theoretical framework that analyzes national societies as parts of a larger stratified sociopolitical and economic system (Shannon 1996). The focus is on the structural features of the larger system itself. It is a world economy with a hierarchical division of labor for the production of different kinds of goods. There are economically and militarily powerful countries in the core, dependent, and dominated regions in the periphery, and a middle sector of countries (the semiperiphery) in which states have intermediate levels of economic and political/military power.

The world market includes both international trade and all the national economies, so the world-system is the whole system, not just international relations. Local, regional, national, international, transnational, and global networks of interaction constitute the world-system. This set of nested and overlapping networks of human interaction is itself located in the biosphere and the physical regimes of the planet Earth, the solar system, our galaxy, and the larger processes and structures of the physical universe. The world-systems perspective is both materialist and institutional. It analyzes the evolution of human institutions while taking account of the constraints and opportunities posed by physics, biology, and the natural environment (Chase-Dunn and Hall 1997).

WORLD-SYSTEMS PERSPECTIVE

The modern world-system is a global set of interaction networks that include all the national societies. But world-systems have not always been global. The modern world-system originated out of an expanding multicore Afro-Eurasian world-system in which the Europeans rose to hegemony by conquering the Americas and using the spoils to overcome the political and economic strengths of contending core regions in south and east Asia (Frank 1998). The result was a global world-system with a single core region. And because capitalism had become a predominant mode of accumulation in the European core, European hegemony further extended commodification and markets to the rest of the world. The consequence was a capitalistic and globalizing world economy in which states and firms were increasingly focused on competitiveness in commodity production for the global market. Commodification was always much more developed in core regions, whereas in peripheral regions, core colonizers used remnants of the tributary modes of accumulation, especially coercive labor control, to mobilize production for profit. Core regions specialized in the production of capital-intensive goods that required skilled and educated labor, and so their class structures and political institutions became more egalitarian and democratic relative to the authoritarianism and much greater internal inequalities of most peripheral and many semiperipheral countries.

The capitalism referred to here is not only the phenomenon of capitalist firms producing commodities but also capitalist states and the modern interstate system that is the political backdrop for capitalist accumulation. The world-systems perspective has produced an understanding of capitalism in which geopolitics and interstate conflict are normal processes of capitalist political competition. Socialist movements are, defined broadly, those political and organizational means by which people try to protect themselves from market forces, exploitation, and domination and to build more cooperative institutions. The sequence of industrial revolutions by which capitalism has restructured production and the control of labor has stimulated a series of political organizations and institutions created by workers to protect their livelihoods. This happened differently under different political and economic conditions in different parts of the world-system. Skilled workers created guilds and craft unions. Less skilled workers created industrial unions. Sometimes these coalesced into labor parties that played important roles in supporting the development of political democracies, mass education, and welfare states (Rueschemeyer, Stephens, and Stephens 1992). In other regions, workers were less politically successful but managed at least to protect access to rural areas or subsistence plots for a fallback or hedge against the insecurities of employment in capitalist enterprises. To some extent, the burgeoning contemporary informal sector provides such a fallback.

The varying success of workers' organizations also had an impact on the further development of capitalism. In some areas, workers or communities were successful at raising the wage bill or protecting the environment in ways that raised the costs of production for capital. When this happened, capitalists either displaced workers by automating them out of jobs or capital migrated to where fewer constraints allowed cheaper production. The process of capital flight is not a new feature of the world-system. It has been an important force behind the uneven development of capitalism and the spreading scale of market integration for centuries. Labor unions and socialist parties were able to obtain some power in certain states, but capitalism became yet more international. Firm size increased. International markets became more and more important to successful capitalist competition. Fordism, the employment of large numbers of easily organizable workers in centralized production locations, has been supplanted by flexible accumulation (small firms producing small customized products) and global sourcing (the use of substitutable components from widely spaced competing producers), production strategies that make traditional labor organizing approaches much less viable.

Theories of social structure provoke a standard set of criticisms. They are allegedly deterministic and downplay the importance of human agency. They are accused of reifying the idea of society (or the world-system), whereas only individual persons are alleged to really exist and to have needs. Structural theories, it is charged, totalize experience and provide ideological covers for domination and exploitation. And they miss the rich detail of locality and period that only thick description can provide.

The world-systems perspective has been accused of all these sins. In this article, I will describe a model of the structures and processes of the modern world-system and propose a project to transform the contemporary system into a democratic and collectively rational global commonwealth. This involves an approach to structure and action first outlined by Friedrich Engels in his *Socialism: Utopian and Scientific* (1935). The point of building a structural theory is to enable us to understand the broad dynamics of social change in the historical system in which we live. This knowledge is potentially useful to those who want to preserve, modify, or transform the historical system. For Engels, the point was to mobilize the working class to humanize and socialize the world. That is also my intention.

The approach developed here assumes a structural model of the world-system, and it identifies the agents who have both the motive and the opportunity to transform the contemporary world-system into a global socialist commonwealth. I also discuss some of the value bases and the organizational issues that surround the project of transformation. By presenting the model in this way, I hope to show the critics of structuralism that structural theories need not be deterministic, nor need they undermine social action. By positively stating the model and its implications for action, I hope to get those who would be critical of the modern system to focus on the problems of scientifically understanding and transforming that system.

The scientific approach to world-system transformation needs to avoid the teleological elements of much of Marxism. The ideology of progress has been used to glorify both capitalism and socialism. Progress is not an inevitable outcome of forces that are immanent in the world. The idea of progress only means that many humans can agree about the basics of what constitutes a good life. These are value judgments. But by making these assumptions explicit, we can determine whether social change really constitutes progress as defined.

Inevitabilism also needs to be renounced. Human social change is both historical and evolutionary, but there is nothing inevitable about it. Indeed, another big asteroid or a human-made ecological catastrophe could destroy the whole experiment. Teleology is the idea that progress is inevitable because it comes out of the nature of the universe, or the nature of history, or some other powerful source. For many Marxists, the proletariat has been understood to be the agency of progress. It is important to disentangle the scientific from the unscientific aspects of this idea. Workers may have interests that are compatible with and encourage the development of a more humane system, but that is not the same as being a magical source of historical progress. Teleology, inevitabilism, and eschatology are powerful bromides for the mobilization of social movements, but they are deceptive and counterproductive when the prophesied utopia fails to arrive. What is needed is an open-ended theory of history that can be useful for practitioners of the arts of transformation. The world-systems perspective can serve this purpose.

THE SPIRAL OF CAPITALISM AND SOCIALISM

In core countries, certain sectors of the working classes were able to mobilize political power and raise wages through trade unions and socialist parties. This was made possible by core capital's need for skilled and educated labor. The relatively more democratic political institutions and the development of welfare programs were mainly based on the political efforts of skilled and organized workers (Rueschemeyer, Stephens, and Stephens 1992). In some core countries, the relative harmony of class relations was supplemented by the extraction of profits from peripheral regions and the availability of cheap food and raw materials provided by core domination and exploitation of the periphery.

At some times and places, the movements of core workers took a more radical turn and threatened the political hegemony of capital, but the long-run outcome in the core states was not socialist revolution but rather the construction of social democratic welfare states or the sort of business unionism that emerged in the United States.

In the periphery, colonial elites used coerced labor (serfdom, slavery, indentured servitude) to produce commodities for export to the core. But resistance in the periphery from peasants and workers, as well as nationalist movements supported by small middle-class groups, led to effective anti-imperialist coalitions that were able to achieve decolonization and the rudiments of national sovereignty. These movements created anti-imperial class alliances that after World War II, often utilized socialist ideology. But most of the resultant regimes remained quite dependent on neocolonial relations with capitalist core states. Radical challenges to capitalism in most of the periphery were easily disrupted by overt or covert intervention. Vietnam was a significant exception.

In the world-system framework, the Communist states represented efforts by popular movements in the semiperiphery and the periphery to transform the capitalist world-system into a socialist world-system but also to catch up with core capitalism in terms of economic development. These efforts largely failed because they were not able to transcend the institutional constraints of the capitalist world economy and because the capitalist core states were spurred to develop new technologies of production, political/military control, and global market and political integration in response to the challenges posed by the Communist states. The long-run relationship between capitalism and anticapitalist movements is a spiral in which the contestants provoke each other to ever-greater feats of mobilization and integration (Boswell and Chase-Dunn 2000).

In some countries in the semiperiphery, radical challenges to capitalism were able to take state power and to partially institutionalize socialist economic institutions. There were great limitations on what was possible despite the fact that there were true revolutions of workers and peasants in Russia, China, Cuba, Yugoslavia, Korea, Albania, and Vietnam.

Socialism in one country was not what the Bolsheviks had in mind. They thought that there would be a world revolution against capitalism after World War I, or at least a revolution in Germany. The decision to hang on in Russia despite the failure of radical regimes to come to power elsewhere may have been a grave mistake. It required the use of both socialist ideology and substantial coercion simply to maintain Communist state power and to mobilize industrialization, urbanization, and education to catch up with core capitalism. This contradiction was already apparent in the time of Lenin. Stalin did not look back.

It was the military part of this equation that was probably the most costly economically and politically. Military-style mass production became the model for the whole "socialist" economy in Russia (Boswell and Peters 1990). Building and supporting a Soviet army that was capable of halting the advance of Germany in World War II meant further concentration of power in the Communist party, the complete elimination of democracy within the party, and the use of the Communist International as purely the instrument of Russian international interests. The humiliation of the Hitler-Stalin pact and its reversal branded Communism as a form of totalitarianism equivalent to fascism in the minds of millions of democratic socialists all over the globe, as well as playing into the hands of the ideologues of capitalism.

Chirot (1991) and Lupher (1996) argued that Stalinism was mainly a continuation of Russian bureaucratic patrimonialism or oriental despotism. I reject this sort of institutional determinism. I see both structural constraints and historical possibilities. The authoritarian outcome of the Russian revolution was not predetermined, but it was greatly conditioned by Russia's semiperipheral location and the military and economic forces that were brought to bear from the capitalist core states. I agree with Hobsbawm (1994) that this does not excuse the Stalinist repression, but my analysis leaves open the possibility of past and future systemic transformation, while the continuationist frame sees only the end of history.

The Chinese, Cuban, Korean, Yugoslavian, Albanian, and Vietnamese revolutions benefited somewhat from the political space opened up by the Soviet Union. The idea that there was a real alternative to the end of history in the capitalist version of the European Enlightenment was kept alive by the existence of the Soviet Union, despite its grave imperfections. The Chinese, Cuban, Korean, Yugoslavian, Albanian, and

Vietnamese revolutions were able to learn from Russian mistakes to some extent and to try new directions and make mistakes of their own. The most obvious example was Mao's turn to the peasantry. While the Bolsheviks had treated peasants as a conservative foe (despite Lenin's analysis), thus putting the party at odds with the majority of the Russian people, Mao embraced the peasantry as a revolutionary class. The later revolutions also benefited from the maneuverability that Soviet political/military power in the world-system made possible.

The regimes created in central and eastern Europe by the Red Army after World War II were a different breed of cat. In these, socialist ideology and Stalinist development policies were imposed from outside, so they were never politically legitimate in the eyes of most of the population. This major structural fact varied to some extent depending on the strength of preexisting socialist and Communist forces before the arrival of the Red Army. The Soviet Union justified its intervention in terms of proletarian internationalism and creating a buffer zone against the Germans. While the geopolitical justification was plausible from the Russian point of view, it did not help to justify the regimes of the eastern European countries with their own populations. And the noble ideal of proletarian internationalism was besmirched by its use as a fig leaf for setting up these puppet regimes.

Jozsef Borocz's (1999, Table 1) analysis of these eastern and central European "comprador" regimes detailed the many compromises that the Soviet overlords introduced to increase internal legitimacy. But because of the origin of these regimes in world geopolitics, the legitimacy problem was insoluble. Russian tanks crushed revolts, but the basic problem of legitimacy eventually led to the overthrow of every one of these regimes as soon as Gorbachev lifted the Soviet fist.

POLITICAL IMPLICATIONS
OF THE WORLD-SYSTEMS
PERSPECTIVE

Thus, class struggles and anti-imperial movements have been important shapers of the institutional structures of modern capitalism for centuries. The waves of globalization of capitalism in the twentieth century were stimulated in important ways by the challenges posed by the Leninist parties and the Communist states. Contrary to the view that history has ended, anticapitalist movements will continue to emerge in response to expanding and intensifying capitalist development. The most recent wave of transnational economic integration and the political ideology of neoliberal restructuring, downsizing, and competitiveness is provoking workers, peasants, women, indigenous groups, and defenders of the biosphere to mobilize. Some of the resulting movements may employ localist and nationalist organizational structures to protect against market forces and transnational capital, but retreat into xenophobic nationalism is likely to be a recipe for another round of world war. The only effective response is to organize "globalization from below"—transnational social movements with the goal of building an Earthwide collectively rational and democratic commonwealth.

The age of U.S. hegemonic decline and the rise of postmodernist philosophy have cast the liberal ideology of the European Enlightenment (science, progress, rationality, liberty, democracy, and equality) into the dustbin of totalizing universalisms. It is alleged that these values have been the basis of imperialism, domination, and exploitation and, thus, they should be cast out in favor of each group's asserting its own set of values. Note that self-determination and a considerable dose of multiculturalism (especially regarding religion) were already central elements in Enlightenment liberalism.

The structuralist and historical materialist world-systems approach poses this problem of values in a different way. The problem with the capitalist world-system has not been with its values. The philosophy of liberalism is fine. It has quite often been an embarrassment to the pragmatics of imperial power and has frequently provided justifications for resistance to domination and exploitation. The philosophy of the Enlightenment has never been a major cause of exploitation and domination. Rather, it was the military and economic power generated by capitalism that made European hegemony possible.

To humanize the world-system, we may need to construct a new philosophy of democratic and egalitarian liberation. Of course, many of the principal ideals that have been the core of the Left's critique of capitalism are shared by non-European philosophies. Democracy in the sense of popular control over collective decision making was not invented in Greece. It was a characteristic of all nonhierarchical human societies on every continent before the emergence of complex chiefdoms and states (Bollen and Paxton 1997). My point is that a new egalitarian universalism can usefully incorporate quite a lot from the old universalisms. It is not liberal ideology that caused so much exploitation and domination. Rather, it was the failure of real capitalism to live up to its own ideals (liberty and equality) in most of the world. That is the problem that progressives must solve.

A central question for any strategy of transformation is the question of agency. Who are the actors who will most vigorously and effectively resist capitalism and construct democratic socialism? Where is the most favorable terrain, the weak link, where concerted action could bear the most fruit? Samir Amin (1990, 1992) contended that the agents of socialism have been most heavily concentrated in the periphery. It is there that the capitalist world-system is most oppressive, and thus peripheral workers and peasants, the vast majority of the world proletariat, have the most to win and the least to lose.

On the other hand, Marx and many contemporary Marxists have argued that socialism will be most effectively built by the action of core proletarians. Since core areas have already attained a high level of technological development, the establishment of socialized production and distribution should be easiest in the core. And organized core workers have had the longest experience with industrial capitalism and the most opportunity to create socialist social relations. I submit that both "workerist" and "Third Worldist" positions have important elements of truth, but there is another alternative that is suggested by the comparative world-systems perspective: the semiperiphery as the weak link.

Core workers may have experience and opportunity, but a sizable segment of the core working classes lack motivation because they have benefited from a nonconfrontational relationship with core capital. The existence of a labor aristocracy has divided the working class in the core and, in combination with a large middle stratum, has undermined political challenges to capitalism. Also, the long experience in which business unionism and social democracy have been the outcome of a series of struggles between radical workers and the labor aristocracy has created a residue of trade union practices, party structures, legal and governmental institutions, and ideological heritages that act as barriers to new socialist challenges. These conditions have changed to some extent during the past two decades as hypermobile capital has attacked organized labor, dismantled welfare states, and downsized middle-class workforces. These create new possibilities for popular movements within the core, and we can expect more confrontational popular movements to emerge as workers devise new forms of organization (or revitalize old forms). Economic globalization makes labor internationalism a necessity, and so we can expect to see the old idea take new forms and become more organizationally real. Even small victories in the core have important effects on peripheral and semiperipheral areas because of demonstration effects and the power of core states.

The main problem with Third Worldism is not motivation but opportunity. Democratic socialist movements that have managed to obtain state power in the periphery either have been overthrown by powerful external forces or have forced them to abandon most of their socialist program. Popular movements in the periphery have most usually been anti-imperialist class alliances that have often succeeded in establishing at least the trappings of national sovereignty, but not socialism. The low level of the development of the productive forces in the periphery has made it difficult to establish socialist forms of accumulation, although this is not impossible in principle. It is simply harder to share power and wealth when there is very little of either. But the emergence of new democratic regimes in the periphery will facilitate new forms of mutual aid, cooperative development, and popular movements once the current ideological hegemony of neoliberalism has thoroughly broken down.

SEMIPERIPHERAL
DEMOCRATIC SOCIALISM

In the semiperiphery, both motivation and opportunity exist. Semiperipheral areas, especially those in which the territorial state is large, have sufficient resources to be able to stave off core attempts at overthrow and to provide some protection to socialist institutions if the political conditions for their emergence should arise. Semiperipheral regions (e.g., Russia and China) have experienced more militant class-based socialist revolutions and movements because of their intermediate position in the core-periphery hierarchy. While core exploitation of the periphery creates and sustains alliances among classes in both the core and the periphery, in the semiperiphery, an intermediate world-system position undermines class alliances and provides a fruitful terrain for strong challenges to capitalism. Semiperipheral revolutions and movements are not always socialist in character, as we have seen in Iran. But when socialist intentions are strong, there are greater possibilities for real transformation than in the core or the periphery. Thus, the semiperiphery is the weak link in the capitalist world-system. It is the terrain on which the strongest efforts to establish socialism have been made, and this is likely to be true of the future as well.

On the other hand, the results of the efforts so far, while they have undoubtedly been important experiments with the logic of socialism, have left much to be desired. The tendency for authoritarian regimes to emerge in the Communist states betrayed Marx's idea of a freely constituted association of direct producers. And the imperial control of eastern Europe by the Russians was an insult to the idea of proletarian internationalism. Democracy within and between nations must be a constituent element of true socialism.

It does not follow that efforts to build socialism in the semiperiphery will always be so constrained and thwarted. The revolutions in the Soviet Union and the People's Republic of China have increased our collective knowledge about how to build socialism despite their only partial successes and their obvious failures. It is important for all of us who want to build a more humane and peaceful world-system to understand the lessons of socialist movements in the semiperiphery and the potential for future, more successful, forms of socialism there.

Once again, the core has developed new lead industries—computers and biotechnology—and much of large-scale heavy industry, the classical terrain of strong labor movements and socialist parties, has been moved to the semiperiphery. This means that new socialist bids for state power in the semiperiphery (e.g., South Africa, Brazil, India, Mexico, and perhaps Korea) will be much more based on an urbanized and organized proletariat in large-scale industry than the earlier semiperipheral socialist revolutions were. This should have happy consequences for the nature of new socialist states in the semiperiphery because the relationship between the city and the countryside within these countries should be less antagonistic. Less internal conflict will make more democratic socialist regimes possible and will lessen the likelihood of core interference. The global expansion of communications has increased the salience of events in the semiperiphery for audiences in the core, and this may serve to dampen core state intervention into the affairs of democratic socialist semiperipheral states.

Some critics of the world–systems perspective have argued that emphasis on the structural importance of global relations leads to political "do–nothingism" while we wait for socialism to emerge at the world level. The world–systems perspective does indeed encourage us to examine global-level constraints (and opportunities) and to allocate our political energies in ways that will be most productive when these structural constraints are taken into account. It does not follow that building socialism at the local or national level is futile, but we must expend resources on transorganizational, transnational, and international socialist relations. The environmental and feminist movements are now in the lead, and labor needs to follow their example.

A simple domino theory of transformation to democratic socialism is misleading and inadequate. Suppose that all firms or all nation-states adopted socialist relations internally but continued to relate to one another through competitive commodity production and political/military conflict. Such a hypothetical world–system would still be dominated by the logic of capitalism, and that logic would be likely to repenetrate the socialist firms and states. This cautionary tale advises us to invest political resources in the construction of multilevel (transorganizational, transnational, and international) socialist relations lest we simply repeat the process of driving capitalism to once again perform an end run by operating on a yet larger scale.

A DEMOCRATIC SOCIALIST WORLD-SYSTEM

These considerations lead us to a discussion of socialist relations at the level of the whole world-system. The emergence of democratic collective rationality (socialism) at the world-system level is likely to be a slow process. What might such a world-system look like and how might it emerge? It is obvious that such a system would require a democratically controlled world federation that can effectively adjudicate disputes among nation-states and eliminate warfare (Goldstein 1988). This is a bare minimum. There are many other problems that badly need to be coordinated at the global level: ecologically sustainable development, a more balanced and egalitarian approach to economic growth, and the lowering of population growth rates.

The idea of global democracy is important for this struggle. The movement needs to push toward a kind of popular democracy that goes beyond the election of representatives to include popular participation in decision making at every level. Global democracy can only be real if it is composed of civil societies and national states that are themselves truly democratic (Robinson 1996). And global democracy is probably the best way to lower the probability of another war among core states. For that reason, it is in everyone's interest.

How might such a global commonwealth come into existence? The process of the growth of international organizations, which has been going on for at least 200 years, will eventually result in a world state—if we are not blown up first. Even international capitalists have some uses for global regulation, as is attested by the International Monetary Fund, the World Bank, and George Soros (1998). Capitalists do not want the massive economic and political upheavals that would likely accompany collapse of the world monetary system, and so they support efforts to regulate ruinous competition and "beggar-thy-neighborism." Some of these same capitalists also fear nuclear holocaust, and so they may support a strengthened global government that can effectively adjudicate conflicts among nation-states.

Of course, capitalists know as well as others that effective adjudication means the establishment of a global monopoly of legitimate violence. The process of state formation has a long history, and the king's army needs to be bigger than any combination of private armies that might be brought against him. While the idea of a world state may be a frightening specter to some, I am optimistic about it for several reasons. First, a world state is probably the most direct and stable way to prevent nuclear holocaust, a desideratum that must be at the top of everyone's list. Second, the creation of a global state that can peacefully adjudicate disputes among nations will transform the existing interstate system.

The interstate system is the political structure that stands behind the maneuverability of capital and its ability to escape organized workers and other social constraints on profitable accumulation. While a world state may at first be dominated by capitalists, the very existence of such a state will provide a single focus for struggles to socially regulate investment decisions and to create a more balanced, egalitarian, and ecologically sound form of production and distribution.

The progressive response to neoliberalism needs to be organized at national, international, and global levels if it is to succeed. Democratic socialists should be wary of strategies that focus only on economic nationalism and national autarchy as a response to economic globalization. Socialism in one country has never worked in the past, and it certainly will not work in a world that is more interlinked than ever before. The old forms of progressive internationalism were somewhat premature, but internationalism has finally become not only desirable but also necessary. This does not mean that local, regional, and national-level struggles are irrelevant. They are just as relevant as they always have been. But they need to also have a global strategy and global-level cooperation lest they be isolated and defeated. Communications technology can certainly be an important tool for the kinds of long-distance interactions that will be required for truly international cooperation and coordination among popular movements. It would be a mistake to pit global strategies against national or local ones. All fronts should be the focus of a coordinated effort.

W. Warren Wagar (1996) has proposed the formation of a "World Party" as an instrument of "mundialization"—the creation of a global socialist commonwealth. His proposal has been critiqued from many angles—as a throwback to the Third International and so forth. I suggest that Wagar's idea is a good one, that a party of the sort he is advocating will indeed emerge, and that it will contribute a great deal toward bringing about a more humane world-system. Self-doubt and postmodern reticence may make such a direct approach appear Napoleonic. It is certainly necessary to learn from past mistakes, but this should not prevent our debating the pros and cons of positive action.

The international segment of the world capitalist class is indeed moving slowly toward global state formation. The World Trade Organization is only the latest element in this process. Rather than simply oppose this move with a return to nationalism, progressives should make every effort to organize social and political globalization and to democratize the emerging global state. We need to prevent the normal operation of the interstate system and future hegemonic rivalry from causing another war among core powers (e.g., Wagar 1992; see also Bornschier and Chase-Dunn 1998). And we need to shape the emerging world society into a global democratic commonwealth based on collective rationality, liberty, and equality. This possibility is present in existing and evolving structures. The agents are all those

who are tired of wars and hatred and who desire a humane, sustainable, and fair world-system. This is certainly a majority of the people of the Earth.

In conclusion, the main point is that the semiperiphery remains the weak link of global capitalism—the structural region where the contradictions between core and periphery and between classes intersect powerfully to generate antisystemic movements. But Terry Boswell and I have also argued that the post-Communist societies are less likely than other semiperipheral countries to generate strong support for future democratic socialist movements (Chase-Dunn and Boswell 1999). Also, I do not expect antisystemic movements to take state power through revolutionary upheavals again. Rather, the much larger proletariats of the non-post-Communist semiperipheral countries and the availability of support from allied groups in the core and the periphery will make it possible for these movements to win legal elections. This path will have a much better chance of avoiding the pitfalls of authoritarianism and war. That is why I am optimistic about the prospects for democratic socialism. But as before, socialism in one country will not work. The semiperipheral socialist governments of the future will necessarily have to join the transnational movements for globalization from below.

References

Amin, Samir. 1990. *Delinking: Towards polycentric world*. London: Zed Press.

———. 1992. *Empire of chaos*. New York: Monthly Review Books.

Bollen, Kenneth A., and Pamela M. Paxton. 1997. Democracy before Athens. In *Inequality, democracy and economic development*, edited by Manus Midlarsky, 13-44. Cambridge, UK: Cambridge University Press.

Bornschier, Volker, and Christopher Chase-Dunn, eds. 1998. *The future of global conflict*. London: Sage.

Borocz, Jozsef. 1999. From comprador state to auctioneer state: Property change, realignment and peripheralization in post-state-socialist Central Europe. In *States and sovereignty in the global economy*, edited by David A. Smith, Dorothy Solinger, and Steven Topik, 193-209. London: Routledge.

Boswell, Terry, and Christopher Chase-Dunn. 2000. *The spiral of capitalism and socialism: Toward global democracy*. Boulder, CO: Lynne Reinner Publishers.

Boswell, Terry, and Ralph Peters. 1990. State socialism and the industrial divide in the world-economy: A comparative essay on the rebellions in Poland and China. *Critical Sociology* 17 (1): 3-35.

Chase-Dunn, Christopher, and Terry Boswell. 1999. Postcommunism and the global commonwealth. *Humboldt Journal of Social Relations* 24 (1-2): 195-219.

Chase-Dunn, Christopher, and Thomas D. Hall. 1997. *Rise and demise: Comparing world-systems*. Boulder, CO: Westview.

Chirot, Daniel, ed. 1991. *The crisis of Leninism and the decline of the Left: The revolutions of 1989*. Seattle: University of Washington Press.

Engels, Friedrich. 1935. *Socialism: Utopian and scientific*. New York: International.

Frank, Andre Gunder. 1998. *Reorient: Global economy in the Asian age*. Berkeley: University of California Press.

Goldstein, Joshua. 1988. *Long cycles: Prosperity and war in the modern age*. New Haven, CT: Yale University Press.

Hobsbawm, Eric. 1994. *The age of extremes: A history of the world, 1914-1991*. New York: Pantheon.

Lupher, Mark. 1996. *Power restructuring in China and Russia*. Boulder, CO: Westview.

Robinson, William I. 1996. *Promoting polyarchy: Globalization, US intervention and hegemony*. Cambridge, UK: Cambridge University Press.

Rueschemeyer, Dietrich, Evelyn Huber Stephens, and John D. Stephens. 1992. *Capitalist development and democracy*. Chicago: University of Chicago Press.

Shannon, Richard Thomas. 1996. *An introduction to the world-systems perspective*. Boulder, CO: Westview.

Soros, George. 1998. *The crisis of global capitalism*. New York: Pantheon.

Wagar, W. Warren. 1992. *A short history of the future*. Chicago: University of Chicago Press.

———. 1996. Toward a praxis of world integration. *Journal of World-Systems Research* 2 (1). Retrieved from http://csf.colorado.edu/wsystems/jwsr.html.

ANNALS, *AAPSS*, **581**, May 2002

Beyond the Tobin Tax: Global Democracy and a Global Currency

By MYRON FRANKMAN

ABSTRACT: The twin phenomena of erratic changes in foreign exchange rates and massive international flows of funds have been important elements in the instability of the world economy since the breakdown of the Bretton Woods system. The much-discussed Tobin Tax proposal on foreign exchange transactions is one response to these disturbances, but it addresses symptoms, not causes. James Tobin recognizes that a world currency with supporting institutions would be preferable. A world of competing currencies imposes a uniform policy template on countries in much the same way that the nineteenth-century gold standard did. The case is made here that a global currency not only offers a solution to the current impasses but also is a necessary component in the shaping of a global democracy, which will restore scope for diversity to the world's constituent parts.

Myron Frankman has been a member of the McGill University Department of Economics and Centre for Developing Areas Studies in Montreal since 1967. He holds a Ph.D. in economics from the University of Texas at Austin. His recent work focuses on institutional responses to globalization within a framework of global democratic federalism.

Let us suppose that all countries had the same currency, as in the progress of political improvement they one day will have. . . . So much of barbarism, however, still remains in the transactions of the most civilized nations that almost all independent countries choose to assert their nationality by having to their own inconvenience and that of their neighbors, a peculiar currency of their own. (Mill 1865, II:175-76)

Canaries were once used in underground mines to warn of impending danger. Today, we who live on the surface in the full (now dangerous) light of the sun have countless warning signs that should spur us to act, among which are disappearing species, holes in the ozone layer, falling water tables, rising sea levels, increasing income inequality, periodic financial contagion, and a rise in the incidence of civil wars. If life (as we know it) on Earth is to continue throughout the twenty-first century and beyond, humanity will need to engage in institutional innovation on a major scale. The rules of the Westphalian state system, of the Bretton Woods system, and of the Washington consensus of the 1980s and 1990s are no longer appropriate, if they ever were, to maintain the peace between the peoples of the world. The scale changes associated with changes in transportation, communications, certain types of production, and human impact on the Earth call out for changes in the scale of institutional arrangements to ensure the enjoyment of human security for the world's people. As long as nations do not meet as equals and the voice of the people is ignored, the functional internationalism that characterizes our fragmented approach to global governance is no longer sufficient.

Once again, as during the epoch of the gold standard, the free market ideal is invoked to provide a unifying overlay for global order. As Karl Polanyi (1957) remarked of the earlier period, "currency had become the pivot of national politics. . . . Men and women everywhere appeared to regard stable money as the supreme need of human society" (p. 24). He went on to describe the pervasive hold of this template on societies:

It would be hard to find any divergence between utterances of Hoover and Lenin, Churchill and Mussolini, on this point. Indeed the essentiality of the gold standard to the functioning of the international economic system of the time was the one and only tenet common to men of all nations and all classes, religious denominations, and social philosophies. It was the invisible reality to which the will to live could cling, when mankind braced itself to the task of restoring its crumbling existence. (P. 25)

Currency is still the pivot of national politics, and the foreign exchange rate remains the key pressure point for the application of external influence, should commitment to the demands of the system waver. It would appear that 150 years after Mill (1865) advanced the idea of a world currency, so much of barbarism still remains in international interactions that talk of such an eventuality has not made it onto the political agenda.

Local and global democracy cannot flourish in an increasingly interdependent world where the balancing of external payments and exchange rate management remain central national policy considerations. The need for countries with separate currencies to compete tends to impose a uniform policy template on countries. A global currency as part of a framework of global democratic institutions offers the promise of restoring the scope for diversity to the constituent parts of the global landscape.

THE UNFULFILLED PROMISE OF FREE TRADE

Today's most active global project is not that of shaping solidarity but rather that of extending the domain of free trade and free markets. Partisans of this political agenda argue, based on the theory of comparative advantage, that overwhelmingly favorable outcomes can be expected to result from the opening of a country's markets to free trade: income differentials between countries are expected to diminish. In the most elaborate theoretical expression of the free trade model, wages in two countries trading exclusively with each other will equalize (as will the returns to the owners of capital) without international migration (or movement of capital) (Samuelson 1949).

The past fifty years have been a period of rapid expansion of world trade and have shown a general tendency toward the opening of external markets. It is appropriate to ask whether the equality-increasing promise of free trade has been realized on a global scale. While no definitive test of assumption-ridden

abstract economic models is possible, there is sufficient evidence to suggest that free trade on its own has failed to produce the outcome that is its principal justification. To cite but a few signs of growing income inequality, the United Nations Development Programme's (UNDP's) (1999) *Human Development Report 1999* reported that the ratio of the income share of the one-fifth of the world's people living in the richest countries to that of the one-fifth living in the world's poorest countries has gone from 30:1 in 1960, to 61:1 in 1991, to 86:1 by the late 1990s and that the assets of the world's three richest individuals exceeded the combined GNP of the 600 million people living in the world's poorest countries (p. 3). Rather than comparing the richest and poorest countries, the more appropriate ratio would require data relating the income of the richest 20 percent of the world's people with that of the world's poorest 20 percent, regardless of place of residence. An estimate of the latter published by the UNDP (1992) in its *Human Development Report 1992* gave the figure for people (140:1) as more than twice that for countries (65:1) in 1988 (p. 36).

There seems to be a means-ends confusion in the espousal of free trade. If the real objective is that of reducing the divergence in income differentials and free trade is merely a vehicle for doing so, then it seems appropriate that either other policies must accompany free trade or a different means must be sought. Within nations, we have a long tradition of trying to offset the income- (and power-) concentrating effects of market activity with combinations of regulation, taxation, and expenditure. Living together sustainably and in peace would seem to require that such offsets be established at the global level.

CAPITAL MOBILITY AND THE GOLDEN STRAIGHTJACKET

Creating a world of capital mobility has been the mission of the International Monetary Fund (IMF) during the past two decades, even though no provision for such an initiative is contained in the Articles of Agreement of the Fund. As many high-ranking government officials and even heads of state are economists, pursuit of capital liberalization has not always required the fund to exercise its leverage on indebted states. The power of hegemonic discourse paves the path. In the Panglossion world of Thomas Friedman (1999), what countries are being asked to do is to don a golden straightjacket, a garment that we produce in exchange for the (minor) sacrifice of a measure of sovereignty. Missing from the arguments for liberalizing trade and capital flows is any hint that substantial regressive changes in distribution of income are the necessary consequences.

Courses in international economics are customarily taught in two parts: international trade and international payments. Trade is the realm of the pure (or barter) theory. Exchange-rate changes are not part of trade theory, and prices are expressed in terms of how much of one good exchanges for another. When payments are taken up,

economists deal with formal models where small changes are assumed to prevail and where the ever-present caveat "other things being equal" is a reasonable first approximation. Here one reads sanguine discussions about balance-of-payment adjustment, a process by which exchange-rate changes will lead to a reallocation of productive resources, thereby reestablishing an equilibrium situation. The practices of the IMF itself originally reflected the fair weather assumptions of exchange rate theory: that a single small devaluation would be sufficient for a country to reallocate resources in a timely manner to attain a new equilibrium rate and the country could sail on undisturbed on a tranquil sea of economic relations between countries.

One can question the adequacy of such analyses (and associated policy recommendations) in a world in which the value of daily foreign exchange transactions is in the trillions of U.S. dollars and where the ratio of the annual value of currency sales to the value of world exports exceeds 100:1 (Bank for International Settlements 1999). In this world, exchange-rate change is more likely to be driven by capital flows than by trade transactions. What sense is there when exchange rates between the world's major currencies change by a larger percentage in one day (which often reverses itself) than they did during the two decades from 1950 to 1970? For example, in the twenty years from 1950 to 1970, the value of the Japanese yen appreciated relative to the U.S. dollar by a mere 1 percent. In contrast, during the period from 7 March to 5 June

2001, there were eight occasions when the yen-dollar day's end exchange rate changed by at least 1 percent. Far more significant was an increase of more than 80 percent in the number of yen per dollar from 79 in 1995 to 145 in 1998 (Goldstein 1999). These changes can be thought of as equivalent to erratic variations in taxes (subsidies) on all foreign transactions.

Worse yet, in the context of developing countries, it is not uncommon for the price of the local currency to increase relative to the U.S. dollar by 50 percent or more within a single year. The figures in Table 1 for countries, other than the industrial country members of the Organization for Economic Cooperation and Development, with populations of 25 million or more provide a clear indication of the instability that has plagued the poorer countries of the world in the past two decades. To keep the table relatively uncluttered, for instances wherein the ratio of exchange-rate change during the period indicated exceeded 10,000 (even exceeding 1 trillion in the case of Brazil and the Democratic Republic of the Congo), I have substituted a symbol (>>) for the actual numbers. With the exceptions of South Korea and Thailand, where the exchange rate merely doubled (roughly) during two decades, and Myanmar, which has retained external controls, the record is overwhelmingly one of successive major shocks that doubtless have distorted, rather than efficiently allocated, resources.

The oft-quoted remark by John Maynard Keynes (1936) about speculation is particularly applicable for

TABLE 1

RATIO OF CHANGES IN END-OF-YEAR EXCHANGE RATES (ORIGINALLY EXPRESSED IN HOME CURRENCY UNITS / U.S.$)

	1990/ 1980	2000/ 1990	2000/ 1980
Algeria	3.1	6.2	19.0
Argentina	>>	1.8	>>
Bangladesh	2.2	1.5	3.3
Brazil	>>	>>	>>
China	3.4	1.6	5.4
Colombia	11.2	3.8	42.9
Democratic Republic of the Congo	>>	>>	>>
Egypt	2.9	1.8	5.3
Ethiopia	1.0	4.0	4.0
India	2.3	2.6	5.9
Indonesia	3.0	5.0	15.3
Iran	0.9	34.6	31.3
Kenya	3.2	3.2	10.3
Korea	1.1	1.8	1.9
Mexico	180.2	2.3	411.6
Morocco	1.9	1.3	2.5
Myanmar[a]	1.0	1.0	1.0
Nigeria	16.5	12.2	201.4
Pakistan	2.2	1.3	2.8
Peru	>>	6.8	>>
Philippines	3.7	1.8	6.6
Poland	206.3	4.4	899.7
Russia[b]		67.9	
South Africa	3.4	3.0	10.2
Tanzania	24.0	4.1	98.2
Thailand	1.2	1.7	2.0
Turkey	32.6	229.8	7482.1
Ukraine[b]		849.1	

SOURCE: International Monetary Fund (1988, 1994, 2001).

NOTE: >> = greater than 10,000. Data for Vietnam, which is not a member of the International Monetary Fund, are not reported here.

a. Figures for Myanmar reflect that its currency is fixed in terms of SDRs (special drawing rights).

b. Russia and Ukraine: rate change from 1992 to 2000.

most of the less developed countries: "the position is serious when enterprise becomes a bubble on a whirlpool of speculation. When the capital development of a country becomes a by-product of the activities of the casino, the job is likely to be ill done" (p. 159).

After the collapse of the fixed exchange rate component of the Bretton Woods system in the early 1970s, Robert Triffin (1986) referred to the scandal of the existence of a nonsystem. Equally scandalous are both the nonsystem where the poor peoples of the world are progressively marginalized by a framework that concentrates gains in the hands of the few and the general lack of attention by either scholars or policy makers to the role of exchange rate adjustment in the generation of inequality.

Apart from capital controls, suggested policy responses to the problems related to market instability arising from capital mobility have taken divergent approaches ranging from a tax on foreign exchange transactions, proposals for reforming the international financial architecture, and "dollarization." All are essentially variations of within-the-box thinking on market themes with little or no direct attention given to distributional issues.

THE TOBIN TAX

The Tobin Tax on foreign exchange transactions, originally proposed by James Tobin in 1972 (Tobin 1974) and then reiterated in 1978 (Tobin 1978), is an example of a partial measure originally proposed for a single purpose, that of discouraging speculative international financial transactions. The proposal was first

rescued from oblivion by those who began to see the tax as a major source of funding for international development. Various estimates indicated that fabulous sums could be realized on the assumption that the tax, which was intended to dampen financial flows, would in fact not do so (were the tax to be successful, the flows, and with them the revenues from the tax, would diminish). Such data as are available on the, by now, at least $2 trillion of average daily foreign exchange transactions, which are published at intervals of three years by the Bank for International Settlements, undoubtedly underestimate the degree of currency transactions insofar as not all financial centers participate in the survey. Even at 0.1 percent per transaction (0.5 percent is commonly suggested for the tax) and assuming the value of transactions actually taxed would be one-half of the current value, annual revenues would still amount to more than one-third of a trillion dollars, more than the combined amount of private capital flows and net official development assistance to the less developed countries in 1998.

As the dangers of capital hypermobility became palpable, Tobin's argument for throwing sand in the wheels of international finance became the object of serious consideration both among economists and policy makers. The capital flight stampedes from Mexico, Indonesia, and South Korea, among others, in the past decade helped sustain interest in a transaction tax on foreign exchange deals. Ironically, these extreme circumstances are also instances where exchange-rate changes (anticipated and actual) were of such a magnitude that a transaction tax of 0.5 percent on currency conversion would hardly have been a deterrent.

The Tobin Tax proposal addresses symptoms, not causes. If exchange rates that are subject to variation are at the heart of capital hypermobility, then a tax would at best mitigate the problem in certain contexts. Tobin, himself, has made it clear that a world currency with supporting institutions would be preferable:

A permanent single currency, as among the 50 states of the American union, would escape all this turbulence. The United States example shows that a currency union works to great advantage when sustained not only by centralized monetary authorities but also by other common institutions. In the absence of such institutions, an irrevocably unique world currency is many decades off. (UNDP 1994, 70)

FLEXIBLE RATES: REFORMING THE INTERNATIONAL FINANCIAL ARCHITECTURE

Following the east Asian financial crisis of 1997-1998, a frenzy of discussion of reforming the international financial architecture was launched. At least four different sets of recommendations emerged from these deliberations. The Joint Economic Committee of the U.S. House of Representatives and Senate commissioned a study by a group headed by Allan Meltzer (International Financial Institution Advisory Commission 2000). The New York–based Council on Foreign Relations com-

missioned an independent task force under the direction of Morris Goldstein (1999); the IMF (2000) and the United Nations (1999), not be left out, also produced reports.

At the conclusion of extended reflection on a new financial architecture, we find reaffirmation of the (preexisting) theological divisions between advocacy of fixed and flexible as one of the outcomes of the debate. Flexible rates are clearly gaining the upper hand and are endorsed by the Meltzer Commission, the Goldstein Task Force, and the IMF. As the Goldstein (1999) report put it, "The Currency Regime: Just Say No to Supporting Pegged Exchange Rates." Yet this is likely to skew activities even more toward the traded goods sector, particularly export goods, and as with the exchange rate discourse in general, it ignores the income distribution effects of what for many Third World countries will simply be a situation of continuously living with depreciating rates. As always, discussion of external payments focuses either at the rarefied level of abstract macroeconomic variables or on the interests of the elite actors directly affected by external transactions. George Soros, a member of the Goldstein Commission, in a dissenting view took exception to a "bias that permeates the report": precisely that of favoring those at the center of the global capitalist system and the disadvantaging of the economies at the periphery (Goldstein 1999).

The last major episode of experimentation with patching up the fixed exchange rate aspect of the Bretton

Woods system in the 1960s and early 1970s led to the creation of the largely stillborn Special Drawing Rights, to swaps between central banks, to a gold pool, to crawling peg exchange-rate regimes, and ultimately to a partial demonetization of gold and generalized floating rates between industrial countries. Indeed the latter is one of the weaknesses of the current system, a point addressed by yet another Goldstein report dissent, which included among its adherents C. Fred Bergsten, George Soros, and Paul Volcker. They spoke of "the complications for the conduct of any sensible exchange rate policy by emerging-market economies when the exchange rates [dollar, euro, yen] among their major trading partners move so erratically" (Goldstein 1999). And so the latest round in the debate leaves us with proposals that urge more tinkering to make an outmoded system work; as Roy Culpeper (2000) observed, the focus tends to be on plumbing, rather than architecture, whatever the rhetoric may be.

FIXED RATES: DOLLARIZATION

Countries that have endured successive economic crises may well be ripe to consider something completely different. There is no shortage of easy-to-apply miracle cures on offer. Full dollarization (defined as the use of a foreign currency by another country) is just such a form of snake oil cure that may be worse than the disease. This goes beyond the notion of an ostensibly irrevocable peg to the U.S. dollar (as in

Argentina), to actually abandoning one's currency. If resorting to an inflationary monetary policy is an irresistible urge for a nation's policy makers, a logical solution might seem to be the abandonment of the national currency. However, dollarization without any compensatory transfers is a sure recipe for either crisis or pauperization in the countries signing up. There may be a short honeymoon brought by stability of economic relations, but more likely than not, deflation, unemployment, and political tension will follow.

In support of dollarization, proponents shamefacedly invoke Panama as a paragon of the advantages to be had through dollarization. The authors of the IMF's pamphlet on full dollarization invoke the example of Panama twice and refer to it within the same sentence as being "the only sizable country with a history of using a foreign currency" and of being "fairly small" (Berg and Borensztein 2000, 5). This "sizable" country, with a population of 3 million, also happens to have one-quarter of its population living on less than $2 per day. The only distributional costs of dollarization that are commonly identified are the insignificant one-time cost to the dollarizing country of buying up local currency in circulation and the loss of the seigniorage that results from the difference between the face value of currency and its cost of production.

Whatever ails the economy, dollarization is said to be the cure. Proponents of dollarization have even been working overtime to sell this idea in Canada. At least one recent study projects a 37 percent increase in GDP that would follow Canada's adoption of the U.S. dollar (Hunter 2001). Missing from the dollarization scenario are considerations of both equity and control, democratic or otherwise. In the Canadian context, mention is occasionally made of the possible creation of a thirteenth Federal Reserve district and bank; for smaller countries, voice is assumed to be irrelevant. Moreover, the default setting that has been promoted by central bankers and the IMF is that of the indispensability of *central bank independence*, a term used so often that it even has its own acronym, CBI. Independence from whom? An apolitical policy is an oxymoron. CBI is nothing more than a smoke screen substituting elite-technocrat control for democratic rule, the apparent necessity of which springs from the failings of our current system of a multitude of separate currencies.

In fact, the benefits held out for full dollarization (avoidance of currency crises, closer integration, avoidance of inflationary finance) are also the benefits that would apply to a world currency. Dollarization is the solution of political simplicity: no elaborate negotiations, no compromises, and no institution building are required. A world money, in contrast, if it is to avoid the pitfalls of our jerry-built currency system, must be the fruit of major commitment and major effort to build global democratic federalism, as was the case with the building of European federalism and the creation of the European Union and the euro.

GLOBAL CURRENCY AND GLOBAL DEMOCRACY

Europe is providing a trial-and-error pilot project for the world. At the time of this writing, twelve of the fifteen members of the European Union have agreed to abandon their national currencies and by many accounts are reaping the benefits of this change, which go well beyond considerations of the euro-dollar exchange rate. The appropriate next step is to work toward a global currency and not to create regional currencies that will still remain within the framework of national competitiveness—a system of domination rather than cooperation.

The *Economist* made the case for a world currency at least twice during the past thirteen years. It addressed the question editorially on 9-15 January 1988 and proclaimed on the cover of that issue, "Get Ready for a World Currency." Ten years later, in "One World, One Money" (1998), it renewed its statement in support of a single world currency, finding all the post–east Asian crisis proposals to be far too modest in light of the circumstances. In the author's words, "in difficult times, people are allowed, even encouraged, to think the unthinkable," which for the author was a "global currency union" (One world, one money 1998). Readers were reminded of Richard Cooper's (1984) endorsement of a single world currency:

A one-currency regime is much too radical to envisage in the near future. But it is not too radical to envisage 25 years from now, and indeed some such scheme or its functional equivalent, will be necessary to avoid retrogression into greater reliance on barriers to international trade and financial transactions. Moreover, it is useful to have a "vision," . . . some idea of where we would like to get to provides a sense of direction for the next steps. (P. 181).

Cooper's (1984) target date of 2009 may not be so far-fetched. As the *Economist* went on to note, if the euro succeeds, "the case for a global currency union will seem much more interesting" (One world, one money 1998). The important distinction in the case of the euro is that it is not a disembodied market solution but rather one that is clearly embedded in a sociopolitical context of democratic decision making, where offsets to adverse market outcomes can, in principle, be implemented.

Inertia has beset us for too long. Diagnoses are made and the next (giant) step seems clear, but analysts are too much the realists to embrace the logical conclusion. The nation continues to be the default setting for many in considering policy options. Barry Eichengreen's (1994) *International Monetary Arrangements for the 21st Century* seems to suffer from this mental impediment. His book starts with a quote by Richard Cooper, the last sentence of which is, "Exchange rates can be most credibly fixed if they are eliminated altogether, that is, if international transactions take place with a single currency" (cited in Eichengreen 1994, ix). Eichengreen goes on to say, "The argument of this book is that contingent policy rules designed to hit explicit exchange rate targets will no longer be viable in the twenty-first century" (p. 4). Well? In fact, there is

no chapter in Eichengreen's book on a world currency, no entry for *world currency* or a suitable synonym in the index. Incredibly, while James Meade (1940) devoted a full chapter to a world currency to be put in place after the Second World War, Eichengreen, given a century-long interval to contemplate, seemed unable or unwilling to detach himself from today's realities to explore the implications of a leap of imagination involving major institutional innovation.

CONCLUSION

Currencies are one symbolic element of our imagined national communities: a vestige of sovereignty that some of us resist parting with, even when the largest share of our transactions is increasingly electronic. Indeed, as far as the receipt of income is concerned, it is unlikely that anyone reading these lines receives a periodic cash payment in compensation for service rendered to an employer. And yet we struggle mightily, as Mill (1865) observed, to preserve separate currencies. As our consciousness of the interconnection of circumstances from the local to the global grows daily, so does our inclination to reexamine the default settings that limit our options. We are aware that national governments, while not impotent, are limited in their abilities to serve the needs of their citizens. A reflection of this awareness can be found in the title of a recent op-ed piece on the benefits of (European) federalism by Timothy Garton Ash (2001): "Joining the Continent To Unite the Kingdom."

The Utopian rarely spells out convincingly, if at all, how we get from here to there. As the *Economist* (One world, one money 1998) noted, "find the answer to that and the idea [of a global currency] would be thinkable." The first step in getting from here to there is to challenge assumptions, suggest alternatives, and open discussion. The path in democracies is rarely predictable, and in the fullness of debate even the best ideas are often improved. What would a country require to willingly abandon an exchange rate? In Europe, a satisfactory answer to that question has been found for most, but not all, of the European Union members. What is necessary is not only a fuller appreciation of the limits of having a separate currency but convincing commitments to provide compensation to those disadvantaged by market outcomes. Perhaps the most attractive prospect of deeper political and economic integration is that of retaining and rebuilding local diversity and control that has been compromised by the imperatives of the golden straightjacket and the complementary requirement that each nation pay its own way through export promotion.

The acceptance of a single world currency requires the renunciation of many nationalist pretensions, both symbolic and real. Whether the discussion relates to free trade, the role of markets exchange rate arrangements, or other economic policies, unless there is serious democratically controlled global policy innovation, the outcome will likely be a situation where the devil takes the hindmost, as is currently the case.

Economic management for a stable world that does not threaten its own survival requires us to begin in earnest on the next stage of institutional innovation: the reality of a world money and the institutional framework that goes with it.

Building national imagined communities required ingenuity and sustained effort over lengthy periods. For those who have added a European identity to their basket of loyalties, the possibility of adding at least one more allegiance should appear to be a plausible project. For most of the rest of us, this is likely to seem an unthinkably giant step. Nonetheless, imagining a world community and building world-scale democratic institutions may well be the only peaceful and sustainable way out of our increasingly strife-prone global race to the bottom.

References

Ash, Timothy Garton. 2001. Joining the continent to unite the kingdom. *New York Times*, 17 June.

Bank for International Settlements. 1999. *Central bank survey of foreign exchange and derivatives market activity 1998*. Basle, Switzerland: Bank for International Settlements. Retrieved from http://www.bis.org/publ/r_fx98finaltxt.pdf.

Berg, Andrew, and Eduardo Borensztein. 2000. *Full Dollarization: The pros and cons*. Economics issues 24. Washington, DC: International Monetary Fund.

Cooper, Richard. 1984. A monetary system for the future. *Foreign Affairs* 63 (fall): 166-84.

Culpeper, Roy. 2000. Systemic reform at a standstill: A flock of "G's" in search of global financial stability. Ottawa,

Canada: North-South Institute. Retrieved from http://www.nsi-ins.ca/download/Gs_eng.pdf.

Eichengreen, Barry. 1994. *International monetary arrangements for the 21st century.* Washington, DC: Brookings Institution.

Friedman, Thomas L. 1999. *The Lexus and the olive tree.* New York: Farrar, Straus and Giroux.

Goldstein, Morris. 1999. *Safeguarding prosperity in a global financial system: The future international financial architecture.* Report of an independent task force. Washington, DC: Institute for International Economics.

Hunter, Justine. 2001. US dollar could lift our economy 37%. *National Post,* 19 May 19.

International Financial Institution Advisory Commission. 2000. *Report.* Retrieved from http://www.house.gov/hec/imf/meltzer.htm.

International Monetary Fund (IMF). 1988. *International financial statistics yearbook.* Vol. 41. Washington, DC: International Monetary Fund.

———. 1994. *International financial statistics yearbook.* Vol. 47. Washington, DC: International Monetary Fund.

———. 2000. *Report of the acting managing director to the International Monetary and Financial Committee on progress in reforming the IMF and strengthening the architecture of the international financial system.* Retrieved from http://www.imf.org.external/np/omd/2000/report.htm.

———. 2001. *International financial statistics yearbook.* Vol. 54. Washington, DC: International Monetary Fund.

Keynes, John Maynard. 1936. *The general theory of employment, interest and money.* London: Macmillan.

Meade, James E. 1940. *The economic basis of a durable peace.* New York: Oxford University Press.

Mill, John Stuart. 1865. *Principles of political economy.* 5th London ed. New York: D. Appleton.

One world, one money. 1998. *Economist,* 26 September-2 October, 80.

Polanyi, Karl. 1957. *The great transformation.* Boston: Beacon.

Samuelson, Paul. 1949. International factor-price equalisation once again. *Economic Journal* 59 (June): 181-97.

Tobin, James. 1974. The new economics one decade older. *Eliot Janeway Lectures, 1972.* Princeton, NJ: Princeton University Press.

———. 1978. A proposal for international monetary reform. *Eastern Economic Journal* 4 (3-4): 153-59.

Triffin, Robert. 1986. Correcting the world monetary scandal. *Challenge* 28 (January/February): 4-14.

United Nations. 1999. *Towards a new international financial architecture: Report of the Task Force of the Executive Committee on Economic and Social Affairs of the United Nations.* New York: United Nations.

United Nations Development Programme (UNDP). 1992. *Human development report 1992.* New York: Oxford University Press.

———. 1994. *Human development report 1994.* New York: Oxford University Press.

———. 1999. *Human development report 1999.* New York: Oxford University Press.

ANNALS, *AAPSS*, **581**, May 2002

Neoliberalism and the Regulation of Global Labor Mobility

By HENK OVERBEEK

ABSTRACT: Globalization involves the international expansion of market relations and the global pursuit of economic liberalism. The essential factor in this process is commodification, including the commodification of human labor. Globalization integrates an increasing proportion of the world population directly into capitalist labor markets and locks national and regional labor markets into an integrated global labor market. We are on the threshold of global initiatives to shift the balance even further, especially regarding the management of global migration flows. The answer cannot be a return to strictly national forms of migration control and should not be a complete capitulation to market-driven regulation of migration. One possible answer is a new, multilateral, democratically screened, global migration regime to set forth and guarantee the general principles governing the regulation of transnational migrations, ensure proper coordination between regional and national migration regimes, and call into existence new institutional forms of transnational democratic governance.

Henk Overbeek is an associate professor in international relations at the Free University, Amsterdam. He received his master's degree and Ph.D. at the University of Amsterdam, where he taught international politics between 1976 and 1999. He is also an adjunct professor at Webster University in Leiden. His research interests are primarily in international political economy. He is coeditor of the RIPE Series in Global Political Economy *(Routledge) and serves on the international editorial board of the* Review of International Political Economy. *His publications include* Global Capitalism and National Decline: The Thatcher Decade in Perspective *(1990),* Restructuring in the Global Political Economy *(editor, 1993), and* The Political Economy of European (Un)Employment *(forthcoming).*

GLOBALIZATION is a sociopolitical project involving the "worldwide application of laissez-faire principles" (Munck 2002 [this issue]). Yet the principles of laissez-faire are unevenly applied to different categories of commodities in the global political economy today. The zeal with which the free movement of goods is pursued through the World Trade Organization (WTO), or the free movement of capital promoted by the International Monetary Fund (IMF), is contrasted by the hostility of most governments and international organizations toward the free movement of labor.

A closer look at the real nature of the globalization project will reveal that this paradox entails no contradiction. After all, the globalization project is about the freedom of capital to maximize its accumulation potential, not about libertarian ideals.

Second, this article investigates the emerging global and regional regulatory structures whose purpose it is to accommodate capital's freedom to accumulate as far as it concerns the movement of labor. It will be argued that these new modes of governance are characterized by their informal and disciplinary nature, thus demonstrating the severely negative implications for democratic accountability of those involved in policy making.

The final argument of this article will be that there is a contradiction between untrammeled commodification on one hand and emancipation from bondage and deprivation on the other. To prevent the regulation of global migration from privileging deeper commodification over emancipation, transparency and accountability in the institutional setup are indispensable. The article advocates consensual multilateralism instead of de facto bilateralism.

NEOLIBERAL GLOBALIZATION AND MOBILITY

Neoliberal globalization is both process and project. While it is important to emphasize the role of agency in globalization, it is equally important to understand the process of structural transformation involved. Globalization is a dialectical phenomenon simultaneously circumscribed by agency and structure mutually constitutive of each other, or to borrow Robert Cox's (1981) phrase, a "historical structure." Viewed in this way, globalization consists in the dialectic between the expansion of market relations on one hand and the pursuit of economic liberalism on the other. In its late twentieth/early twenty-first century manifestation, globalization is reaching new highs, or should we say new depths.

Globalization entails a qualitative transformation in the political, economic, cultural, strategic, and technological worlds around us of which I mention three elements: the compression of time and space, the rise of a market-oriented neoliberal politico-economic order, and the transition in world politics from the bipolar cold war order of system rivalry to the present unipolar NATO-American order.

The essential moving factor of this process is the expansion of the market: ever more people, countries, and regions are incorporated into the global market economy (expansion as geographic widening), and more and more spheres and dimensions of human existence are invaded by market relations and subordinated to the pursuit of private profit (expansion as deepening).

This deepening commodification takes place through three interrelated processes, namely, the transnationalization of production, the globalization of financial markets, and the tendential emergence of a global labor market. The first two aspects of what is commonly called globalization are abundantly documented in much of the globalization literature. These aspects, although by no means beyond dispute, need not be addressed here. For the purposes of this contribution, it is more relevant to focus on the third element.

In their path-breaking study of the new international division of labor of the 1970s, the German researchers Fröbel, Heinrichs, and Kreye (1977) observed an accelerating relocation of labor-intensive production processes from the older industrial economies to low wage countries in Asia and Latin America. Three preconditions made this relocation drive possible: the existence of a sheer inexhaustible reservoir of cheap labor in large parts of the Third World, new production technologies' making it possible to separate the labor-intensive parts of the production process from the capital-intensive parts, and new transport and communication technologies' facilitating the coordination of dispersed production and assembly

establishments. The authors concluded that "the conjuncture of these three conditions . . . has created a single world market for labor power, a true worldwide industrial reserve army, and a single world market for production sites" (p. 30, author's translation). Crucial for this argument is that as a consequence of the rapid development of new communication and information technology, foreign direct investment (FDI) became a functional alternative not only to trade but also to labor migration. (Mobility of capital can substitute for the mobility of goods and labor power.)

In the core of the global system, in the Organization for Economic Cooperation and Development (OECD) countries, globalization has transformed the economy from a Fordist model (with mass production and mass consumption sustained by one or another form of welfare state) into a model of flexible accumulation (with lean production and just-in-time delivery supported by a competition state). This has had the fundamental consequence for the labor market of establishing a "core-periphery" structure within the advanced capitalist economies (Cox 1987), reflected particularly in the "peripheralization" of labor in the global cities (cf. Harris 1995; Sassen 1996a). One element of this has been the reemergence of domestic labor, another the reappearance of sweatshop production in the garment industry:

There exists within New York, the global city, a substantial growing segment of the labor force whose conditions of production resemble those of the labor force in the Third World. . . . Sweatshops in New York are the logical consequence of the global restructuring of production in the garment industry and the consequent competition for jobs between segments of the global reserve of labor. (Ross and Trachte 1983, 416)

These developments go hand in hand with, and are enhanced by, a neoliberal offensive of deregulation, liberalization, and flexibilization. While undermining the bargaining power of organized labor and helping to depress wage demands, it simultaneously creates and/or reinforces the demand for various forms of unskilled and semiskilled labor, employed under increasingly precarious conditions (Cox 1987; Sassen 1996a; Castells 1998). Undocumented immigration is quite functional from this perspective. The employment of undocumented foreign labor has thus in many cases become a condition for the continued existence of small- and medium-size firms, creating a substantial economic interest in continued (illegal) immigration (Brochmann 1993, 119-20; see also Papademetriou 1994, 27).

In more peripheral areas of the world (e.g., Africa, eastern Europe, and Central America), the two most important changes since the mid-seventies (often interacting) have been the debt crisis, the ensuing imposition of structural adjustment policies, and the end of the cold war. The Structural Adjustment Programs of the IMF and the World Bank and the withdrawal of military and economic assistance by the superpowers both resulted in a substantial reduction of external sources

of finance available for redistribution by the state. In many cases, this seriously affected the ability of governments to co-opt rivaling elites into the power structure, resulting in serious social and political crises, economic disasters, and regime change or state collapse. These complex processes largely explain the surge in forced movements of people since the mid-seventies across the globe, in search of protection and in search of a new and better life (cf. Cohen and Deng 1998; Loescher 1993; United Nations High Commissioner for Refugees 1997; Zolberg, Suhrke, and Aguayo 1989). In other cases, governments of Third World countries have turned to other sources of external income and have become intricately involved in the business of promoting outward migration of skilled workers and professionals. Through workers' remittances, the inflow of hard currency is thus increased. Worldwide, remittances have surpassed development aid as a source of foreign exchange. In 1995, worldwide remittances ran to $70 billion; in the same year, development aid total ran to $66 billion (World Bank 1997). India and Egypt are two examples of countries in which the government has taken an active role in this trade. In the 1970s, the Egyptian government "planned to expand the output of teachers in order to supply 14,000 of them to the oil-producing countries" (Harris 1995, 151). The Indian government recently announced plans to spend $650 million to double India's current annual output of 100,000 information technology graduates by

2002 and reach 500,000 by 2005 (Chanda 2000).[1]

These developments in various parts of the world show that globalization indeed integrates an increasing proportion of the world population directly into capitalist labor markets and locks national and regional labor markets into an integrated global labor market. The mechanisms that produce this effect are of three kinds.

First, we witness various forms of commodification of labor power, which was not previously bought and sold on "free" labor markets. We can think of three forms in particular:

- incorporation of previously disconnected areas (primarily former socialist economies but also the remaining precapitalist societies on the outskirts of the modern world) into the capitalist world market,
- continuing proletarianization of the world's population through urbanization and the disintegration of subsistence economies in the Third World and through increasing labor market participation in the industrial economies, and
- privatization of economic activities within capitalist societies previously organized outside the market.

Second, nationally or regionally bounded labor markets are increasingly integrated by the internationalization of production. The importance of this new form of internationalization as contrasted with the earlier phases of globalization in which commercial capital and money capital moved across borders cannot be overstated. Whereas money capital imposes an abstract and indirect discipline on labor, FDI directly reproduces capitalist relations of production within the host countries (Poulantzas 1974).[2] Transnational production has indeed become by far the most important engine of accumulation in the global economy, as is confirmed by a few key statistics:

- After a slowdown in the early 1990s, direct investments were growing explosively in the closing years of the century. As a consequence, the share of foreign investment inflows in world gross fixed capital formation has grown rapidly, from 1.1 percent in 1960 via 2.0 percent in 1980 to 7.4 percent in 1997 (United Nations Conference on Trade and Development [UNCTAD] 1994, 1998).
- By 1997, total assets of foreign affiliates of transnational corporations stood at $12.6 trillion. Sales by foreign subsidiaries reached $9.5 trillion (UNCTAD 1998, 2). In addition to FDI, through strategic alliances and other nonequity arrangements, transnational corporations gain control over assets and markets that are not measured in the statistics.
- In 1960, worldwide sales by foreign affiliates of transnational corporations were smaller than world exports, but in 1997, they stood at 148 percent of world exports (UNCTAD 1998, 2).
- One-third of world exports are exports of foreign affiliates (UNCTAD 1998, 6).
- Transnational corporations have a strong impact on the shape of the world economy: "they organize the production process internationally: by placing their affiliates worldwide under common governance systems, they interweave production activities located in different countries, create an international

intra-firm division of labor and, in the process, internalize a range of international transactions that would otherwise have taken place in the market" (UNCTAD 1994, 9).

- The rapid expansion of FDI is increasingly tied up with the explosive increase in mergers and acquisitions in the world. The total value of cross-border mergers and acquisitions in 1997 was approximately $342 billion (up from less than $100 billion in 1992), representing 58 percent of FDI flows (UNCTAD 1998, 19-20).
- Cross-border mergers and acquisitions are mostly concentrated within the developed world, thus reinforcing tremendously the process of transnationalization, the rapidly intensifying interpenetration of the economies (capital markets but also labor markets) of the OECD countries.

Third, nationally or regionally bounded labor markets are further integrated by increased international labor mobility in its various forms:

- the spread of transnational corporations brings with it increased international mobility of top- and intermediate-level managers and executives;
- the internationalization of services (engineering, advertising, software development) creates increased international mobility of technical and commercial experts;
- the combination of more restrictive immigration policies and labor market flexibilization and deregulation in the OECD countries creates increased opportunities for illegal immigration (increasingly through the intervention of organized crime); and

- the economic and political crisis of the state in many Third World countries and the resulting intensification of social and ethnic conflicts swell the ranks of international refugee movements and the outward flow of migrant workers.

With the tendential formation of a global labor market and the increased labor mobility it implies, the question of the international regulation of that mobility has gradually become a more prominent issue on the international agenda. Before we can turn to a discussion of the emerging framework for the regulation of global migration, however, we must briefly address some general issues of global governance in the neoliberal age.

GLOBALIZATION
AND GOVERNANCE

Changes in production organization and location have been accompanied by attempts at the political and ideological levels to create more transnational forms of governance. The key elements of the emerging structure of global governance can be summarized as follows (see Cox 1987; Gill 1995; McMichael 1996):

1. emerging consensus among policy makers favoring market-based over state-managed solutions,

2. centralized management of the global economy by the G-7 states, and

3. implementation and surveillance by multilateral agencies such as the World Bank, the IMF, and the WTO.

The key development in this respect is the reconfiguration of the state. State forms and functions are being transformed under the impact of, but in turn itself furthering, globalization. Global restructuring leads to (or implies) the creation of additional formal and informal structures of authority and sovereignty besides and beyond the state. With globalization and the progression of the neoliberal ideology, there has also been a strengthening of (quasi-) authoritarian structures and practices and an assault on established forms of progressive or Left popular participation. In the core areas of the world economy, this discipline appears in the shape of voluntary programs of competitive deregulation and austerity that are codified and constitutionalized in such arrangements as the Economic and Monetary Union stability pact or the WTO liberalization regime.

In peripheral areas, the discipline of the market is often externally imposed through the financial power exercised by the IMF and the World Bank, which was tremendously intensified after the debt crisis of the 1980s.

In the context of globalization, the functions of the state dealing with transnational processes are increasingly performed transnationally by a variety of state, interstate, and nonstate institutions. The state is no longer the proverbial Westphalian nation-state in which sovereignty and territoriality are exclusively combined. Indeed, the "unbundling" of sovereignty and territoriality (Ruggie 1993, 165) makes it possible for governments to circumvent the need to account for the international agreements they conclude in their own national parliaments. It has also created a greater space for social forces outside the state to become involved in new forms of regulation. The boundaries between public and private regulation and between national and international relations are becoming increasingly blurred, and policy formation in international contexts is increasingly informalized, opening up the channels of governance to nongovernmental organizations of various kinds. In a reference to the manifestation of this tendency in the area of migration policy, Saskia Sassen (1996b) observed that "we are seeing a *de facto* transnationalizing of immigration policy" in which there is "a displacement of government functions on to non-governmental or quasi-governmental institutions and criteria for legitimacy" (pp. 1, 24). It is to this particular area of global governance that we now turn.

THE EMERGENCE OF A
NEOLIBERAL FRAMEWORK FOR
THE MANAGEMENT OF MOBILITY

In the postwar order, international labor migration was hardly regulated. This provided a sharp contrast with the regulatory framework for financial relations (IMF, Bank for International Settlements) and for international trade (GATT). To be sure, there are international organizations that are concerned one way or another with the international mobility of people, such as the International Labor Organization, the International Organization for

Migration, and of course the United Nations High Commissioner for Refugees. However, the regime they form (if we may call it that) has been far weaker than the financial and trade regimes. Several explanations are possible for this state of affairs. For one, as is often observed in the migration literature, the sovereign state is assumed to be unwilling to relinquish control over who crosses its borders: "Since the development of the modern state from the fifteenth century onward, governments have regarded control over their borders as the core of sovereignty" (Weiner 1995, 9). The argument does not convince, because state sovereignty has never been absolute, nor is this an argument that would apply exclusively to migration as opposed to other cross-border traffic such as trade. A second possible explanation is the modest scale of international migration in the twentieth century. The United Nations estimated the world's foreign-born population for 1995 at 125 million or about 2 percent of the world's population (UNCTAD/International Organization for Migration 1996). Finally, during the post-1945 decades of embedded liberalism, foreign labor was available in surplus quantities, and as a consequence, states did not need to compete for scarce sources when organizing their recruitment schemes in the 1960s and 1970s (Zolberg 1991, 309, 313-4).

With the effects of globalization on the mobility of people becoming stronger, the call for an effective international migration regime also gained strength (for a survey, see Ghosh 2000). Four effects stand out:

- the growth of asylum migration to the OECD countries;
- the growing demand for cheap unskilled labor, the growth of illegal labor immigration, and the increasing involvement of organized crime with smuggling people across borders;
- the shortage of highly skilled labor in the OECD in sectors such as information and communication technology; and
- the increased mobility of upper-level managers in transnational corporations.

As a result, two seemingly contradictory tendencies are visible in the ongoing policy discussions, namely, the effort to control and reduce asylum migration and illegal migration and the call (especially since the mid-1990s) to liberalize forms of migration that are deemed economically desirable. To understand better how this contradiction translates into regulation, we must briefly analyze the interface between the various forms of factor mobility in the global economy, especially in the Americas and in Europe.

The idea of mobility is, as we have seen, usually associated with the movement of capital more than of people. In the Americas, some twenty bilateral agreements have been signed since 1990 that serve to liberalize trade and investment between South, Central, and North American countries. Here the emphasis is primarily on the subordination of migration management to the needs of capital. In Europe, the significance of arrangements facilitating the mobility of capital within the region (primarily the completion of the

Single Market and the flexibilization of labor markets) has overshadowed the number of initiatives which European capital developed in peripheral economies. Nevertheless, in the framework of increasing cooperation and economic aid, the European Union has signed a series of accession and association agreements with countries of central and eastern Europe, with the Mediterranean countries, and with the remaining states of the former Soviet Union. These agreements all have in common a number of regulations with respect to the freedom of movement of people insofar as this movement is connected to capital mobility. Freedom of establishment, freedom to migrate to set up businesses as self-employed individuals, and nondiscrimination (national treatment) of legally established firms, workers, and their families (cf. Niessen and Mochel 1999) are the key elements.[3] These rules about national treatment for investments and labor tend to have repercussions on labor markets, on industrial policies, and on judicial systems. The movement of capital requires some mobility of people as well, for labor market purposes, but also for access to land and to markets. Especially relevant here is the movement of professionals and business people whose professions are related to trade in services. Their movement is encoded in bilateral or trilateral treaties, regional agreements (NAFTA, European Economic Area), and global agreements (General Agreement on Trade in Services [GATS]) (see Ghosh 1997; OECD Système d'observation permanente des migrations 1998).

In addition to the formal arrangements the European states (east and west) have developed, there is a parallel system of informal consultations on migration issues, the so-called Budapest Group.[4] The origins of the Budapest Process go back to the events leading up to the fall of the Berlin Wall in 1989 and the disintegration of the Soviet Union. The primary objective of the consultations was to discuss measures for checking illegal migration from and through central and eastern Europe. Much emphasis was put on the need to strengthen the surveillance of borders, the conclusion of readmission agreements, and the harmonization of visa policies. Technological and financial aid was promised. During follow-up meetings, the themes that would dominate subsequent conferences became clear: criminalization of trafficking and improvement of police forces and border controls, imposition of carrier sanctions on airlines, exchange of information, conclusion of readmission agreements, and financial assistance to the central and east European countries (which were in reality the targets of these measures given their deficient or totally absent relevant legislation and policies). The statutory meeting of the Budapest Group (December 1993) reconfirmed these objectives and decided that the group would comprise senior officials from all participating states, making the Budapest Group into the only pan-European discussion forum for these issues. The issue of visa approximation was taken up at a special meeting in Portoroz (Slovenia) in September 1998. The harmonization of visa policies is to be achieved by the central and east European states aligning their policies with those of the European Union member states. In recent years, the Budapest Group has also set up an elaborate monitoring system to keep track of the progress with the implementation of agreed measures, thus acquiring a very real influence over national policy making.

In the Americas, most of the regional integration processes ignore or sidetrack the question of the movement of people. This is the case with the Mercado Común del Sur (Southern Cone Common Market), with NAFTA, and with the series of bilateral treaties on free trade in the region. Yet despite limited state regulations, labor migration represented a significant dimension of transborder economic activities, controlled mostly by the private sectors. The Puebla Process, which started in 1996 under the name Regional Conference on Migration (RCM), marks a significant step in the regionalization trend in migration control.[5] Officially, the direct trigger of the RCM was the population conference in Cairo in 1994, but it was also linked to the plans for the Free Trade Area of the Americas, which is to extend the liberalization of national economies to Central and South America. The immediate initiative for the Puebla Process came from Mexico, a country facing important pressures from both its northern partners, particularly the United States, to control the flows of people crossing the border and from its southern neighbors in the form of transit migration. The RCM's plan of action, adopted in 1997 during its second annual meeting in Panama, focused on information gathering as well as on five areas of activities: (1) the formulation of migration policies (both emigration and immigration) that would respond to the commitments of the conference, (2) migration and development, (3) combating migrant trafficking, (4) collaboration for the return of extraregional migrants, and (5) human rights. Most of the work of the RCM has been devoted, since then, to the combating of migrant trafficking while the area of activity that received the least attention was the formulation of harmonized migration policies. Yet paradoxically, some form of coordination of these policies does take place, but indirectly, notably through the promotion by the RCM of transborder and labor market cooperation schemes.

There is obviously a clear analogy between the Puebla Process and the Budapest Process in terms of which issues are central to their work. They share, in particular, emphases on the coordination of visa and migration policy, on the combating of illegal trafficking, and on the promotion of a system of readmission agreements. These informal modes of governance fulfil very specific functions. They first of all serve as channels for communication between policy makers, experts, and interested third parties. This is especially important for those countries (e.g., several of the Commonwealth of Independent States countries) whose officials have little or no direct contact with their counterparts in the OECD world. Beyond that, they further serve to socialize the officials, experts, and policy makers of peripheral states into the existing epistemic communities in the migration field within the OECD, and they help to moor the policy reforms desired by the OECD partners within the associated states: migration policies deemed desirable by the OECD partners are thus locked in within the dependent states. Finally, in the case of the relationship between the European Union and a number of the central and east European states involved, the Budapest Process is clearly complementary to the ongoing accession process and prepares the ground, in the area of the regulation of people's mobility, for ultimate full membership of the European Union.

These neoliberal forms of mobility controls will not disappear with political changes in countries at the receiving end. Because of their inclusion into regional frameworks of integration, these mechanisms become locked in, and it would be extremely costly, both economically and politically, not to respect them (Gill 1998). Accordingly, states become more accountable to external than to internal forces. States are made responsible for maintaining the direction or the orientation taken by the regional system and to upholding the principles or social purpose of the agreements signed. Both the Budapest Process and the Puebla Process have developed mechanisms to strengthen these tendencies and to monitor the compliance of the participating states. Particular emphasis is placed in both contexts on the selective criminalization of migration.

In fact, the selective criminalization of specific forms of migration and the privileged treatment of other types of mobility is functional not only in the context of proliferating neoliberal labor market reforms but also in the context of redrawing the boundaries of the regions concerned. Both in the case of the Americas and in the case of Europe, we observe the restructuring of regional hierarchies. Certain countries or regions are gradually integrated into the OECD heartland (Mexico, Central Europe, and possibly in the long run, Turkey). These countries are themselves becoming destination countries for migrants from the outer layers of the emerging new regional geohierarchies (just as a decade ago the southern European countries made the transition from migrant-sending to migrant-receiving countries against the background of their integration into the hegemonic structures of the West). Other countries are recast in the role of dependent (semi-) peripheries, whose migrant workers are admitted to the heartland countries only on the strictest conditions, and who are themselves burdened with the task of policing their borders with the external world whose people can come in only as illegal migrants (and in decreasing measure as asylum seekers) (cf. van Buuren 1999).[6]

To summarize this section, Neoliberal restructuring of the global economy involves both the deepening and the widening of market relations and the transformation of governance structures. Labor has a specific role in this process: because international labor migration is only one way in which global capital can access the emerging global labor market, the emerging global regime for labor involves both the disciplining of labor and the selective freeing of the mobility of labor. There is clearly a tension between regulating migration under the auspices of global neoliberalism on one hand and upholding the values of democratic governance on the other. When we turn to discuss the contours of a possible new comprehensive framework for the regulation of global migration in the next section, we shall therefore emphasize the importance of democratic multilateralism as a safeguard against downward harmonization through disciplinary neoliberal policy competition.

IMPLICATIONS FOR A FUTURE MULTILATERAL AGREEMENT ON MIGRATION

We have, in the preceding analysis, argued that the contemporary migration issues must be viewed against the backdrop of globalization. Likewise, if we want to speculate on the contours of a future international migration regime, let us first look at the implications of globalization for such an enterprise.

First, unless an effort is made to address the underlying causes, especially of all forms of involuntary migration, any effort to create an international migration convention will inevitably result in the codification of the existing extremely restrictive immigration practices of most of the countries of destination. The international community (this often abused eulogism) must address the structural inequities in the global political economy producing and/or reproducing poverty among two-thirds of the world's population (such as unequal exchange, the dumping of agricultural surpluses, etc.). It should also look very critically at the global arms trade that fuels many of the refugee-producing conflicts around the globe. Especially where arms trade and neocolonial political interference with (if not initiation of) regional and local conflicts by major powers coincide, the results have been disastrous.

Second, the particular character of globalization as a process of deepening commodification and as a project of privileging the market over public regulation suggests that to be democratic and responsive to the needs of all people, certain fundamental principles must underlie any regulatory project. It is, first, of crucial importance that the trend to further commodification is reversed and that essential spheres of human life are wholly or partly decommodified. This implies also that we must reassert the primacy of public governance as opposed to the market-led governance, which neoliberalism advocates for those areas where the interests of capital predominate. Finally, these new forms of public governance of global processes must provide for democratic decision making and grassroots participation, not just at the national and international levels but also in transnational settings. At the national level, the institutions to implement democratic control and popular participation exist, at least in principle if not everywhere in practice, in the form of political parties, parliaments, and legal systems. At the international level, we have the institutions and practices of traditional diplomacy, including the framework of the United Nations system, to guarantee the representation of all sovereign states in the process. Notwithstanding its many shortcomings, it should be obvious that the United Nations is preferable as a framework for worldwide agreements to other frameworks. This is so whether these are international but with representation based on economic strength (such as the IMF or the WTO) or whether they are bilateral and skewed toward the strongest economic power (as in the bilateral negotiations between the European Union and the individual candidate-members on their terms of entry).

In such a new, democratic, multilateral context, we might envisage the creation of a comprehensive international migration framework convention. The purpose of this convention is to set forth and guarantee the general principles governing the regulation of transnational migrations, to ensure a sufficient degree of coordination between regional and national migration regimes, and to deal with those migratory movements that cannot be covered in a regional setting. There are three major components in such a regime.

1. The institutional framework to be developed at the world (and regional) level must be democratic, that is, transparent and responsive to the needs of migrants as well as to those of the participating states. The organizational forms for such an enterprise are still to be developed; they will need to find a balance between facilitating grassroots participation and democratic representation, which is often lacking in the literature singing the praises of global civil society and of transnational nongovernmental organizations.

2. The asylum and refugee framework providing the basis for the existing international refugee regime (i.e., the 1951 Geneva Convention and the 1967 New York Protocol) must be amended to take account of the changed nature of international refugee movements. Here the proposals put forward by Zolberg, Suhrke, and Aguayo (1989) may serve as a starting point. They propose to introduce as the central principle "the immediacy and degree of life-threatening violence" (p. 270) to afford protection to the "victims" on an equal footing with the more common subjects of present asylum law, the "activists" and the "targets." The asylum policies of the OECD countries deserve special mention here: these tend to produce illegal immigrants in large numbers through the practice of denying official status to asylum seekers who cannot be returned to their countries of origin because of humanitarian concerns.

3. An equivalent framework for voluntary migration (permanent and temporary) must be created in which states undertake to bring their national and regional immigration policies in accordance with an internationally negotiated set of minimum criteria formulated to safeguard the interests of migrants as well as the interests of the signatory states. The existing provisions of international

labor organization conventions and the GATS should be incorporated into such a framework or replaced by it where they conflict with the fundamental principles set out above. One important principle to be obeyed here is that the legal position of long-term residents must be improved. Both the return of migrants to their home countries and their effective integration into the host society are obstructed by their insecure status (i.e., by the difficulty in many host countries of obtaining full membership in the welfare state and by the difficulties they encounter on return to their home countries). These problems could be substantially reduced, for instance, by expanding the possibilities for dual citizenship or by allowing reimmigration with full retention of rights in case of failed return migration.

On the basis of such a comprehensive set of principles, regional migration conventions can then create the institutional and operational settings for their practical implementation. It is plausible that only in regional settings will it be possible to develop effective instruments to deal with such undesirable developments as the increasing role of organized crime in the trafficking of people (and drugs and arms). As with Prohibition in the 1930s, an exclusively repressive policy only raises the price of the prohibited goods (in this case access to the labor markets of the OECD countries) without substantially reducing the flow. These regional regimes might be expected, depending on specific circumstances, to incorporate regional development, educa-

tional and employment initiatives, preferential trade agreements, effective measures against trafficking in people, agreements on the readmission of illegal migrants, arrangements for temporary labor migration, quota for permanent immigration, return migration schemes, and improvement of the legal position of migrants in host countries. An integral and comprehensive approach is essential. If certain elements, such as temporary labor provisions, are realized in isolation from the other elements and principles, such schemes are bound to serve only the interests of the employers looking for cheap workers. Public governance of these processes must guarantee the balance between the various elements of the conventions.

This article has put forward that there is a possibly irreconcilable tension between commodification on one hand and emancipation and deprivation on the other. The present trend in the global economy is to privilege private market forces over public regulation. We are presently on the threshold of global initiatives to shift this balance even further, especially with respect to the management of global migration flows. This article maintains that the answer cannot be a return to strictly national forms of migration control and should not be a complete capitulation to market-driven regulation of migration. Polanyi's (1957) "double movement" is now, more than ever, operative at the global level, and this implies that we must actively develop global forms of social protection (complementing, not replacing, national forms) to counter the destructive effects of deepening commodification. Resisting the subordination of international labor markets to the neoliberal regimes of the WTO (via GATS and the Multilateral Agreement on Investment) must be an integral component of the struggle for a more democratic global economic order.

Notes

1. Remittances in India indeed cover more than half of the negative balance of international trade. At the same time, India has illiteracy rates of some 35 percent for men and more than 60 percent for women (World Bank 1997).

2. Financial globalization, that is, the emergence and growth of global financial markets, is identified by many as the hallmark of globalization. From the perspective of the overall transnationalization of the circuits of productive capital, the role of global finance is in a sense secondary, namely, to keep the system together and to lock the spatially dispersed sites of production and accumulation into one global system. We will therefore not discuss this here.

3. Note that national treatment is also one of the founding principles in the aborted Multilateral Agreement on Investment and the GATS.

4. By 1997, the Budapest Group encompassed thirty-six European states (including among the republics of the former Soviet Union the three Baltic states, Belarus, Ukraine, Moldova, and the Russian Federation), Australia, Canada, and the United States, as well as the Central European Initiative, the Council of Europe, the European Union Council Secretariat, the European Commission, the Intergovernmental Consultations on Asylum, Refugee and Migration Policies, the International Center for Migration Policy Development (functioning as the secretariat of the Budapest Group), the International Organization for Migration, Interpol, the United Nations High Commissioner for Refugees, the International Civil Aviation Organization, and the United Nations Commission on Crime Prevention. For more information as well as sources on the work of the Budapest Group and also of the Puebla Process, the reader is referred to Pellerin and Overbeek (2001).

5. The Puebla Process involved the participation of ten countries of Central and North America (Belize, Canada, Costa Rica, El Salvador, Guatemala, Honduras, Mexico, Nicaragua, Panama, and the United States). A few countries and international organizations were invited as observers: Colombia, the Dominican Republic, Ecuador, Jamaica, and Peru, as well as the Economic Commission for Latin America, the United Nations High Commissioner for Refugees, and the International Organization for Migration.

6. Of course, this process of regional hierarchization intersects with processes of geostrategic rivalry being played out partly in the same region, such as NATO intervention in Kosovo, the involvement of several Western interests in the Caucasus, and most recently the entry of Western forces in central Asia through the war in Afghanistan.

References

Brochmann, G. 1993. "Fortress Europe"—A European immigration regime in the making? In *Migration: The politics of contemporary population movements*, 117-32. Papers presented at the Sampol Conference 1993, University of Bergen, Norway, 21-22 September.

Castells, M. 1998. *The information age: Economy, society and culture III: End of millennium*. Oxford, UK: Blackwell.

Chanda, Nayan. 2000. The tug of war for Asia's best brains. *Far Eastern Economic Review*, 9 November. Retrieved from http://www.feer.com/_0011_09/p038innov.html.

Cohen, R., and F. M. Deng. 1998. *Masses in flight: The global crisis of internal displacement*. Washington, DC: Brookings Institution.

Cox, R. W. 1981. Social forces, states and world order: Beyond international relations theory. *Millennium: Journal of International Studies* 10 (2): 126-55.

————. 1987. *Production, power and world order: Social forces in the making of history.* New York: Columbia University Press.

Fröbel, F., J. Heinrichs, and O. Kreye. 1977. *Die neue internationale Arbeitsteilung. Strukturelle Arbeitslosigkeit in den Industrieländern und die Industrialisierung der Entwicklungsländer.* Hamburg, Germany: Rowohlt.

Ghosh, B. 1997. *Gains from global linkages: Trade in services and movements of persons.* New York: Macmillan.

————, ed. 2000. *Managing migration. Time for a new international regime?* Oxford, UK: Oxford University Press.

Gill, S. 1995. Globalisation, market civilisation, and disciplinary neoliberalism. *Millennium: Journal of International Studies* 24 (3): 399-423.

————. 1998. European governance and new constitutionalism: Economic and monetary union and alternatives to disciplinary neoliberalism in Europe. *New Political Economy* 3:1, 5-26.

Harris, N. 1995. *The new untouchables: Immigration and the new world worker.* London: Penguin.

Loescher, G. 1993. *Beyond charity: International cooperation and the global refugee crisis.* Oxford, UK: Oxford University Press.

McMichael, P. 1996. *Development and social change: A global perspective.* Thousand Oaks, CA: Pine Forge Press.

Munck, Ronaldo. 2002. Globalization and democracy: A new "great transformation"? *Annals of the American Academy of Political and Social Science* 581:10-21.

Niessen, J., and F. Mochel. 1999. *EU external relations and international migration.* Brussels, Belgium: Migration Policy Group.

Organization for Economic Cooperation and Development Système d'observation permanente des migrations. 1998. *Trends in international migration.* Paris: Organization for Economic Cooperation and Development.

Papademetriou, D. G. 1994. At a crossroads: Europe and migration. In *Migration and the new Europe,* edited by K. A. Hamilton, 12-36. Washington, DC: Center for Strategic and International Studies.

Pellerin, H., and H. W. Overbeek. 2001. Neo-Liberal regionalism and the management of people's mobility. In *Social forces in the making of the new Europe,* edited by A. Bieler and A. Morton, 137-57. Houndmills, UK: Palgrave.

Polanyi, Karl. 1957. *The great transformation: The political and economic origins of our time.* Boston: Beacon.

Poulantzas, N. 1974. *Les classes sociales dans le capitalisme aujourd'hui.* Paris: Le Seuil.

Ross, R., and K. Trachte. 1983. Global cities and global classes: The peripheralization of labor in New York City. *Review* 6 (3): 393-431.

Ruggie, J. G. 1993. Territoriality and beyond: Problematizing modernity in international relations. *International Organization* 47 (1): 139-74.

Sassen, S. 1996a. *Losing control? Sovereignty in an age of globalization.* New York: Columbia University Press.

————. 1996b. *Transnational economies and national migration policies.* Amsterdam: IMES.

United Nations Conference on Trade and Development (UNCTAD). 1994. *Transnational corporations, employment and the workplace: An executive summary.* New York: United Nations.

————. 1998. *World investment report 1998: Trends and determinants.* New York: United Nations.

United Nations Conference on Trade and Development/International Organization for Migration. 1996. *Foreign direct investment, trade, aid and migration.* Current studies series A, no. 29, Unctad/DTCI/27. Geneva: United Nations.

United Nations High Commissioner for Refugees. 1997. *The state of the world's refugees: A humanitarian agenda*. Oxford, UK: Oxford University Press.

van Buuren, J. 1999. Quand l'Union européenne s'entoure d'un cordon sanitaire. *Le Monde Diplomatique* (January):6-7.

Weiner, M. 1995. *The global migration crisis: Challenge to states and to human rights*. New York: HarperCollins.

World Bank. 1997. *World development report: The state in a changing world*. Washington, DC: World Bank.

Zolberg, A. R. 1991. Bounded states in a global market: The uses of international labor migrations. In *Social theory for a changing society*, edited by P. Bourdieu and J. S. Coleman, 301-25. Boulder, CO: Westview.

Zolberg, A. R., A. Suhrke, and S. Aguayo. 1989. *Escape from violence: Conflict and the refugee crisis in the developing world*. Oxford, UK: Oxford University Press.

ANNALS, *AAPSS*, **581**, May 2002

Agents, Subjects, Objects, or Phantoms? Labor, the Environment, and Liberal Institutionalization

By DIMITRIS STEVIS

ABSTRACT: The liberal institutionalization of world politics has engendered a vibrant debate over its form and its content. The proposals range from those aiming at the democratization of international institutions to those that aim to modify them at the margins. This contribution proposes that the democratization of social institutions has both an internal (within an organization or sector) and an external (in relation to whole political economy) dimension. Not surprisingly, unions and environmentalists have limited influence on international institutions when compared to corporations and liberal economic ministries. There is enough evidence, however, that liberal elites are advocating the selective inclusion of liberal unionists and environmentalists at the expense of social unionists and environmentalists. In addition to other responses, social unions and environmentalists should make internal democratization a priority and should utilize domestic fora, where unions and environmentalists have more access and resources, in a manner that embeds domestic tactics within inclusive internationalist strategies.

Dimitris Stevis teaches international politics at Colorado State University. His research interests focus on international labor and environmental politics and policy with an emphasis on their social purpose. He is currently working on a book on international labor politics (with Terry Boswell of Emory University) and preparing a project on unions and the environment. His most recent work has appeared in Strategies, Environmental Politics, Research in Political Sociology, *and* International Political Economy of the Environment: Critical Perspectives, Volume 12 *of* IPE Yearbook, *which he coedited.*

ONE of the prominent issues of our era is the nature and powers of international institutions. There is quite a variety of opinions on the subject, but two sets of proposals motivate this contribution. First, various egalitarian social entities, including unions, environmentalists, and some governments have long called for the democratization of these institutions (see O'Brien et al. 2000; International Confederation of Trade Unions [ICFTU] 2000). Second, during the past ten years or so, there has been a proliferation of calls for more humane international institutions from organizations and individuals that have been at the forefront of liberalization (see Tanzi, Chu, and Gupta 1999; Salinas de Gortari and Mangabeira Unger 1999; Organization for Economic Cooperation and Development [OECD] 1997; Schwab and Smadja 1996).

INTRODUCTION

The general goal of this contribution is to examine the position of labor and the environment in contemporary international institutionalization in a manner that allows us to distinguish institutional arrangements that deepen social policies and democracy from those that seek to manage or divert discontent and legitimate a liberal world order. Thus, a more specific goal is to propose an analytic scheme and employ it to map both the internal (within an organization or sector) and the external (with respect to whole political economy) dimensions of democratization, a second specific goal of the contribution. The third goal is to compare the standing of unions and environmental organizations in international institutionalization.

In the part that follows, I outline the analytic scheme for the study of the democratization of social relations and a related heuristic typology that aims to communicate the degree to which social entities influence a social order, in this case international institutionalization. The third and fourth parts examine labor and the environment in terms of the analytical scheme and the typology proposed. The last part compares the two cases and suggests key strategic challenges faced by social unionists and social environmentalists.

THE DEMOCRATIC
CONTENT OF INTERNATIONAL
INSTITUTIONS

The conventional view of international institutionalization focuses on formally international organizations and rules. Various analysts have suggested, correctly in my view, that international institutionalization consists of both domestic and international components. Stated differently, we need a more sociological approach to the state and the domestic-international interface (Halliday 1987; Cox [1991] 1995). No global or regional organization approximates the autonomy and authority of the state at this point. If federal systems are to serve as our guides, moreover, authority will always be organized in multitiered ways. This is well understood by business. As Egan and Levy (2001) have suggested, businesses are not attached to international fora but rather choose fora tactically. One may add that the cosmopolitanism of capital is predicated on its success at limiting the cosmopolitan reach of workers. To disregard domestic arenas, particularly of key countries, is tantamount to abandoning not only the arenas where most international policies are shaped but also the arenas where much international authority is exercised. Alternatively, to concentrate exclusively on international fora is to overestimate their actual authority in the world political economy. The problem, in my view, is not the use of domestic arenas but their use in ways that recognize that they are integral parts of international institutionalization rather than independent of it.

The democratization of international institutions has become the object of a vibrant debate. Some analysts doubt that international organizations and institutions, more broadly, can be democratized and suggest that they are important for other good reasons. Others believe that it is possible and desirable to democratize international politics through cosmopolitan or republican mechanisms (see Shapiro and Hacker-Cordón 1999a). In addition to debates over the possibility and forms of international or global democracy, there are also debates about its content. Some analysts advocate a minimalist procedural approach while others call for the integration of substantive criteria into any definition of the concept (see Shapiro and Hacker-Cordón 1999b). I share the view that democracy consists of both procedural and substantive elements and no procedural

rules would survive deep cleavages in substantive priorities.[1]

In this vein, every institution, including every democratic one, delineates explicitly or implicitly which social entities can have voice and what kinds of choice are considered legitimate and feasible. The rules of voice cannot tell us how democratic a policy is without understanding what types of choice are feasible within a policy's parameters. Similarly, the rules of choice are an inadequate guideline to democracy if affected parties cannot participate in their elaboration and implementation. In general, the issue is not whether procedure or substance is more important but how concatenations of procedural and substantive rules engender and regulate social relations.[2]

Democracy implies more participation by subaltern groups, participation that can challenge the substantive rules that make them subaltern. A policy is more democratic to the degree that it undoes structural inequities, in the process undoing the relations that produce these inequities and thus leading to the transformation of the social entities engendered by these unequal relations. The pursuit of ideal forms of procedure, in my view, should not stand in the way of recognizing that various procedures can enhance the openness and lessen the inequities of international institutions. Similarly, the instruments of choice may also vary. The criterion should be the degree to which various instruments challenge structural inequities rather than some atavistic hostility or attachment to particular instruments (Young 2000, chap. 7).

I propose to examine voice and choice in simple terms. Accordingly, I ask two very related questions in each case. First, Who has voice or choice (of any type)? and second, What kind of voice or choice do they have? The first question allows us to ascertain whether some groups or categories of people (or natural entities) have no voice and whether some choices are illegitimate or unfeasible—in short, these questions allow us to identify the boundaries between outsiders and insiders and place the internal-external democracy issue at the forefront. The second question allows us to examine the depth or strength of the voice or choice of the various insiders, that is, the degree to which they can affect politics and policies by virtue of the procedural and substantive rules that variably empower or constrain insiders.

In the case of voice, I utilize the simple distinction between agenda setting, policy making, and policy implementation. Participation in all of these arenas, particularly policy making, is evidence of strong voice. In terms of choice, I employ a simple distinction between redistribution, mitigation, and allocation. Accordingly, *redistribution* refers to policies that aim at the transfer of resources and powers to hitherto weaker groups, *mitigation* refers to the use of substantial resources to ensure stability and avoid massive failures affecting the weaker, and *allocation* refers to the orderly distribution of benefits and obligations without regard for structural inequities. I believe that omitting the discussion of implementation and allocation at this point will not affect the central argument.

On the basis of this operationalization, I propose a heuristic typology to map and communicate the different positions that various stakeholders can occupy in an institutional arrangement. Accordingly, I believe that we can distinguish stakeholders in terms of agents, subjects, objects, and "phantoms."[3] One of the goals of this typology is to underscore the diversity of positions, something that cannot be captured by the subject-object dichotomy common in international law (Cutler 2001; Stevis 1999). On this basis, it is also possible to show how fractions within social categories can occupy different positions, forcing us to examine democratization both internally and externally.

Agents in this spirit are stakeholders who have strong voice and strong choice. In terms of the criteria just mentioned, they can play a policy-making role (as well as policy implementation and agenda-setting roles), and the range of choices available empowers rather than constrains them. Subjects are entities who have no or limited policy-making power but can participate in policy implementation and agenda setting. While the range of choices within which they can operate is shaped more by others than themselves, it is possible that they can use their subjecthood to affect the operation of the institution and also become agents. Objects are entities who are regulated but have no policy-making or implementation powers

TABLE 1
THE DEMOCRATIC CONTENT OF INSTITUTIONS

	Narrow Voice	Broad Voice
Narrow choice	Military policies Hyperliberal industrial relations Polluter pays (extreme versions)	Privatization of welfare Hyperliberal markets
Broad choice	Soviet redistribution	Scandinavian social democracy Precaution (German version)

and may have marginal influence on the public agenda. Basically, then, objects are regulated as a result of the activities of agents and subjects. This category is somewhat more complicated than the previous two inasmuch as I can think of at least two major subcategories of objects; that is, objects such as children, nature, or monuments may be regulated for their protection, or objects such as slaves or wild animals that prey on household pets may be regulated to discipline them. Finally, phantoms are entities that are produced by the social processes at hand but have neither voice nor choice and, often, no one to speak on their behalf. In some cases, this may be the result of conscious marginalization strategies, as has been the case with women and undocumented workers during parts of history. In other instances, these may be entities in the interstices of world political economy or obscured to us due to our blinders, as may be the case with temporary workers in academia or nonphotogenic species.

It seems to me that entities with more policy-making voice are likely to have more power in the shaping of substantive rules, precisely because it takes power to become a policy maker. Yet there is no perfect correspondence between voice and choice because these are matters of historical legacies and political contestations. As a result, the democratic content of a specific policy or a whole social order cannot be derived solely by the rules of voice or choice; rather, it requires the examination of their historical concatenations. Table 1 offers some historical examples that approximate simple analytical combinations between voice and choice.

VOICE IN GLOBAL LABOR AND ENVIRONMENTAL POLITICS

Who has voice?

The majority of the world's working people are not organized or represented in any fashion (Harrod 1987). As a result, arrangements between capital and protected labor may be intentionally or unintentionally exclusionary. It has also been capital's strategy to devolve standing to workers as individuals or to advocacy organizations rather than unions, for example, European Works Councils and most codes of conduct.

The issue is somewhat more complex with the environment. When dealing with the impacts of environmental harm on people or property, the problem is not much different from that of labor. Because of the prominence of scientific/technical, service, and advocacy organizations, however, we should investigate whether representative environmental organizations or individuals affected by environmental harm also have voice. In the same sense that the prominent role of unions may obscure the unprotected workers, the prominence of advocacy organizations may obscure the voices of representative environmental organizations or unorganized citizens.

Various ecologists would also argue that nature has standing and should be included. This claim presents serious theoretical and practical problems precisely because nature must be taken into account and because nature cannot speak for itself. For the purposes of this contribution, suffice it to say that naturalist arguments do not provide us with an unassailable criterion (Stevis 2000). This is not an argument that social justice will abut in ecologically sound actions anymore than socialism will automatically undo sexism or racism (see Young 1990 on various forms of inequities). It is an argument that naturalism cannot replace questions of social power and uneven responsibility when dealing with nature.

What kind of voice?

Agenda setting. Unions and environmentalists are actively contesting the international social regulation agenda (O'Brien et al. 2000; Seattle: December '99? 2000;

Williams 2001). For much of the post–World War II era, unions in the core and parts of the semiperiphery have influenced the foreign policy agendas of their own governments, but their access has become more tenuous during the past twenty years, particularly when their priorities conflict with those of liberal alliances or economic integration. At the global level, they have certainly played a role in shaping the International Labor Organization's (ILO's) agenda over the years, and they can be credited with the breadth of topics that the organization has dealt with. Unions from industrial countries have also influenced the OECD's agenda at the margins but continue to be unsuccessful at the World Trade Organization and the International Monetary Fund. Finally, the Global Compact, a wholly prescriptive proposal, does recognize them as legitimate partners. What makes the Compact interesting for unions and environmentalists is the fact that it brings together corporate elites, the United Nations Secretariat, unions, environmentalists, and human rights advocates. In that sense, it may presage some form of global corporatism, albeit one that does not challenge the primacy of capital (see United Nations 2001).

At the regional level, the ability of unions to shape the North American labor agenda is extremely limited. In the case of the European Union, the European Trade Unions Confederation can play a more consequential role both through the Social Dialogue and through its access to the Commission (see Stevis and Boswell 2001).

Unions have certainly sought to influence the agenda of corporations, with limited success, partly due to intralabor divisions. Yet there are farsighted corporate elites who would welcome collaboration with unions to improve productivity, consumption, and industrial peace and provided that these initiatives did not affect their flexibility and discretion.

A number of international environmental organizations have a prominent role in contesting the broad agenda of multilateral environmental negotiations. The formal agendas, however, are less in the direction of social environmentalist priorities and more of a compromise between liberal state agencies, firms, and some liberal environmentalists (Williams 2001; Bernstein 2000), a trend underscored at the fourth World Trade Organization ministerial conference. At the regional level, environmental organizations have prominent if circumscribed roles in both North America and Europe. Some environmental organizations do have some influence on the North American agenda through access to the Commission for Environmental Cooperation, keeping in mind that the commission cannot adopt binding regional policies. The Green Group of the European Parliament has some influence on the agenda of the European Union (Stevis and Mumme 2001, 26-34). Finally, environmental organizations have been active in trying to shape the agendas of corporations. It is still not clear whether the responses of firms are mostly public relations exercises or genuine, if limited, reforms.

Policy making. Policy makers include those entities who play a predominant role in shaping the formal policy-agenda (to be distinguished from the general discourse about the issue) and participate in the elaboration of policies.[4] The arena where some unions have consequential voice is also that of domestic politics and, to a lesser degree, foreign policy. Their often considerable domestic and foreign influence has been increasingly constrained by liberal economic ministries. Yet the fact that unions do often have significant policy-making capacity in domestic politics suggests that this is an arena that they cannot afford to abandon, particularly in light of the hybrid nature of international institutionalization.

At the global level, the impact of unions through the ILO is very limited, a situation that goes back to the establishment of the organization. Member countries pay no price for the nonratification of ILO conventions—something that is not the case with the international trading or financial arrangements. Unions from the industrial world also have a marginal consultative status at the OECD and have been consulted by financial agencies in an effort to deal with the impacts of structural adjustment. At the regional level, unions have no policy-making rights in North America but do have some, albeit limited, in the European Union through the Social Dialogue (for a comparison, see Stevis and Boswell 2001).

At the private level, framework agreements involving international trade secretariats—the sectoral international union organizations—

and particular corporations (ICFTU 2000, 101) may develop into something more formal, but at this point they are very general and discretionary. Finally, unions have been rather hesitant to participate in codes of conduct or standards for various reasons, including the voluntarism of these codes, and the patchwork of labor rules that they include (ICFTU 2000, 99-100; Pearson and Seyfang 2001).

Environmental organizations and parties also influence domestic politics and foreign policies. The absence of corporatist arrangements similar to various types of industrial relations does limit their influence at those levels. At the global level, the United Nations Environment Programme is a weak agency, and it does not seem that future environmental intergovernmental organizations will be tripartite, like the ILO. While some technical/scientific organizations, such as the Intergovernmental Panel on Climate Change and the International Union for the Conservation of Nature, do have some influence in specific policies in their capacity as scientific advisors, they are not policy makers. Environmental advocacy organizations often have a high profile in the negotiation of multilateral environmental agreements, the basic form of environmental policy, but do not have corresponding policy-making powers.

At the regional level, the role of environmentalists varies. In the European Union, there is nothing similar to the Social Dialogue, but environmentalists can affect policy making through the Green Group of the European Parliament. In North America, liberal environmentalists have accepted a marginal role through the North American Agreement for Environmental Cooperation, which, however, discourages regional policies.

At the private level, environmental organizations have also been hesitant to accept unilateral codes of conduct; but more so than unions, environmentalists have participated in bilateral arrangements with corporations, whether in the crafting of codes of conduct and standards or through other policy arrangements. Some of these arrangements are clearly controlled by firms or are very narrow in coverage and goals; the most counterhegemonic are resolutely opposed or undermined by business (for various cases, see Newell 1999; Murray and Raynolds 2000).

CHOICE IN GLOBAL LABOR
AND ENVIRONMENTAL AFFAIRS

Who has choice?

The contemporary world of union politics remains diverse, but it is not as diverse as it has been in the past (Stevis 1998). Radical unions (syndicalists, anarchists, Communists) have been historically denied access to policy making or have been allowed to participate only after modifying their goals. In short, it is fair to say that choices that envision the structural reorganization of the political economy are less prominent, with social democratic views among them being the more prominent ones. At the same time, however, we must recognize that some existing labor policies are important achievements and, in any event, create path dependencies of their own. It is for these reasons that neoliberal alliances would like to see the policy debate reduced to one between business unionists and personnel managers. These views have been around for a long time, but it is important to note that, today, calls for the abandonment of unions altogether are taken more seriously than talk of unions as instruments of social change.

The same situation is developing in environmental affairs where social environmentalists and deep ecologists are increasingly challenged by business or liberal environmentalists. The most characteristic case is that of the German Greens and their move to the center. In a similar fashion, Greenpeace, with all its imaginative tactics, has also moved toward naturalism. Many of the most prominent international and national organizations have also come to terms with some kinds of market mechanisms. More so than in the case of labor, however, and reflecting the recent history of the environmental movement, the differences between social environmentalists and business environmentalists remain to be settled, but the preferences of liberal elites are clearly in favor of business environmentalism.

What kind of choice?

Redistribution. Compared to the best examples of the social welfare state, there are no international policies or organizations that aim at equity through redistribution (for intergovernmental organization policies, see Deacon 1997). One of the legacies of the work of the ILO is the social clause consisting of core labor rights and standards that unions have sought to attach to international economic agreements (Tsogas 2001, chaps. 3 and 7; ICFTU 2000, 44-45). Without underestimating the significance of inserting such a clause into otherwise liberal arrangements, we should note that neither the clause nor the whole broad spectrum of the ILO's conventions challenge the decision-making rights of corporations or the desirability or primacy of capitalism. At the regional level, also, there are no major comprehensive redistributive policies whose aim is to enhance the position of labor. The most prominent efforts are to be found in the European Union, and they deal with certain types of working conditions and gender. Most important, European Union labor regulation excludes key collective rights from its policy domain (Stevis and Boswell 2001, 344).

Precaution is arguably the environmental principle that has the most significant redistributive implications, in terms of both power and resources. According to the German version of the precautionary principle, no activity should take place until there is reasonable certainty that it will not cause environmental harm (Stevis 2000, 73-74). Clearly, taking this principle to the extreme would result in stasis. The point, however, is that the precautionary principle places the responsibility on the initiator to prove the environmental soundness of its activities and gives all other stakeholders the right to demand and approve such assurances. Compared to the polluter pays or prevention principles, it is certainly much more equitable.

As with the move away from radical egalitarian forms of unionism, there has also been a move away from radical precautionary environmentalism. In its stead, we are witnessing the proliferation of business environmentalism whose aim is to marshal the forces of the market to serve the environment (Bernstein 2000). The general acceptance of emission trading and other market instruments to deal with climate change may have been a necessary compromise under the circumstances, but it is also evidence of the victory of liberal environmentalism and can well lead to more global inequities.

Mitigation. While the more radical egalitarian proposals have been marginalized, there has been a proliferation of proposals for international social regulation from various neoliberal organizations and leaders. There are no significant mitigation policies at the global level as far as labor is concerned. What we do encounter, however, are policy proposals to provide a broad safety net that would include working people. The attitudes and priorities of the United Nations Development Program are probably the most far-reaching among these policy proposals. The World Bank has long emphasized its commitment to alleviating poverty, albeit in the process of deepening market forces (e.g., World Bank 2000). More recently, the OECD has also initiated a dialogue over the

need for preserving social cohesion while preserving economic flexibility (OECD 1997). Both the World Bank and the OECD have also paid closer attention to workers, albeit as individuals and factors of production. Finally, the International Monetary Fund has also raised the issue of its social responsibilities (Tanzi, Chu, and Gupta 1999). To the policies of these intergovernmental organizations we should add the World Economic Forum. Its organizers have long realized the destabilizing effects of hyperliberalism (Schwab and Smadja 1996), and in the past few years, they have started inviting union leaders and promoting the Global Compact.

The same process is evident with respect to the environment. Increasingly, various intergovernmental organizations (particularly the World Bank and the OECD but also the Food and Agriculture Organization) have come to terms with the need for environmental policies. Under the intellectual leadership of the OECD, there has developed a liberal environmentalist consensus that like labor, aims to combine economic flexibility, growth, and environmental protection (Bernstein 2000; Williams 2001). Central to this tendency is the use of the market and persuasion more than binding policies.

Environmental opinions remain divided on the matter, but there are many environmental organizations and business organizations, such as the Business Council for Sustainable Development and the World Economic Forum, that have accepted the wisdom of reforming the system through what has been called "weak ecological modernization" (Williams 2001; on ecological modernization, see Mol and Spaargaren 2000). While the "strong ecological modernization" approach would demand the questioning of many of these processes and reject some of them as inherently harmful and undemocratic, weak ecological modernization takes a more benign approach toward the ability and willingness of industry to improve its environmental record and do so out of self-interest.

CONCLUSION
AND PROSPECTS

Parallel or divergent trajectories?

Where do labor and the environment fall in international institutionalization? Are their situations significantly similar or different? As noted earlier, any answer to these questions must be sensitive to the fact that not all workers and people affected by environmental harm are organized or powerful. As a result, it is possible that various elements within each social category may be situated differently. This, I believe, is the most important lesson from the point of view of democracy. One does not have to be hostile to unions or environmental organizations to recognize that some have served to create phantoms through their own practices; for example, some unions have excluded women or other categories of people while some environmentalists are virulently Malthusian and nativist. In our days, however, most unions are aware of

this situation and at least recognize its practical and moral implications. Many of them, in fact, have sought to change their own politics through various policies dealing with gender, ethnicity, migration, racism, and so on (see ICFTU 2000). The same applies to many environmental organizations, although in my view, many of them have not made a satisfactory transition from naturalism to social environmentalism. On balance, unions and environmental organizations, with all of their diversity and shortcomings, have been at the forefront of opening political discourse and deepening democracy. While nativism does continue to emerge from within their ranks, business elites and their state allies continue to remain among the strongest opponents to democracy.

What about the kinds of voice that unions and environmental organizations have in international public policy? I believe that it is fair to say that unions and environmental organizations are agents marginally at most, compared to firms and even some churches. Labor and environmental state agencies, through which labor and environmentalist priorities could be channeled, are routinely subjugated to liberal economic ministries. Unions and environmental organizations also have limited subjecthood, particularly when compared to corporations. Corporations, for instance, are able to pursue their rights through various dispute resolution mechanisms and rights embedded within domestic and international law. I have suggested that unions and environmentalists have and should use domestic means, but I also recognize that national and international rules limit the reach of domestic means in the areas of labor and the environment.

Clearly, unions and environmental organizations are objects both in the sense that they can contest the international agenda and because their limited agency and subjecthood casts them at the receiving end of regulation. In fact, the most significant international labor or environmental policy proposals are those that protect groups of workers (such as children) or species (such as endangered species) and those that discipline workers (such as the prohibition of solidarity strikes).

On balance, then, unions and environmentalists are primarily objects of world politics while many categories of workers and aspects of the environment are phantoms.[5] The significant activism of environmental organizations in global fora and the relative silence of unions may manifest differences in political, strategic, or tactical priorities but are not evidence of significantly different positions.

Broadening and deepening democracy

What, then, are the challenges for unions and environmentalists? Much depends on one's benchmark. I do not believe in a golden era of social democracy or pristine nature from which we have fallen. I do think, however, that the past creates path dependencies that are difficult to redirect. In this sense, any successes that liberal alliances will have in the future will not take us back to the nineteenth century. One reason this

will not happen is the resilience and functions of the welfare state and the environmental state. Another reason is that liberal alliances must pay the cost of hegemony, and that involves enticing some significant subalterns to join. While we may disagree with business unionists or environmentalists, they are unionists and environmentalists, and they do have a more socially regulated vision of the world. So the issue is not one of falling from grace from more democratic times but one of not taking democracy far enough. With those comments in mind, what are the prospects for international unions and environmental organizations in terms of the struggle for more democracy?

The ability of unions and environmentalists to contest the international agenda and some significant achievements in domestic politics suggest to me that it is only a matter of time before they achieve subjecthood and agency in world politics. In light of the differences within these movements, however, and in light of the emergence of farsighted corporate elites, the possibility of inclusion of liberal (and not so liberal) segments from within labor and environmentalists, at the expense of social unionists and environmentalists, is very strong. Internal differences among nonhegemonic social categories have played, and will continue to play, an important role in the organization of the political economy because they facilitate the formation of hegemonic alliances led by segments of capital and the state and at the expense of more radical or reformist options. In short, then, the future of democracy will have to be contested both internally and externally.

I do not believe that unions and environmentalists should abstain from efforts at deepening external democracy until they have solved the question of internal democracy. In fact, I believe that unions and environmentalists cannot afford to bypass public authority. I do believe, however, that a key challenge for unions and environmental organizations is to enhance democracy within their respective domains because success in that regard will also serve to strengthen these movements in terms of numbers, discourse, and political effectiveness. What I am envisioning here is not only seeking out more workers and environmentalists nor simply allying across movements. I am also suggesting that egalitarian social movements must internalize the values now associated with other social movements. Unions, for example, must integrate environmental or gender priorities into their internal and external practices and confront the reasons they have been slow in doing so.[6]

In terms of external democracy, unions and environmentalists are well served by recognizing the duality of international institutionalization. Choosing where to place the emphasis in these networks of power should be a matter of tactical and strategic choices rather than a doctrinaire politics of emphasizing one over the other. The major challenge is the embedding of appropriate domestic and international tactics and strategies into a democratic and internationalist politics. How unions and environmentalists deal with the plight of migrants under the recent rise of xenophobia and authoritarianism in parts of the core is a good place to begin and a good criterion by which they can be evaluated.

Notes

1. In the language of rights, *democracy* refers to profound political, economic, and social rights (Marshall [1963] 1964, chap. 4). On democracy I draw on the works of Bachrach and Botwinick (1992), Iris Young (1990, 2000), Boswell and Chase-Dunn (2000), and Picciotto (2001).

2. This approach is informed by various accounts of social welfare policies such as Marshall ([1963] 1964), Furniss and Mitchell (1984), Esping-Andersen (1990), Cox ([1991] 1995), Deacon (1997), and Misra (1999).

3. Social entities are routinely some or all of these things, depending on policy arena and issue. The distinguishing characteristic is that some are only phantoms most of the time while others have a great deal of agency.

4. Corporations participate in policy making because of structural power and preferential access and because they are often the only entities who can provide the information for standardization or technical issues (Gerth 1998). Transnational corporations also engage in intercorporate agreements that shape the organization of the world political economy, on the basis of international or global rules legitimated by states (Bowman 1993; Cutler, Haufler, and Porter 1999). In a sense, these powers are allowed and legitimated by the state, yet this does not imply that any state can turn around and undo these rules on a wholesale basis. In short, these rules are foundational for state-society relations rather than discretionary allowances by the state.

5. In the area of labor, the proposed policies of the International Labor Organization have narrowed the realm of total phantoms but have not exhausted it.

6. I am not insinuating here that particular organizations must try to deal with all political issues. I am suggesting, however, that

single-issue politics is not the same as particularistic politics.

References

Bachrach, Peter, and Aryeh Botwinick. 1992. *Power and empowerment: A radical theory of participatory democracy.* Philadelphia: Temple University Press.

Bernstein, Stephen. 2000. Ideas, social structure and the compromise of liberal environmentalism. *European Journal of International Relations* 6 (4): 464-512.

Boswell, Terry, and Christopher Chase-Dunn. 2000. *The spiral of capitalism and socialism: Toward global democracy.* Boulder, CO: Lynne Rienner.

Bowman, Scott. 1993. The ideology of transnational enterprise. *Social Science Journal* 30 (1): 47-68.

Cox, Robert. [1991] 1995. The global political economy and social choice. In *Approaches to world order,* edited by R. W. Cox with T. J. Sinclair, 191-208. Cambridge, UK: Cambridge University Press.

Cutler, A. Claire. 2001. Critical reflections on the Westphalian assumption of international law and organization: A crisis of legitimacy. *Review of International Studies* 27:133-50.

Cutler, A. Claire, Virginia Haufler, and Tony Porter. 1999. Private authority and international affairs. In *Private authority and international affairs,* edited by A. Claire Cutler, Virginia Haufler, and Tony Porter, 3-28. Albany: State University of New York Press.

Deacon, Bob, with Michele Hulse and Paul Stubbs. 1997. *Global social policy: International organizations and the future of welfare.* London: Sage.

Egan, Daniel, and David Levy. 2001. International environmental politics and the internationalization of the state: The cases of climate change and the multilateral agreement on investment. In *The international political economy of the environment: Critical perspectives.* Vol. 12 of *IPE Yearbook,* edited by D. Stevis and V. J. Assetto, 63-83. Boulder, CO: Lynne Rienner.

Esping-Andersen, Gosta. 1990. *The three worlds of capitalism.* Princeton, NJ: Princeton University Press.

Furniss, Norman, and Neil Mitchell. 1984. Social welfare provisions in western Europe: Current status and future possibilities. In *Public policy and social institutions,* edited by Harrell R. Rodgers Jr., 15-54. Greenwich, CT: JAI.

Gerth, Jeff. 1998. Where business rules: Forging global regulations that put industry first. *New York Times,* 9 January, national edition, C1.

Halliday, Fred. 1987. State and society in international relations: A second agenda. *Millennium: Journal of International Studies* 16 (2): 215-29.

Harrod, Jeffrey. 1987. *Production, power and the unprotected worker.* New York: Columbia University Press.

International Confederation of Trade Unions (ICFTU). 2000. *Globalising social justice: Trade unionism in the twenty-first century.* Brussels, Belgium: International Confederation of Trade Unions.

Marshall, T. H. [1963] 1964. *Class, citizenship and social development.* Garden City, NY: Doubleday.

Misra, Ramesh. 1999. Beyond the nation state: Social policy in an age of globalization. In *Transnational social policy,* edited by C. Jones Finer, 29-48. Oxford, UK: Blackwell.

Mol, A.P.J., and G. Spaargaren. 2000. Ecological modernization theory in debate: A review. *Environmental Politics* 9 (1): 17-49.

Murray, Douglas, and Laura Raynolds. 2000. Alternative trade in bananas: Obstacles and opportunities for progressive social change in the global economy. *Agriculture and Human Values* 17:65-74.

Newell, Peter, ed. 1999. Globalization and the governance of the environment. *IDS Bulletin* 30:3.

O'Brien, Robert, Anne M. Goetz, Jan A. Scholte, and Marc Williams. 2000. *Contesting global governance: Multilateral economic institutions and global social movements.* Cambridge, UK: Cambridge University Press.

Organization for Economic Cooperation and Development (OECD), ed. 1997. *Societal cohesion and the globalizing economy: What does the future hold?* Paris: Organization for Economic Cooperation and Development.

Pearson, Ruth, and Gill Seyfang. 2001. New hope or false dawn? Voluntary codes of conduct, labor regulation and social policy in a globalizing world. *Global Social Policy* 1 (1): 49-78.

Picciotto, Sol. 2001. Liberalization and democratization: The forum and the hearth in the era of cosmopolitan post-industrial capitalism. *Law and Contemporary Problems* 63 (4): 157-78.

Salinas de Gortari, Carlos, and Roberto Mangabeira Unger. 1999. The market turn without neoliberalism. *Challenge* 42 (1): 14-33.

Schwab, Klaus, and Claude Smadja. 1996. Davos: Mondialisation et responsabilité sociale. *Le Monde*, 17 July, 10.

"Seattle: December '99?" 2000. *Millennium: Journal of International Studies* 29 (1): 103-40.

Shapiro, Ian, and Casiano Hacker-Cordón, eds. 1999a. *Democracy's edges.* Cambridge, UK: Cambridge University Press.

———, eds. 1999b. *Democracy's value.* Cambridge, UK: Cambridge University Press.

Stevis, Dimitris. 1998. International labor organizations, 1864-1997: The weight of history and the challenges of the present. *Journal of World-Systems Research* 4 (1): 52-75. Available from http://csf.colorado.edu/wsystems/jwsr.html.

———. 1999. Agents, subjects, objects and phantoms: Form and purpose in international policies. Paper presented at the International Studies Association convention, Washington, DC, February.

———. 2000. Whose ecological justice? *Strategies* 13 (1): 63-76.

Stevis, Dimitris, and Terry Boswell. 2001. Labor policy and politics in international integration: Comparing NAFTA and the European Union. In *The politics of social inequality*, edited by B. Dobratz, L. Waldner, and T. Buzzell, 335-64. Amsterdam: JAI/Elsevier.

Stevis, Dimitris, and Stephen Mumme. 2001. Rules and politics in international integration: Environmental regulation in NAFTA and the EU. *Environmental Politics* 9 (4): 20-42.

Tanzi, Vito, Ke-young Chu, and Sanjeev Gupta, eds. 1999. *Economic policy and equity.* Washington, DC: International Monetary Fund.

Tsogas, George. 2001. *Labor regulation in a global economy.* Armonk, NY: Sharpe.

United Nations. 2001. *The global compact.* New York: United Nations. Available from http://www.unglobalcompact.org.

Williams, Mark. 2001. In search of global standards: The political economy of trade and the environment. In *The international political economy of the environment: Critical perspectives.* Vol. 12 of *IPE Yearbook*, edited by D. Stevis and V. J. Assetto, 39-61. Boulder, CO: Lynne Rienner.

World Bank. 2000. *World development report 2000/2001: Attacking poverty.* New York: Oxford University Press.

Young, Iris M. 1990. *Justice and the politics of difference.* Princeton, NJ: Princeton University Press.

———. 2000. *Inclusion and democracy.* New York: Oxford University Press.

ANNALS, *AAPSS*, **581**, May 2002

Globalization of Production and Women in Asia

By DONG-SOOK S. GILLS

ABSTRACT: Globalization of production represents a new organization of production processes, accompanied by technological advances and neoliberal ideology, which emphasizes the separation of politics from economics. Emanating from these changes, labor relations are being altered, in particular by world trends of the flexibilization and feminization of labor. Women's labor constitutes a foundation of the international competitiveness of most Asian countries. The forces of economic globalization expose women in Asia to diverse mechanisms of exploitation in complex ways. There is no single pattern but rather an array of complex ways in which gender hierarchy, national capital, foreign capital, and the state negotiate and adapt to globalization. Women's social movements have been part of the social actions that have strengthened the counterhegemonic movements against capital-led economic globalization. Women's labor is an important social force that can resist neoliberal global trends and contribute to an alternative globalization based on democratization and greater social inclusion.

Dong-Sook S. Gills is a senior lecturer in sociology at the University of Sunderland in the United Kingdom. She gained her doctorate in sociology from the University of Sheffield. She is a member of the International Advisory Council of the TODA Institute for Global Peace and Policy Research and a faculty affiliate at the Globalization Research Centre, University of Hawaii. Her most recent publications include Women and Triple Exploitation in Korean Development *(1999, Macmillan),* Globalization and Strategic Choice in South Korea: Economic Reform and Labor *(coauthored with Barry Gills) (2000, Cambridge University Press), and* Women and Work in Globalising Asia *(coedited with N. Piper) (2002, Routledge).*

ONE of the most important aspects of contemporary restructuring processes in the global economy is the discord between the liberal ideology that propels economic globalization and the politics of labor rights. The present model of globalization emphasizes the strength of economic rationalism at the ideological level and operates through globalization of production in practice. This trend of economic globalization demands a critical assessment of its impact on labor.

GLOBALIZATION: STRUCTURE
AND AGENCY

While globalization as a concept is often overstated by enthusiasts, notably by neoliberal writers, others claim that there has been no qualitative change in international economic relations. Even if we accept that the fundamental structure of the world economy has not significantly altered, however, there have certainly been noticeable changes that affected the ways in which our contemporary societies are organized. These include the trends toward increasing market liberalization, greater specialization in production, and higher mobility of capital, goods, and labor around the globe. Most notably, globalization of production has been a key element in the reshaping of the world economy with visible impact on our daily lives. Globalization of production represents new organization of production processes, backed up by new technologies. Emanating from these changes, labor relations are being altered, in particular, to world trends of the flexibilization and feminization of labor.

In general, globalization can be traced as a set of multidimensional processes, encompassing many arenas of ideology, economy, politics, and culture. Perhaps globalization in the cultural arena is more visible and immediate to our everyday life, for example, transborder exchange through music, fashion, food, films, and television. Nevertheless, these are only symptoms of globalization, not globalization itself. In fact, the symptoms of globalization are often (mis)interpreted as being globalization itself, or even as the main parameters of current globalization. It is such a (mis)perception that leads the debate to focus on the globalization of mass-media images and to the argument that globalization is a comprehensive transformation of our lives. This type of interpretation of globalization tends to ignore structural aspects of globalization while privileging the symbolic aspects (Waters 1995).

By contrast, the debate on economic globalization, for example, concerning international competitiveness, liberalization, and the global financial markets, focuses on the economic structure and tends to ignore agency as an important factor. To date, much of the debate on economic globalization in the mainstream has been separated from people, for example, as if financial crisis did not have a direct relevance to the lives of ordinary people. It is therefore important to find a balance between emphasis on structure on one hand and on agents (people) on the other and to avoid exaggerating the independence of the symbolic arena. This is not to say that globalization processes in different social arenas are entirely separate from each other. On the contrary, they are tightly interrelated processes. The globalization of Disney culture, for example, might at first appear to be a purely cultural process. However, this happens through material exchange that entails the global expansion of trade in Disney films, *Aladdin* T-shirts, *Lion King* pencil cases, Mickey Mouse story books, and so on. At the same time, global trade of these wares involves globalization of production, which enables the expansion of Disney in the global market. The production (the material) and the symbolic (the ideational) are not at all separated in the process of globalization but tightly integrated.

The globalization of production provides industry with a higher degree of mobility and flexibility not only in its production process but also in industrial relations vis-à-vis labor. In this example of globalization of Disney culture, the *101 Dalmatians* T-shirts are sewn by workers in Haiti for as little as 12 cents an hour (MacAdam 1998), thus providing a cheap global product to the global market. Alternatively, the work could be subcontracted to a sweatshop in Los Angeles that will offer competitive costs (even compared to Haiti) by employing migrant workers (often illegal) at below the legal minimum wage. This globalization of production thus in turn brings forward the question of international labor rights and standards and universal human rights issues, which reside firmly in the political arena. This brief case study of Disney culture illustrates how different, and sometimes seemingly independent, processes of globalization—that is, cultural globalization, financial and economic globalization, and political globalization—are closely tied together in reality. The underlying structure of globalization, even the cultural and symbolic manifestation, is revealed to be largely economic.

Moreover, the logic of globalization cannot be one of globalization itself, of technology alone, or merely of a new ideology, à la Giddens or Castells (Giddens 1990, 1996; Castells 1996). The logic of globalization, as a set of social processes, is mainly derived from the logic of capitalism. The central logic of capitalism is to maintain and expand the process of capital accumulation. The increase in the level of global exchange and flows of materials, people, and ideas can largely be accounted for and explained within the framework of capital accumulation. This is not to put forward a reductionist interpretation of globalization to attribute every aspect of social change to capitalist market expansion. Rather, it is to emphasize the fact that the main driving force of economic globalization is the logic of capitalism and that economic globalization is at the forefront of the globalization processes, as presented above in the example of the globalization of Disney culture. This has important implications in adopting methodological perspectives and constructing analytical frameworks in our overall understanding of globalization. When globalization is understood as multi-

dimensional processes led by economic globalization and the logic of
capitalism, then we do not need to
reinvent the wheel. There is no need
to try to imagine a postmodern world
as yet, and certainly not a
postmodern global world, because
the global logic in question is certainly not postcapitalist.

In sum, the historical forces of
globalization are mainly derived
from the logic of capitalism. Globalization itself is a set of dynamic social
practices that bring social change. In
this framework, the social relations
of globalization are based on the
requirements of capital accumulation, while adapting to technological
advances. While recognizing the
primary tendencies of economic globalization through which labor is
"victimized," both economic reduc-
tionism and technological determinism should be questioned. The
globalization of production hinges on
many changes: in the ways financial
markets are integrated and regulated, the ever-increasing liberalization of trade, and the relentless
expansion of the flexibilization of
labor. Clearly, these changes are supported by technological innovations,
in particular in the area of information and communication technology,
affecting the logistics and viability of
these new practices. As the invention
of the telegraph, railroads, and
steamships supported the expanding
nineteenth-century production system, the Internet and satellite communications have a supportive function in the present economic
reorganization. However, these new
technological advances should not be
taken as overwhelming determinants of economic restructuring
but only as its adjutants. Technological change is not globalization, only
an aspect of it.

Likewise, analysis of women's
labor in globalization should not simply be a description of their suffering.
There are two axes of analysis
involved in women's labor and globalization: one is of women as victims
of the economic process; the other is
the potential for women as subjects
of the process. When women are perceived as an agency in the globalization process, they become a social
force capable of acting in their own
interest. This, in turn, brings our
attention back to our understanding
of the relationship between the politics and economics of globalization,
or the political economy of
globalization.

As the factory system of industrial
production increased the rate of
exploitation and control of labor in
the nineteenth and twentieth centuries, it also brought workers together
and stimulated the trade union
movement. Similarly, as the current
trend of globalization of production
brings about an intensification of the
exploitation of labor, it also acts as a
stimulus to new forms of organization and resistance, in particular
global social movements. Today's
"global factory" and the new environment of global communications mean
that global networking can emerge
as a practical tool of resistance and
organization. This reveals not only
the contradictions of globalization
but also the dialectic nature of trend
and countertrend in globalization
(Gills 2000). In other words, globalization elicits counterglobalization

on a global scale, which induces alternative globalization movements in which labor and women play a critical role.

GLOBAL PRODUCTION AND WOMEN IN ASIA

The past experience of many developing countries, including those that adopted the World Bank's structural adjustment programs, has demonstrated that when overriding policy priority is given to gaining international competitiveness and the promotion of exports, less attention is given to the promotion of the welfare of the general population and particularly of labor. Indeed, the emphasis on international competitiveness and export promotion often supplants explicit policy measures against poverty and social inequality. In most cases, it appears that export promotion tends to induce further suppression of labor rights, combined with low wages. In the absence of any substantial increase in domestic consumption via a higher wage structure, the export promotion policies primarily benefit business interests. The labor practices now prevailing in the ever more ubiquitous free export processing zones (EPZs) around the world are a prime example of this tendency. For most countries in the developing world, with a low level of industrial capacity, promotion of exports is gained at the expense of labor, most notably of women.

With the restructuring of the world economy since the 1970s, governments in Asia have been competing for the favors of transnationally mobile capital. There has been an upsurge of free EPZs and free trade zones in which social and environmental standards are lowered while social subsidies to capital are increased, for example, through offering financial and other investment incentives by the host governments (Hoogvelt and Puxty 1997; Thomas 1997). The general historical outcome of this process has been an increase in the rate of exploitation of labor. Therefore, it represents a general redistribution of wealth and resources from labor to capital. That is, through the extension of both international competition and the mobility of capital, the tendency of an increased flow of wealth and resources from labor to capital has been intensified, rather than the trickle down of wealth from capital to labor taking place. As a result, rather than global wealth redistribution, there is further global wealth concentration.

As was the case in the recent history of the industrializing miracle economies, such as the Four Asian Tigers, women's labor continues to play a crucial role in the contemporary liberalization and restructuring of Asia's economies. Women are becoming increasingly active in both the rural and the urban economy, and their labor constitutes the ultimate foundation of international competitiveness of most Asian countries. Women are a direct source of cheap labor, especially in export manufacturing industries, whether as formal, informal, or casual labor. Among the workers of the world, women are all too often the most vulnerable and the most exploited during the so-called adjustment or restructuring processes.

Transnational companies are the main agents that facilitate the globalization of production. These corporations are responsible for 80 percent of foreign direct investment and are the main employers in some 850 EPZs in developing countries, with a workforce that has been estimated at around 27 million (United Nations Conference on Trade and Development 1994; International Labor Organization [ILO] 1998). Women's labor is central to these export factories that produce or assemble commodities for the global market. Female employment in EPZs is significantly higher than national average female employment in many developing economies. In major exporting countries in Asia, for example, in Malaysia, the Philippines, South Korea, and Sri Lanka, the share of women in employment in EPZs is more than 70 percent while women account for only 30 to 40 percent of overall employment in these countries (Kasugo and Tzannatos 1998). According to a study of nine electronics factories in one industrial park in Thailand, among the well-paid managerial-level employment, only 4 percent is female, while 88 percent of shop-floor workers are women (Theobald 2001). In China, women constitute an average 85 percent of the total workforce in state-owned cotton mills in the export sector (Zhao and West 2001). According to data from the Bangladesh Export Processing Zones Authority, in 1996, 70 percent of the employees in the Chittagong EPZ were women. This figure illustrates the point that the pattern of national industrial development, in the context of globalization of production, is being sustained by a predominantly female labor force in many Asian countries.

However, the ways in which women's labor is adopted in global production in Asia is very distinctive from the situation of women workers in core developed countries. Women in these global factories are subjected to a particular set of social relations that are related to the distinctive nature of global factories and the political economies of industrializing Asian countries. To a large extent, the labor experiences of many Asian women can be explained by the particular nature and the role of foreign capital (mostly transnational companies) in Asia. Core capital, in the form of foreign direct investment, as it operates in developing countries, is not strictly comparable to its role within the core states from which this capital originates. Accordingly, the social relations of capital and labor in the developing countries are quite different from those prevailing in the core countries. Therefore, Asian women workers in global production are a special category of labor that is not only different from men in general but also different from women workers in the developed economies.

Conventional wisdom says that foreign direct investment brings jobs and therefore prosperity and progress—for labor and especially for women. However, while the expansion of the export manufacturing sector through foreign capital investment does provide further opportunities to increase employment and exports for many countries in Asia, it also involves excessive competition to attract and maintain foreign direct investment. This in turn creates a tendency toward increase in the level of labor exploitation, via lower wages and longer working hours, with very little job security. In some cases, the minimum wage in the EPZs is lower than the national minimum wage, and many EPZs are excluded altogether from the scope of national labor laws. According to an ILO report, "the classic model of labor regulation is extremely rare in EPZs." In other words, workers in EPZs cannot negotiate binding agreements that regulate their interaction "with a 'floor' or framework of minimum labor standards, and free trade unions and employers (individually or collectively) coming together" (ILO 1998, 21).

Moreover, the footloose nature of globally mobile capital tends to move away from the countries where wages and working conditions have improved, for example, from South Korea, Hong Kong, and Malaysia to less developed economies such as Vietnam, Sri Lanka, Bangladesh, and China. This in turn creates a tendency toward increase in a downward pressure on wages, as expressed in the race-to-the-bottom syndrome. Thus, in global factories, the capital-labor relations for Asian women are becoming more exploitative and oppressive in the process of globalization of production. The flip side of the race to the bottom is the corporations' incessant search for ever-cheaper labor. As a consequence of these two processes, the labor

conditions of many women in contemporary Asia are coming to resemble those of an earlier era of industrialization in the West, characterized by sweatshops, that is, high levels of exploitation.

With increased emphasis on export production in national economic policy and a substantial increase in foreign direct investment in the region, the feminization of the labor force has now been firmly set in motion in many Asian countries. The feminization of labor in Asia is rather unique compared to that type of feminization taking place in the core countries. First of all, in Asia, the feminization of labor is accompanied by a new process of the proletarianization of women's labor. Many of this new pool of Asian women workers who are engaged in industrial production are drawn from the noncapitalist sphere of production, in particular from rural subsistence farming households. As such, many women wageworkers engaged in capitalist production are still a central part of a noncapitalist or nonproletarian household economy located in rural villages. This continued direct link between wage labor in the formal sector and the reproduction of village subsistence economies is a key feature of the political economy of globalization and women's labor in Asia.

Second, while feminization in the West is mainly located in service sector employment, the feminization of labor in Asia is concentrated in the manufacturing and agricultural sectors. While the proletarianization of women's labor in capitalist industries is a visible trend in most Asian countries, nevertheless a large proportion of Asia's women are still engaged in noncapitalist production.[1] Noncapitalist production refers to all activities that do not involve capital-labor relations but are nonetheless both economic and productive. This includes nonwage forms of work in subsistence agriculture, petty trade, community project work, exchange labor, and so on. Many women in Asian countries are engaged in more than one type of work at the same time. For example, they are involved in family farming while simultaneously working in informal and casual economic sectors, such as street vending or subcontracting piecework at home. In this way, they continuously carry out all types of work that fall outside the category of typical wage labor in the Western model of capitalist production. While some jobs in this category generate direct cash income, some do not necessarily remunerate women's labor in money form.

Nevertheless, these kinds of women's work, both paid and unpaid, significantly contribute to maintain the low cost of industrial and capitalist production. Even though women's labor is performed within the noncapitalist sphere of production, it is more often than not still fully integrated into the national economy, which is usually dominated by capitalist relations of production. A unit of economy, say, subsistence farming, may appear to be unrelated to, or separate from, the main capitalist economic system since social relations in the sphere of subsistence family farming are certainly noncapitalist and nonindustrial. Yet farming production is closely linked to the capitalist production system, especially via market exchange, and by its relation to national industrial policy, which affects the valorization of peasant production, usually to its detriment.

Let us discuss how this linkage works. Subsistence farm households sell their agricultural products in the market while they purchase other industrial goods, including farming materials such as fertilizers, pesticides, seeds, and agricultural tools. The relative exchange values of these two types of production (i.e., subsistence production and capitalist production) are set differently, and thus unequal exchange occurs at the expense of subsistence production.[2] When farm goods produced in a noncapitalist mode of production are exchanged in the capitalist market, the hidden value of noncapitalist labor activities is valorized and realized in disguised forms. The value of the farm products—grain, vegetables, fruits, and so forth—is created from two layers of noncapitalist labor. One is the value directly created by nonwage subsistence farming labor in producing the goods, a larger part of which consists of rural female labor. The other is the hidden value indirectly created within the sphere of reproduction, that is, domestic labor. When both parts of this noncapitalist labor are considered, women's labor accounts for the largest portion. In this way, even when it is not directly exploited via capital-wage relations, women's labor in noncapitalist production is subjected to indirect but more intensive exploitation by industrial capital. Rural women's labor activity in newly industrializing economies thus involves an "articulation of modes of production" in which value created in the noncapitalist sphere actually subsidizes the capitalist sphere (Meillassoux 1975).

Globalization of production affects women not only in terms of the increasing number of women workers but also in terms of the quality of their labor conditions. Contrary to Engels's claim,[3] the proletarianization in both manufacturing and service industries and the feminization of labor in Asia do not in themselves necessarily entail the empowerment of women through labor participation in production. Rather, under the present environment of a male-dominated structure of organized labor, feminization tends to weaken labor power in general. What is more, the feminization of labor occurs as a part of the process of flexibilization of labor, and this increasingly pushes women out of the core workforce and into a marginalized group of workers consisting of part-time, temporary, casual, and subcontracted labor. The direct and more immediate result of this process of economic marginalization, which affects perhaps the majority of women in Asia, is exacerbated by the intensified exploitation of their labor. In noneconomic terms, the predominance of neoliberal ideology may dampen what little exists of the sociopolitical movement of women in Asia and act to prevent radical improvement of their lives. Much empirical evidence indicates that economic globalization, in particular globalization of production, brings with it further exploitation

and impoverishment of women rather than their empowerment and emancipation.

The relative absence of substantive political representation of women and their alienation from political organizations inevitably affects women's position in society, including their legal rights. The political exclusion of women in Asia is directly related to the deepening of their economic marginalization and impoverishment. Therefore, along with further deterioration in the economic position of women, political exclusion of women, if it remains unchallenged, yields very little scope for improvement of women's position. Women will not get more claim on the society as a gender group unless specific women's issues are included in the political and social agenda of globalization.

ALTERNATIVE GLOBALIZATION:
DEMOCRATIC SOCIAL INCLUSION
AND WOMEN'S RIGHTS

Globalization is not just the predetermined triumph of Western consumerism, expressed as "the ultimate victory of VCR" by Francis Fukuyama (1992), for instance. Those who promise such a utopia for consumers while insisting on the separation of politics from economics do not take into account the fact that both the representation of power and the competition among conflicting interests in the sphere of politics are conditioned by economic relations. For example, capital-labor relations are not politically neutral, nor do capital and labor share an equal balance of power to begin with. Capital, by holding property and money and wielding considerable expertise and organizational power, begins in an advantageous position vis-à-vis labor. That is, the unequal distribution of material resources undermines equal access to political decisions and the capacity to influence political outcomes. In this sense, the assumption of fair and open political competition and equal political rights, on which formalistic notions of democracy ultimately depend, does not hold for everyone. In reality, due to underlying social inequalities, the political system operates largely in favor of capital rather than labor (Cohen 1991). Put another way, as Galbraith said, nothing so constrains the freedom of the individual as a complete absence of money.

The depoliticization element in the current economic globalization has a direct bearing on democratization, when democratization is understood as a process of social inclusion rather than merely as formal electoral participation. Democratization is a key process that may counter neoliberal globalization and how it ignores and marginalizes labor rights. In this context, democratization is a form of political and social resistance to capital-led globalization, which can be expressed as "counter-globalization" or "alternative-globalization" (Gills 2001). This claim depends on defining democratization in broad substantive terms rather than narrow formalistic terms. Any definition of democracy must include formal political democracy resting on legitimate civilian government and the rule of law, but a substantive definition of democracy goes beyond this narrow conventional understanding. Democracy cannot be constituted only by a formal electoral system, and it needs to meet certain types of redistributive socioeconomic criteria.

The concept of democracy as used typically in the liberal tradition emphasizes the economic freedom or liberty of private property and capital, that is, their independence from public (state) control. The function of the state in this conceptual framework is confined to ensure the individual freedom of capital and the optimum conditions of free market competition. Thus, the role of the state in the economy becomes minimal. It is also on this basis, according to liberalism, that the individual liberty of each citizen is best guaranteed. The concept of Western democracy via a minimalist state grants autonomy to those who already occupy an advantageous position, most notably holders of capital. In the absence of political resistance and intervention, jobs, prices, growth, and the standard of living all rest in the hands of businessmen (Sun 1999). According to Charles Lindblom (1977), the privileged position of business gives capital a louder voice than anyone else's on matters not only of economics but also of politics. The "autonomy of the private corporation" thus becomes "the major specific institutional barrier to fuller democracy." The current trend in globalization is driving toward precisely that goal, that is, increasing the autonomy of the private corporation.

Such a process results in the opposite of broadened social inclusion.

The increased autonomy granted to private capital and corporations exacerbates the process of exclusion. The processes of corporate concentration, megamerger, and oligarchization of global capital occurring in the world today mean that more and more workers and ordinary people will be excluded. The idea of the politics of inclusion is that prosperity for the majority can be brought about only by the inclusion of social forces, in particular of labor, into the state and its decision-making procedures. It also means focusing on redistributional economic policies that favor the weak majority rather than the strong minority. The process of inclusion implies decreasing social inequalities, polarization, and marginalization. Democratization, therefore, requires significant changes in the composition of power, allowing the inclusion of a broad spectrum of social forces into the state, or giving them access to influence the state policy decision-making process. This includes labor, not only organized labor but also unorganized labor, such as women's labor, children's labor, and migrants' labor. The problem of the creation and exclusion of the so-called underclass also has to be dealt with within a more inclusive social-political framework.

Above all, in the argument of democratization, what counts most is whether meaningful social change is actually taking place. In recent years, there has been a tendency toward a co-optive strategy. It is characterized by the convergence of opposition programs until there ceases to be any substantive difference between the alternative and the elite conservative position, be it called "the Third Way" or "New Labour" as put forward by Tony Blair. Such an ideology proclaims that capital-labor relations should no longer be characterized by antagonism but rather by a harmony of interests. This implies the class struggle is an irrelevance in globalized politics and social relations. In other words, in the new globalized world, *Left* and *Right* no longer bear any useful meaning in political discourse. In this way, the state both poses as and acts as the instrument conveying the interests of transnational capital onto national society. To borrow Robert Cox's (1987) term, this is the process of the "internationalizing of the state" in which the key state function is primarily to adjust domestic policies and practices to accommodate the functional requirements of the neoliberal global economy.

In contrast, substantive democratization via a politics of inclusion depends on a decisive shift in the balance of forces in favor of the political inclusion of popular social forces and movements. It strives for expanding and enhancing the political centrality of a progressive program, bringing about the empowerment of new social forces. Such democratization requires the prioritizing of social equity over economic growth. It also requires the will of the state to accept public accountability for the role of protection of societal interests from the depredations of private capital and economic interests. The role of the state therefore becomes central in the politics of globalization. In defense of societal interests, the state must be assumed to be neither merely a neutral mediating institution nor powerless vis-à-vis the forces of globalization. The state is a crucial political actor that facilitates social inclusion and overtly resists undesirable aspects of globalization. Rather than assuming that national policy cannot affect global market forces, the state can retain sufficient independence to exert a powerful influence over domestic outcomes, such as unemployment (Ashton and Maguire 1991) or even capital controls, as some governments in east Asia demonstrated during the Asian financial crisis. For the state to behave in this way, it is true that the first minimum condition is electoral competition, which allows the possibility of popular access to state power. Second, it requires that the party(ies) in government represent and defend the interests of the majority and can be held accountable to or be checked by this majority.

The dynamics in the politics of globalization can be detected in the development of global resistance movements in recent years. For example, Sweatshop Watch and the National Labor Committee, two coalitions based in the United States, represent one type of broad popular social movement. They bring together various campaigners for labor rights, human rights, and legal rights as well as community and religious organizations and university students to battle against sweatshop labor throughout the world. Other similar coalitions include the Maquila Solidarity Network, which promotes cooperation between labor and other social movements in NAFTA countries. The International Center for Trade Union Rights works specifically for the rights of unions and their workers at the international level, while Women Working Worldwide supports women workers through organizing public awareness campaigns and networking efforts. There are many other social organizations active in all parts of the world connected by the Internet. For example, 50 Years is Enough Network organizes a global network of resistance with some twenty-five similar organizations worldwide, including those in Nicaragua, South Africa, the Philippines, India, Senegal, Mauritius, Brazil, Macedonia, Pakistan, and Mexico.

In addition to new types of movements, the traditional union movement is also rejuvenating internationalism, for example, the International Confederation of Free Trade Unions and the International Trade Secretariats (Stevis and Boswell 2000). While these organizations bring together bureaucrats at the top of the organizational structure, others bring the grassroots unionists together for common action, such as the Transnationals Information Exchange (Niemeljer 1996). Labor is organizing worldwide in "the era of globalization," and as new models of solidarity and collective action emerge, they bridge old barriers between North and South (Munck and Waterman 1999).

In the case of women's labor experiences, the complex ways in which gender hierarchy, national capital, foreign capital, and the state negotiate and adapt to the forces of economic globalization expose women to diverse mechanisms of exploitation.

Accordingly, women are responding in a wide range of ways and at different levels. The spectrum of actions by women extends from day-to-day resistance by individuals and informal resistance and support by a group of women to formal organizational actions. The informal organizational resistance includes various social networks based on women's communities, dormitories, workplaces, and even through worldwide Web sites. This type of activity can provide women with moral and material support as well as a foundation on which collective consciousness and actions develop. Such groups as the Union for Civil Liberty and the Friends for Friends Group in Thailand, Women's Shelters, National Network for Solidarity with Migrant Workers, the Working Women's Network in Japan, and various women's support groups and watchdog organizations, including formal organizations in Asian countries, represent different levels and channels of resistance. Trade union movements demanding increased labor rights for women have also gained further momentum in recent years. For example, there has been an unprecedented level of increase in trade union membership during the past few years in Malaysia, while numerous new women's labor unions and organizations were formed after the 1997-1998 financial crisis in spite of the fact that the absolute amount of female employment has been reduced.

It is apparent that there have been various social actions that have strengthened the counterhegemonic movements against capital-led economic globalization. Labor, especially women's labor, is an important social force that can check the power of capital and resist the global trends that encroach on labor rights. Women's movements, however, are now required to be something more than traditional male-oriented labor movements. Cultural norms and values determining women's adverse social position are very much tied to the dominant patriarchal relations within a society. Therefore, any meaningful changes that would raise women's social status will not come about without some form of organized resistance to gender inequality. Rejection of unequal gender relations can only be effectively pursued via organized political-social action. More broadly, social and political responses working for social justice should be based on greater inclusion, including women's rights.

Globalization of production at the expense of women's and workers' rights cannot be maintained without creating volatility that affects both industry and labor. On one hand, such volatility "makes zones less effective as export platforms and limits their potential to attract investment, generate jobs, boost exports and promote broader economic growth" (ILO 1998). On the other hand, further repression of labor as a way of controlling volatility does not offer long-term solutions; rather, it prevents real progress toward democratization. Meaningful democratization can be pushed forward only through a social agenda of redistribution, not only of economic but of political power, between the divided groups within society, which must include gender.

Notes

1. The heavily urbanized and industrialized countries of northeast Asia, such as Japan, South Korea, and Taiwan, and the city-state of Singapore are exceptions. Elsewhere in Asia, from India, through most of southeast Asia, to mainland China, peasant life still predominates.

2. For a detailed discussion of exchange between subsistence and capitalist production, see Gills (1999).

3. Engels presented production relations as the principal factor that conditions the development of society and of social institutions. Along this line of argument, that social production relations determine all power relations, he and subsequent Marxist writers explained women's subordination as the result of their assignment to "unproductive" roles in the domestic sphere.

References

Ashton, D., and M. Maguire. 1991. Patterns and experience of unemployment. In *Poor work: Disadvantage and the division of labor*, edited by P. Brown and R. Scase, 40-55. Milton Keynes, UK: Open University Press.

Castells, M. 1996. *The rise of the network society*. Oxford, UK: Blackwell.

Cohen, J. 1991. Maximising social welfare or institutionalising democratic ideals? Commentary on Adam Prezworski's article. *Politics and Society* 19 (1): 39-58.

Cox, R. 1987. *Production, power and world order: Social forces in the shaping of history*. New York: Columbia University Press.

Fukuyama, F. 1992. *The end of history and the last man*. Harmondsworth, UK: Penguin.

Galbraith, J. 2000. Forward: The social Left and the market system. In *Globalization and politics of resistance*, edited by B. Gills. London: Macmillan.

Giddens, A. 1990. *The consequences of modernity*. Cambridge, UK: Polity.

———. 1996. Globalization: A keynote address. *UNRISD News*:15.

Gills, B. K. 1997. Editorial: Globalization and the politics of resistance. *New Political Economy* 2 (1): 11-15.

Gills, D.-S.S. 1999. *Rural women and triple exploitation in Korean Development*. New York: Macmillan.

———. 2001. Globalization and counter-globalization. In *Women and work in globalizing Asia*, edited by D. S. Gills and N. Piper, 13-29. London: Routledge.

Hoogvelt, A., and A. Puxty. 1997. *Multinational enterprise: An encyclopedic dictionary of concepts and terms*. London: Macmillan.

International Labor Organization (ILO). 1998. *Labor and social issues relating to export processing zones: Report for discussion in the tripartite meeting of export processing zone-operating countries*. Geneva: International Labor Organization.

Kasugo, T., and Z. Tzannatos. 1998. *Export processing zones: A review in need of update*. Discussion paper series 9802. Washington, DC: World Bank.

Lindblom, C. 1977. *Politics and markets*. New York: Basic Books.

MacAdam, M. 1998. Working for the rat. *New Internationalist* 308 (December): 15-17.

Meillassoux, C. 1975. From production to reproduction: A Marxist approach to economic anthropology. *Economy and Society* 1 (1): 93-104.

Munck, R., and P. Waterman, eds. 1999. *Labour worldwide in the era of globalization: Alternative union models in the new world order*. London: Macmillan.

Niemeljer, M. 1996. Grassroots labor internationalism: The transnational information exchange. Unpublished thesis, University of Amsterdam.

Stevis, D., and T. Boswell. 2000. From national resistance to international labor politics. In *Globalization and the politics of resistance*, edited by B. Gills, 150-70. London: Macmillan.

Sun, H. 1999. Democratic consolidation and labor politics. Unpublished paper, University of Newcastle, UK.

Theobald, S. 2001. Working for global factories: Thai women in electronics export companies in the Northern Regional Industrial Estate. In *Women and work in globalizing Asia*, edited by D. S. Gills and N. Piper, 136. London: Routledge.

Thomas, K. 1997. Corporate welfare campaigns in North America. *New Political Economy* 2 (1): 117-26.

United Nations Conference on Trade and Development. 1994. *UNCTAD statistical pocket book*.

Waters, M. 1995. *Globalization*. London: Routledge.

Zhao, M., and J. West. 2001. Adjusting to urban capital: Rural female labor in state cotton mills in China. In *Women and work in globalizing Asia*, edited by D. S. Gills and N. Piper, 169-187. London: Routledge.

ANNALS, *AAPSS*, **581**, May 2002

Predatory Globalization and Democracy in the Islamic World

By MUSTAPHA KAMAL PASHA

ABSTRACT: The rise of Islamic activism worldwide, including the appearance of illiberal politics in Islamic cultural areas (ICAs), is usually seen as a reaction to globalizing modernization. Based on the assumption of an elective affinity between Western cultural assets and liberal democracy, most analysts neglect to see globalization, particularly, in its predatory form, as a constitutive condition of Islamism. Accentuating the cultural divide within ICAs, predatory globalization strives to constrict political space for democratic expression. The growing disconnect between an already fractured political community and an increasingly illegitimate state provides Islamicists the opening to capture key institutions in civil society or to create alternative avenues of communal identity, participation, and civic action. Prospects for building a liberal democratic order hinge mainly on a resolution of the internal dialectic within ICAs. The unstoppable march of predatory globalization, however, appears unlikely to yield either the political space or the historical time to bridge the deep chasm within ICAs.

Mustapha Kamal Pasha is an associate professor of comparative and international political economy in the School of International Service at American University in Washington, D.C. His principal work focuses on the confluence of culture and political economy, particularly in relation to Islamic cultural areas. He is the author of Colonial Political Economy: Recruitment and Underdevelopment in the Punjab *(Oxford) and has widely published in journals, including articles in* Millennium, Alternatives, Studies in Comparative International Development, *and* Journal of Developing Societies. *He served as program chair of the International Studies Association annual convention in Chicago in 2001 and is a recent recipient of a grant to study the role of madrassas (religious schools) in civil society.*

T HE enduring otherness of Islam has long ensured recurrent mockery of its culture and people in Western scholarship and the popular media, with orientalist truisms of inherent Muslim abnormality and excess regularly coloring examinations of the faith, including understandings of the seemingly tortured career of democracy in the Islamic cultural areas (ICAs).[1] Predictably, the reputed failure of Muslims to successfully negotiate modernity and modernization has become a constant motif of representation. Apologetics about Islam, on the other hand, generally express a persistent defensiveness characteristic of the intellectual and political subjection of the Muslim community, an acquiescence to the dominant terms of the discourse, which authorize democratic ideals and their realization as cultural idiom. Accepting these terms, the Western political experience, notably in its institutional form, becomes the universal currency for worldwide circulation, as the current discourse on global democracy suggests. Between ridicule and apologia lies limited analytical space to assess the nature of democracy in ICAs, further circumscribed by dramatic recent events.[2]

Orientalist constructions of Islam and the totalizing logic of predatory globalization (Falk 1999)[3] take the resurgence of Islam in the political and personal spheres of Muslim social life as basically an antimodern phenomenon. These accounts reduce cultural processes in Islamic societies to a revolt against the West or challenges to a universal civilization. Assuming a basic cleavage between a globalizing project and forms of politics that are encoded in a religious idiom, these perspectives reproduce an irreconcilable breach between universalistic claims of the rise of a global society and particularistic forms of political and cultural expression. Suppressed in these accounts is the possibility that social processes in ICAs are not simply about transitions to (Western) modernity but the workings of complex inner dynamics now complicated by globalization. With this leaning, the purpose of this article is to recognize the current phase of Islamism (or the increasing assertion of Islamic idiom into political practice) as both an articulation of internal processes in ICAs and as a constitutive element of neoliberal globalization (Pasha 2000; Pasha and Samatar 1996), not simply a reaction to its predatory instincts.

GLOBALIZATION AND DEMOCRACY

Neoliberals see the movement toward global democratization as both cause and consequence of globalization. Free association of capital and labor intensifies and extends worldwide social connectedness. Open markets and the unfettered spirit of enterprise, in turn, pave the way for democratic politics as institution and practice. Economic globalization, global democracy, and a global commercial culture are closely intertwined. The expansion of the market opens up political spaces. Liberal democracy (synonymous with procedural democracy) facilitates and nurtures the human capacity to realize its natural economic instincts. A global commercial culture shatters barriers of difference and identity (Holton 2000). In this context, neoliberal globalization and liberal democracy are mutually constitutive and reinforcing. Clearly, the density of both globalization and liberalism as complex constructs is subordinated to a self-evident logic: neither the contradictory nor the contested nature of these phenomena are examined. On one hand, liberalism is emptied of its core content, namely, its emphasis on socially self-determined citizenship. On the other hand, neoliberals reduce globalization to homogenization, not recognizing increasing global relatedness as the recognition of hybridization or cultural difference.

Rather than facilitate, predatory globalization threatens liberal democracy in multiple ways. The liberal democratic project as theory and historical experience once premised on the nation(al)-state—a well-marked, territorially distinct political community—is in deep trouble. On questions of political membership, participation, accountability, and legitimacy, the nation-state once effectively served as the principal locus and agency of mobilization and authorization. Both procedural and substantive notions of democracy have hinged on varied concatenations of state-society relations secured within an imagined, but spatially designated, political community. With a rearticulation in the nature of power, authority, and governance afforded by new divisions of labor between capital and the state locally and globally, the dimensions of the liberal democratic state are severely tested. More directly, neoliberal globalization, with its emphasis on diminished state intervention in political economy, except in matters of surveillance and security, facilitates governance, not government. Cross-border flows of people and commodities are difficult to tame, resulting in reduced state capacity to perform its political, not simply functional, role. What is the imagined political community of neoliberal globalization? A tentative answer to this difficult question lies in appreciating the subordination of politics to technical rationality inherent in neoliberalism.

It would be a mistake, however, to neglect new forms of social connectedness on a global scale, often occasioned by the expansion of the global market, but not limited to its logic. Alternative forms of cross-national and cross-cultural interaction may also be entirely consistent with an awareness of human diversity and dignity, a consciousness about the borderless nature of ecological problems, and respect for the rights of the weak and the dispossessed. Some claims of cosmopolitan democracy, therefore, are not without merit, particularly those that recognize the diminishing relevance of notions of nationally articulated popular sovereignty, but also arguments that draw our attention to the indivisibility of global political action and mobilization given time-space compression of social processes. Yet these putative forms of social connectedness are confined mainly to the more prosperous, the affluent, and the better-organized sectors of the global political economy. The parallel structures these new modalities of social relatedness produce are incapable of incorporating the vast majority of the powerless, politically unrepresented or underrepresented quasi-citizens of the world. In the absence of the state that is unable to exercise sovereignty over its own community, a general crisis of representation becomes a distinct possibility.

The contention between predatory globalization and democracy is accentuated within political economy. Once the common purpose is relegated to the exchange principle under a neoliberal order, redefining the role of the state, reliance on private enterprise substitutes the ethical state. And in countries where the state, despite its own predatory instincts, has supervised welfare, neoliberal globalization can spell disaster by inverting the public-private societal equation. With the state's becoming the custodian of global private, not societal, interests and civil society (the realm of private association) given the responsibility to shoulder collective projects, including development and welfare, powerful interests will be allowed to dominate civil society. Liberal democracy, under conditions of inequality, without available redress for the powerless, is not a very sustainable project in the long run. Despite the contradictions that are often cited, Keynesian compromises underscored the necessity of redress to legitimate both democracy and capitalism. The effects of revisions in the Keynesian compact are clearly more pronounced in the marginal

regions of the global political economy.

A major effect of predatory globalization most directly relevant to ICAs is the growing detachment of the nation from the state. If dominant parts of the state collude with global economic forces to stay afloat, the nation must drift and lose cohesion, common purpose, and solidarity. Though this scenario is too dramatic to have factual significance, the growing power of global capital and its institutional complementarity in unaccountable international agencies portends the sign of the times. Once citizenship is radically emptied of political content, it assumes a mere symbolic, procedural, or formal character. This is not to suggest the collapse of liberalism entirely but its radical rearticulation under conditions of flux.

Against the backdrop of predatory globalization, the prospects for building and sustaining liberal democracy in ICAs assumes a tenuous character. To examine this question, however, a short detour on the relation between Islam and democracy in received wisdom seems appropriate.

DEMOCRACY AND ISLAM

Despite ritualistic and polite qualification, the pervasive scholarly sentiment suggests a basic divergence between democracy and Islam. Democracy is ultimately a Western ideal-type; spatial and cultural distance weaken its resemblance to the original[4] (Lewis 1993; Abootalebi 1995). By implication, Westernization (not merely modernization) alone can provide the prerequisites for building a universal civilization in which democratic polities can thrive and realize the promise of liberal enlightenment. According to this modernist claim, some cultures are obviously incompatible with democratic sentiment; their destiny is glued to particularistic political expression. The inclusion of the ICAs as favorite undifferentiated others inhabiting this fixed universe naturally follows: Muslim society of all shades and hues can only fulfill its consecrated fate as broker of antimodern passion, illiberal politics, and religious fervor. Despite the lure of global democracy, the ICAs cannot generate projects of either state or civil society bearing the signature of liberalism: Islamism is sheer continuation of the endless, if sometimes modulated, drama of oriental despotism. And in the context of globalization, it is an open rebellion against the latest phase of modernity.

An initial step toward approaching an alternative reading of the relation between Islam and democracy, especially in the context of global consciousness of societal processes worldwide, perhaps, is to appreciate the possibility that democratic ideals do exist in ICAs; these (alternative) ideals may not be so readily accessible or even recognizable (Moten 1997). Both the historical site of their inception and the form in which democratic aspirations are articulated can elude examination informed by culturalist assumptions (Zartman 1992). Cultural beliefs and institutional inheritances remain crucial determinants of politics, including

democracy (Clague, Gleason, and Knack 2001). And to the degree liberal democracy is equated with particular cultural endowments and orientations, the future of this relation is already determined: arrested political development remains the only probable trajectory for ICAs, released only by externally induced compulsions and opportunities. Advanced modernization or globalization thus can only herald new opportunities to permit an unfreezing of domestic societal processes in ICAs; alternatives to neoliberal globalization are mere acts of resistance. This logic, smuggled from doctrines of political modernization, undergirds much of the recent thinking among neoliberal globalists on building democracy in the ex-colonial world.

A corollary to the empiricism that typically accompanies common sense, neoliberal triumphalism fortifies its claims by assembling cases that provide obvious antithesis to liberal democracy in its varied social and cultural forms. An absence of procedural democracy in many parts of the West's periphery thus lends credence to an array of oft-repeated lines declaring the implausibility of democracy without cultural prerequisites. In the present era, however, not Marx but Keynes now stands between democracy and development. Welfare, equity, redistribution, or ecological justice, not class conflict, allegedly obstruct the inevitable passage to the brave new world of neoliberal globalization. The fate of ICAs is not too difficult to ascertain within this circumscribed horizon.

The official story of incompatibility has familiar sequential parts, beginning with an essentialized view of Islamic culture and civilization, leading to the current phenomenon of militant rage serving as a proxy for the entire civilization. In its abbreviated version, this narrative locates the failure of political liberalism to the totalizing structure of Muslim cosmology and political theory, an unchanged fixture of irrational unwillingness toward recognizing and separating ecclesiastic spheres from the more mundane (Kramer 1993; Lewis 1993). The inseparability of religion and politics in Islam foretells the political fate of its believers. Unable to secure an autonomous realm for building politics and citizenship, Muslims are forever condemned to the purgatory of rendering everything to God what belongs to either God or Caesar. The subsequent historical episodes in Islamic history replay this theme in varied guises: the recognition of a de facto separation between religion and politics (Lapidus 1975) is repeatedly subordinated to the overarching precepts of conformity to the central belief. Despite the appearance of multiple political forms through the centuries in diverse settings (hence the usage of "cultural areas" after "Islamic" in this article), the incompatibility thesis has survived, giving contemporary incarnations of a totalizing religion the status of a utopia (Addi 1992).

On this view, much of the political language of Islam is seemingly possessed by the ghosts of failed past attempts to separate the inseparable. The absence of a true reformation, in part, is explained in this way. Informed and sympathetic scholars are not too far behind authentically orientalist observers of ICAs to deliver the familiar message. Islam brooks no separation between the faith and politics, not even in the face of expediency, colonial onslaughts, and more recent externally induced challenges, the argument goes. Extrapolating from this account, globalization further closes the opening to separate religion and politics, as Islam and its culture become renewed sites and agency of resistance against modernity. In a total reversal in the argument, neoliberal globalists now find ICAs impenetrable to globalization's enlightening mission, given Islam's notorious rigidity in the face of change.

The incompatibility thesis is buttressed by invocation of a so-called paradox of democracy in ICAs. While embracing the procedural accoutrements of Western-style democracy, Islamicists on this reading are opposed to the vision of an open society. Clearly, the range of illiberal politics in ICAs is fairly elastic, including an attitude of exclusionary politics, a disregard for the values of tolerance and respect for political difference, and a program for amending the rules of democratic politics. Depriving uncertain believers of equal participation by curtailing voting rights is a clear example of illiberal politics. The climate of intolerance can be both implicit and explicit as the political platforms of Islamicists suggest, especially on questions of women's rights and minority status. In the face of illiberal pronouncements by Islamicists themselves, the arrival of democracy in ICAs prefaces its demise in the hands of those who deny its liberal promise. Allowing Islamicists the benefits of liberal democracy thus invites political suicide. But blocking Islamicists from participation in the formalized political process equally undermines and delegitimizes the essence of the liberal project itself. This proposed paradox serves as a regular staple to rationalize repression of Islamicists in ICAs, notably Egypt and Turkey, countries with nominal commitments to democracy.

The central inference drawn from the conventional perspective takes Islamism as a form of cultural resistance to globalization or, more poignantly, a repudiation of the basic civilizational principles of enlightenment thought and operation. Hence, the prospect of democracy in the ICAs in the context of globalization is likely to repeat the history of the original mismatch between modernity and Islam. Although some recent diagnoses of democracy's ailing health in the ICAs bend toward more sociologically oriented explanations, the claim of culturally dependent social pathology of ICAs endures; Durkheimian anomie becomes yet another layer above extant neopatrimonial state structures.

Predatory globalization introduces new challenges for democratic construction. The older question of compatibility between Islam and modernity is resurrected with globalization—once modernization, now globalization. But a discussion of globalization's impact on democracy in ICAs must be preceded by a focus of the internal character of social formations in the Islamic world. The actually existing world of Islam, it will become clear, is more fractured politically than conventional readings permit.

A FRACTURED POLITICAL COMMUNITY

Shifting the focus away from an essentialized perspective on Islamic politics entails a recognition of the heterogeneity of ICAs but also their heterodox character internally. To suggest the class nature of ICAs is to rehearse the obvious. Perhaps more relevant for present purposes is the awareness of a cultural divide drawn by access to the accoutrements of a West-centered modernity (especially European languages) and its relative or partial denial to the vast majority. The division, by no means absolute, is not between Westernizing moderates and Islamic militants per se but between centers of privilege and the marginalized periphery structured and stabilized to global cultural capital, in addition to a monopoly of control by elites over material wealth. The distinctly cultural manifestation of social distinction disguises the materiality of its institution, however. Hence, Islamicists are better recognized as repositories of subaltern sensibilities, not irrational opponents of modernity or modernization. The cumulative effect, nonetheless, of past inheritances and contemporary societal dynamics is the growing fragmentation of the imagined Muslim nation, fractured by a practical breakdown in the dialogue between its various cultural parts; the weakening of the state in ICAs heightens national disintegration.

Acknowledging the existence of alternative expressions of the democratic ideal in ICAs also entails a recognition of the national context in which the new Islamists' social movements operate. But the nation is an increasingly fractured political community. The calls for democratic participation by Islamists in the idiom of religion, not liberalism, underscores the rift within ICAs. The question, then, is not of whether Islam and democracy are compatible but of recognizing the process of building a new social order drawn from alternative conceptions of the common good, including the character of political identity. Islam provides ample intellectual resources to articulate alternative visions (Lapidus 1992) but, like other religions, is equally susceptible to "absolutism and hierarchy as well as foundations for liberty and equality" (Esposito and Voll 1996, 7) and, as Esposito and Voll (1996) suggested, a ready source for provisioning ideas of equality and legitimate opposition.

Islamism seeks a reconstitution of state and civil society in ICAs. And it is the form and context in which reconstitution must occur that conditions its relation to democratic principles and practice; there is no inevitability built into the social process. One useful site for analyzing processes of reconstitution lies in the contrasting views on the state and civil society (Zubaida 1992) in ICAs. Islamicists propound several alternative conceptions of civil society, ranging from civil society's equation

with a realm of voluntary association, informal networks, or the market. Similarly, the state is analyzed in ethical, instrumental, or structural terms. Despite variance in the language, parallel (Islamic) concepts suggest the vitality of political discourse. Given the official marginalization of the Islamic discourse in most ICAs, however, informed understandings of state-civil society relations are subordinated to simplified prose. The growing dependency of politics on the popular media further drowns serious conversation.

Another layer in a complex and evolving political process in ICAs is decolonization (Sayyid 1997), especially at the cognitive level: the awareness of the possibility of alternatives to West-centered worlds. The emphasis on Islam is not coincidental but contingent on the indigenization of ideological production and circulation in Muslim civil society. However, the indigenization of knowledge in the context of mass media may not be entirely supportive of inclusionary politics. The circulation of popular opinion without careful reflection or scrutiny may even hamper efforts to fight prejudice, especially in areas of gender equality and the rights of minorities. Celebrations of the nativization of knowledge, therefore, must be carefully read as cautious tales pregnant with unexpected twists and plots.

Despite these disclaimers, the demand for democratization, albeit of an Islamic variant, embodies struggles for empowerment of the many against secular-nationalist elites. These struggles are quite diverse in character. Esposito and Voll (1996) provided a useful typology of Islamicist movements. First, some movements highlight the successful assumption of political power by Islamicists: Iran, through a revolution against secular modernization, and the Sudan, with the development of an Islamic movement and its takeover of the state, provide obvious examples. Then, there are movements centered around political parties willing to operate with recognized rules of the game. The case of the Jamaat-I-Islami in Pakistan, on one hand, and the Angkatan Belia Islam Malaysia, on the other, offer good examples. Finally, there are movements that stand in severe contention to state structures, operating largely outside legal channels. The Islamicist movements in Syria, Morocco, Turkey, Algeria, and Egypt, with many variations among them, illustrate the third kind (Esposito and Voll 1996). Under globalizing conditions, new movements may also be originating, while established ones experience fresh challenges.

Three elements in the social production of Islamism are relevant here: (1) the generally inhospitable climate and attitude of secular-nationalist elites toward Islamicists in general, (2) the breakdown of an internal dialogue between different sectors of society, and (3) the lumpen nature of the Islamic intellectual discourse(s) in ICAs. All three elements contribute to illiberal politics. In the first instance, Islamicists, who generally come from the more marginal sectors of society, are often perceived as the internal other in ICAs, except in national contexts where they have

concentrated political power. The marginal sectors here are defined not simply in economic terms but by a complex process of social layering involving access to cultural capital. Access to Western modernity, despite the shallowness of its articulation, is invariably a basis of privilege and mobility in ICAs. It is against culturally articulated distinction and inequality that marginality becomes recognizable. The presumed resentment of Islamicists directed at Westernizing elites is not a repudiation of modernity per se, as the rhetoric often suggests, but an expression of protest in deeply divided social formations (Deeb 1992). Often, repression of Islamicists is rationalized on the basis of their presumed backwardness or potential menace to the legality of state structures and policy. Calls for equity, fairness, or redistribution once couched in an unfamiliar (Islamicist) idiom immediately invite suspicion and draconian policing. Without openings in the political process, the extremists in Islamicist movements can often prevail in justifying their own exclusionary version of politics.

The breakdown of the internal dialogue also reflects the cultural divergence within ICAs. Even the vocabulary and syntax of communication deployed by secular-nationalists and Islamicists, to simplify a very complex picture, appear incommensurable. Globalization contributes to the growing chasm, acknowledging only those who are conversant with the West-centered forms of expression while ignoring those who speak in more indigenous vernaculars. But the original source of this breakdown is not globalization but a legacy of political and social schizophrenia injected into the cultural fabric of ICAs by colonialism; then by postcolonial secular-nationalist state managers guided by the mythology of modernist progress, economic planning, and social engineering; and now by predatory globalization. The crisis of political representation in most ICAs is a logical outcome of the divergence within Muslim society, reflected in the cultural gulf that separates the powerful from the subaltern.

Finally, the nature of the Islamicist discourse in most ICAs increasingly reveals a lumpen intellectual character. The decline in major centers of intellectual activity in most ICAs, especially the alienation of contemporary discourses from rich currents in Islamic thought, have helped foster political, not philosophical, Islam: an unwavering reliance on formulaic logic in dealing with complex issues, supplemented by linear solutions (Butterworth 1992). Intellectuals better skilled in the art of manipulating the mass media can now enjoy the widest audience. Once the principal vehicle in struggles for decolonization, print capitalism serves the tyranny of common sense. The Islamicists are no strangers to the technical and instrumental aspects of either print capitalism or the telecommunications revolution. Islamicists are moderns, but without the baggage of secularism. Artful use of the new instrumentality of communication especially helps Islamicists bypass formal political channels imposed and closely guarded by secular nationalists. In either case, the result is the oversimplification of social inquiry and a deterioration in reflexive habits of analysis. Against this backdrop, perhaps, the rise in the capacity of Islamicists to influence the nature of the discourses in ICAs, often disproportionate to their meager size, becomes more comprehensible.

The fractured nature of political community in Muslim society in ICAs and pressures of neoliberal globalization combine forces to nurture new forms of exclusionary politics. Globalization theorists recognize Islamism mainly as a reaction to neoliberal globalization. Instead, the attempt to see globalization and Islamism as mutually constitutive avoids the perils of binary constructions of contradictory phenomena. On this alternative reading, the rise of exclusionary politics globally, especially in ICAs, becomes more fathomable.

CONCLUSION

Premised on a logic of inevitability, predatory globalization provides both the context and the pretext for bolstering religious activism in ICAs at two levels. First, it weakens state capacity for secular-nationalists to provide basic social and economic services to a demographically expanding and restless population. Entertaining neoliberal prescriptions for chronic ills further draws state managers in ICAs into global processes over which they exercise diminishing influence. Embracing neoliberalism also means acknowledging the hegemony of global market rationality, its largely homogenized cultural enunciation, liberal institutionalism, and incorporation into a worldwide vortex of social connectedness via telecommunications and the global media. These structural arrangements further polarize the social formation in ICAs, deepening both the economic crisis and the crisis of representation.

On the other side of the equation, political alienation of state managers from their populace becomes the impetus for wider and more elaborate forms of repression and authoritarianism, shrinking an already limited space for political expression and pushing Islamicists further into the clasp of extremism. A source of solace and succor, but also legitimation, religion readily supplies the pretext for the extremist turn in ICAs, as secular legality increasingly correlates statist neglect and malfeasance. This is not a propitious context to either build or consolidate a liberal democratic project; the (alternative) ideal of Islamic democracy in several ICAs seems infinitely more attractive to Muslims under these conditions. Yet this alternative assumes a more rejectionist, and often illiberal, profile given its marginalization within a globalizing context— spurned, mocked, and attacked as a symbol of barbarity or social pathology. Standing outside the preferred world of homogenized cultural space drawn by neoliberal globalization, the complexity of this alternative ideal is compromised by its appearance solely as a grotesque stain on a universal civilization. The growing militancy and rage of some zealous converts to this (alternative) Islamic ideal only validates the lunacy of their project or, in religiously charged prose, the evil that animates random acts of savagery.

Notes

1. The usage of the term "Islamic cultural areas" (ICAs) throughout this article is deliberate. It suggests the plurality of historical and social experience of Muslims, underscoring a nonessentialized viewpoint.

2. The brazen attacks in New York and Washington D.C. by Muslim extremists last September have only deepened the divide separating analysis from caricature; the events of 11 September have confirmed the general image of Islam as a religion of rage, an illiberal, antimodern culture. Given the recent disfigured climate, an informed understanding of the liberal democratic project in ICAs is an obvious challenge.

3. The focus on the "predatory" aspects of globalization include, but are not confined to, the "cumulative effects" of neoliberalism and attendant political choices on human well-being, which are basically negative (Falk 1999, 2).

4. "Liberal democracy," wrote Lewis (1993),

however far it may have traveled, is in its origins a product of the West. . . . No such system has originated in any other cultural tradition; it remains to be seen whether such a system, transplanted and adapted in another culture, can long survive. (P. 93)

References

Abootalebi, Ali R. 1995. Democratization in developing countries: 1980-1989. *Journal of Developing Areas* 29 (4): 507-30.

Addi, Lahouari. 1992. Islamicist utopia and democracy. *Annals of the American Academy of Political and Social Science* 524:120-30.

Butterworth, Charles E. 1992. Political Islam: The origins. *Annals of the*

American Academy of Political and Social Science 524:26-37.

Clague, Christopher, Suzanne Gleason, and Stephen Knack. 2001. Determinants of lasting democracy in poor countries: Culture, development and institutions. Annals of the American Academy of Political and Social Science 573:16-41.

Deeb, Mary-Jane. 1992. Militant Islam and the politics of redemption. Annals of the American Academy of Political and Social Science 524:52-65.

Esposito, John L., and John O. Voll. 1996. Islam and democracy. New York: Oxford University Press.

Falk, Richard. 1999. Predatory globalization: A critique. Oxford, UK: Polity.

Holton, Robert. 2000. Globalization's cultural consequences. Annals of the American Academy of Political and Social Science 570:140-52.

Kramer, Martin. 1993. Where Islam and democracy part ways. In Democracy in the Middle East: Defining the challenge, edited by Yehuda Mirsky and Matt Ahrens. Washington, DC: Washington Institute for Near East Policy.

Lapidus, Ira M. 1975. The separation of state and religion in the development of early Islamic society. International Journal of Middle East Studies 6 (4): 363-85.

———. 1992. The golden age: The political concepts of Islam. Annals of the American Academy of Political and Social Science 524:13-25.

Lewis, Bernard. 1993. Islam and liberal democracy. Atlantic Monthly, February, 89-98.

Moten, Abdul Rashid. 1997. Democratic and Shura-based system: A comparative analysis. Encounters 3 (March): 3-20.

Pasha, Mustapha Kamal. 2000. Globalization, Islam and resistance. In Globalization and the politics of resistance, edited by B. G. Gills. Basingstoke, UK: Macmillan.

Pasha, Mustapha Kamal, and Ahmed I. Samatar. 1996. The resurgence of Islam. In Globalization: Critical reflections, edited by J. H. Mittelman. Boulder, CO: Lynne Rienner.

Sayyid, Bobby S. 1997. A fundamental fear: Eurocentrism and the emergence of Islamism. London: Zed Books.

Zartman, I. William. 1992. Democracy and Islam: The cultural dialectic. Annals of the American Academy of Political and Social Science 524:181-91.

Zubaida, Sami. 1992. Islam, the state and democracy: Contrasting conceptions of society in Egypt. Middle East Report 22 (6): 2-10.

Globalization and Culture: Placing Ireland

By G. HONOR FAGAN

ABSTRACT: Instead of asking how globalization can help us understand Ireland today, this article starts from the premise that Ireland may be useful for an understanding of globalization. Always at a crossroads culturally and through its huge migration overseas, contemporary Ireland is seen as the epitome of a globalization success story. The article examines the constant (re)creation of Irish identity and its complex (re)constitution in the era of globalization. It concludes that if an Ireland did not already exist, globalization theory would have to invent it.

G. Honor Fagan is a lecturer in sociology at the National University of Ireland, Maynooth. Her doctorate was awarded from Miami University, Oxford, Ohio, in 1991. Her current research interests include cultural politics, globalization and culture, civil society, and conflict resolution. She has done field research on early school leavers in Dublin for her book Cultural Politics and Irish Early School Leavers: Constructing Political Identities *(1995) and on women in South African townships. She is currently living in Ireland and researching for a book titled* Globalization and Culture: Repositioning Politics.

I N spite of the criticisms accruing from second-generation globalization studies, the term "globalization" is still surviving as a description of the widening, deepening, and speeding up of global interconnectedness and its impact on social change and social processes on a world scale. Rather than dying off, it appears that the term is becoming increasingly popular with leading politicians now using it as a matter of course to describe the era we live in. Any event that appears on the world scene, for example, the events of 11 September, is now interpreted through the lens of globalization.

INTRODUCTION

At the level of the academy, globalization studies originally heralded the globalization of communications, capital, and culture almost in that order, and the argument was made that these globalization forces were in effect decomposing the nation-state and the distinctiveness of individual societies. This argument was followed immediately by critiques of the notion of an all-encompassing globalization process, and the work in this mode emphasized uneven, complex, and contingent aspects of globalization. This article seeks to position itself outside either of these established approaches to the study of globalization. Where, in general, the trend has been to show how global processes affect the production of single events or social change at the local or national level, I propose to reverse the trend by approaching an explanation of the global with specific reference to the national or local. Basically, I wish to ask the question, What can a study of Ireland do for understanding the phenomenon called globalization? rather than, How can globalization explain modern Ireland? In looking at the specificity of Irish international and national dynamics and the linkages between cultural and economic processes at play in developing or imagining Ireland, we can see tendencies and countertendencies toward globalizing dynamics.

This special issue looks at globalization and democracy, and this article attempts to look at the link between the two by emphasizing the articulation of the cultural and the economic at one and the same time in the production of Ireland in a global era. In short, the argument is that if we are to understand Ireland as a democratic nation, which has produced itself in its current form within and around the dynamics of the global forces of capitalism, then we need to examine the phenomenon of Ireland through an analytical framework of cultural political economy. This should throw light on globalization tendencies and countertendencies from a specific location and, likewise, show how culture implicates itself daily in the democratic processes that have produced Ireland.

The most common reading of Ireland and its current state of development is as a country that has done well in the era of globalization much as it had earlier done badly in the era of imperialism. Has there really been such a turnaround? What dynamics does this uncover that the emerging area of global studies needs to take on board? This article moves toward an answer in three parts: it examines first, the problematic placing of Ireland in the world; second, its constant (re)invention from a cultural political economy approach; and finally, its moving parts on the global scenes—its exiles and diasporas. I hope to contribute an Irish perspective that avoids the difficulties associated with taking either a nationalist or postnationalist approach.

PLACING

We can usually, fairly unproblematically, place a given country in the global order in terms of its economic, political, or strategic importance. Yet with Ireland, there is little agreement. Recently, a historian of the Americas, James Dunkerley (2000), sought to place Ireland "across the Atlantic" as it were. Dunkerley follows the tradition of "Atlanticism" (of Gilroy 1993) but is skeptical of "globalism." However, he argued for "the idea that Ireland is really an American country located in the wrong continent" (p. xxii). It was the Great Famine of the mid-nineteenth century and subsequent mass migrations that, supposedly, converted Ireland from an Atlantic country to an American one. This shift in cultural geography was sustained, according to Dunkerley, by a "superabundance of myth" (p. 37) but also validated by the one million Irish people who became U.S. citizens in the second half of the nineteenth century. From this perspective, it is easy to leap to another end of the century and in an economistic reading place Ireland as an outpost of the Silicon Valley. O'Hearn (1998) argued

that U.S. computer and pharmaceutical companies set the tone for the "Celtic Tiger" that transformed the economic, social, and cultural makeup of the country. Whether the economic growth of the Celtic Tiger set the scene for the cultural makeup of Ireland or the cultural makeup set the scene for the economic growth, we have here an argument that Ireland can be historically and economically placed as an American country or outpost. Recent Irish political and social reaction to the terrorist threat to the United States, coming from conservative and radical politicians alike, seems to confirm the view that Irish leaders and the vast majority of its people wish Ireland to be seen as an island extension of the United States.

However, the American perspective seems to ignore the facts of British colonial rule in Ireland and the prevalence of a neocolonial pattern of development in the years since independence, itself of course geographically incomplete. Not so long ago, the question, "Is Ireland a Third World Country?" (Caherty et al. 1992) could elicit a mainly positive, albeit qualified, response. The colonial legacy is seen as enduring, and all attempts to revise Irish history beyond the nationalist myths are rejected out of hand. For Robbie McVeigh (1998), this move to "decolonise" (or "postcolonise") Irish history is "factually incorrect and intellectually dishonest," and we are enjoined "to address the colonial legacy directly in order to transcend its negative and corrupting consequences" (p. 31). The latter may be simply a truism, but it does point to a blind spot of the new postcolonial proglobalization per-spectives. Perhaps our colonial leg-acy has indeed left the Irish leader-ship and the Irish psyche prone to adopt a subordinate attachment to imperialistic powers. Alternatively, it could have left us with a national consciousness that sees the need to struggle against imperial, or exter-nal, forces. A cultural reading would suggest that both might well be pres-ent at one and the same time. How-ever, to return to the question of plac-ing Ireland, at the economic level, we are certainly not simply a Third World (itself an anachronism) coun-try. The Republic of Ireland is today one of the top performers in the Euro-pean Union—the once poor and underdeveloped Western periphery gave way to a thriving economy and cultural revival in the nineties, albeit with all the inequalities and prob-lematic long-term prospects all thriv-ing economies have. However, in terms of the debate as to whether Ire-land is a First World country of an American variety or a Third World country, rather than adjudicating between these admittedly rather starkly painted alternatives, I would like to use the debate as a marker for the analysis that follows.

First, though, I wish to argue for a slightly different approach to global studies than the one that dominates in the literature. It would seem that from Malcolm Waters (1995, 2001) onward, global studies has been par-celled out into discrete economic, political, social, and cultural domains or levels. While mindful that this may simply be a research or presentation strategy, I would be wary of going back to the old Marxist topographical analogy of levels. Soci-ety is simply not a building with a structure and a superstructure, or roof. This type of structural deter-minism has long since received a decent burial, and we would not really benefit from its resurrection within new global studies. The latter are at their best when they analyze processes and flows, not bound by any determinisms and self-con-sciously eschewing disciplinary boundaries. If the global studies approach is to become a new para-digm in the fullest sense of the word, it will need to shake off the last ves-tiges of disciplinary ownership. In terms of economics, there are signs that Ireland is a satellite of the United States, given its dependency on U.S.-based companies. In terms of politics, there are indications of the same, as Irish leaders rush to sup-port the United States in its current difficulties. Likewise, cultural con-siderations feed into both economics and politics and have to be taken into account in placing Ireland. Hence, my suggestion to merge the political economy and cultural studies approaches.

It would be possible to start off with the recent call by Ngai-Ling Sim (2000) to create a "cultural political economy," which was at once sensi-tive to cultural or discursive dynam-ics and the role of economic and polit-ical factors. Nigel Thrift (2000) has also referred suggestively to the "cul-tural circuits of capital." Thinking about culture in Ireland (the Irish pub, Irish film, U2, Riverdance) and the new capitalism (software compa-nies, the e-economy) has made me even more conscious of the need to build an integrated cultural political economy. The cultural element is clearly part and parcel of the Celtic Tiger, and the economic element certainly has a strong cultural component. From the critique of political economy (not its existing disciplinary forms) and from a reflexive cultural studies (not an unthinking application), we may derive a critical optic that is adequate for the study of the complex reality we call Ireland today. All I would add is the need for a historical approach, only sketched here given constraints of length, which is necessary to make any sense of the current situation. This is, of course, a contested historical terrain, and my rendering is not the only one possible.

INVENTING

Cultural critic Declan Kiberd (1995) once wrote that "if Ireland had never existed, the English would have invented it" (p. 9). One could add, conversely, that because England existed, Ireland was forced to invent itself, much as what the West knows as the Orient and Islam are inseparable from Western discourses. It is common now to understand that nationalism is indeed, in Hobsbawn's words, an "invented tradition" (Hobsbawn and Ranger 1983) or an "imagined community" (Anderson 1983). However, it would seem that in the era of globalization, this approach has great validity for Ireland in particular. What passes for Irish culture today—the musical dance show Riverdance, the supergroup U2, or the ubiquitous global Irish pub—does not spring

from the eternal wells of the Irish soul. Rather these phenomena are, to a large extent, manufactured by the global cultural industry. They reflect fully all of the hybridity, syncretism, and even arguably the postmodernism typical of the cultural political economy of globalization. If globalization can be said to have produced a "world show case of cultures" (Featherstone 1995, 13), then on this stage, Ireland has achieved a paradigmatic position. Ireland today, or at least Dublin, is witnessing a culture-led process of regeneration and insertion into globalization in terms more favorable than could be expected from its economic weight. In fact, the two may well be linked—it is perhaps because of Ireland's economic lightness that it may have gone into overdrive in terms of its cultural production.

Historically, Ireland gained its partial independence from Britain in 1921. It was not until the Wall Street crash of 1929 and the Great Depression of the 1930s that a consistent path of inward-oriented growth began. While De Valera's notions might today smack of right-wing romantic isolationism, his industrialization policies did lay the basis for a more independent development strategy in Ireland. This process of conservative modernization can be compared to the "passive revolution" Antonio Gramsci (1971) analyzed in Italy: a case of "molecular changes which in fact progressively modify the pre-existing composition of forces and hence become the matrix of new change" (p. 109). That new process of change occurred in the late 1950s, as protectionism gave way to free trade and inward-oriented growth turned into outward-oriented growth. As T. K. Whitaker (1973), the architect of the post-1958 turn toward foreign loans and investments, put it at the time, "there is really no choice for a country wishing to keep pace materially with the rest of Europe" (p. 415). So, Ireland joined the European Economic Community in 1973, and the removal of protectionism proceeded at full pace.

When Ireland "joined" Europe in 1973, it was very much as a poor relation and major beneficiary of all the structural funds made available for less developed regions. It seemed that Ireland was exchanging self-reliance for dependency in a willful shift away from the independence movement ethos. As Denis O'Hearn (1998) put it, "a country which had virtually clothed and shod itself in 1960 imported more than 71 per cent of its clothing in 1980" (pp. 41-2). This shift away from indigenous industry toward transnational investment operated across the board. It coincided with a period in which U.S. transnational corporations were seeking profitable, high-tech locations, particularly ones that would offer them access to the lucrative European market. The outward-oriented growth orientations led to mass unemployment as national industries collapsed, but by the 1990s, a new era of prosperity seemed to begin. Officially, the boom began in 1994, when in an obscure European investment assessment bulletin, the U.S. investment bank Morgan Stanley asked, perhaps tongue in cheek, whether there was a new Celtic Tiger about to join the family of east Asian tiger economies.

So the Celtic Tiger (the myth feeding the real economic advances) emerged just when globalization was beginning to make itself felt in earnest. This does not mean that globalization produced the Celtic Tiger, whose origins lay, as we saw in the bare outline, in a series of economic transformations going back to the 1920s. And while the Irish boom may be real enough, it has its limits: growth rates are half those experienced in east Asia during the growth phase, and its sustainability is seriously in question given the limited base of the growth sector. Dependency on the whims and market susceptibility of the transnational sector (essentially the computing and pharmaceutical sectors) is even greater than in the 1970s insofar as in the mid-1990s, this sector accounted for three-quarters of value added in manufacturing. A handful of computer companies, such as the giant processor manufacturer Intel, literally hold the key to sustained growth rates in Ireland. As the United States now moves into a slowdown if not a full-blown recession, the Celtic Tiger is beginning to look distinctly more fragile than it did a couple of years ago. Indeed, by late 2001, the Irish growth rate was officially described as flat.

Going back to Ireland as an American country and Ireland as a Third World country, what can we now say? Ireland does seem to be very much an American state, given its reliance on U.S. investments and its unthinking support for U.S. militarism abroad. Yet Ireland is very much still a Third

World country in terms of its conditions of structural dependency. Ireland is perhaps more accurately described in terms of hybridity though, meaning mixed temporalities and a process of uneven development. This cutting-edge technology coexists with traditional social relations to a large extent. Luke Gibbons (1988) wrote a while back that "the IDA [Irish Development Authority, which helped bring in foreign investment] image of Ireland as the silicon valley of Europe may not be so far removed after all from the valley of the squinting windows" (p. 218), the latter an image of traditional rural Ireland. This image of uneven but combined development may serve as a useful and evocative backdrop for our analysis of the cultural political economy of contemporary Ireland.

Observers of the contemporary cultural scene in Ireland are impressed by its dynamism. Conservative politician Gemma Hussey (1995) in her book *Ireland Today* referred to a "new exuberance of self-expression which the country has never seen before" and noted the "new Irish appetite for expression of its own identity" (pp. 470-71). We get a picture of a pristine and whole national identity proudly reasserting itself. Insularity is left behind as Ireland enters the world scene but remains in touch with its traditions. Hussey remarked how "traditional music has been revived in its many forms, and enthrals tourists as much as Irish people, who are themselves, amazed by its richness" (p. 484). From the touching tones of the travelogue, we receive an image of tradition largely uncontaminated by

unpleasant associations with a colonial past or a fierce anti-imperialist struggle. Faced with the "inexorable weakening of the Irish language" (p. 471), which Hussey seemed to see as the main repository of tradition, Ireland has been able to avoid "the pressure of Anglo-American media" (p. 471) and construct for itself the eminently valuable commodity known as contemporary Irish culture.

From the Left of the political spectrum, we get a not dissimilar reading of Irish cultural political economy. Thus, Denis O'Hearn (1998) in his book *Inside the Celtic Tiger* referred to "Ireland's cultural revival throughout the Western world [which] was evidenced in the popularity of the musical Riverdance" (p. 117) and also made an explicit link between "an apparently vibrant economy and a confident culture" (p. 57). As with Hussey (1995), the parameters of the nation-state are taken for granted, and one could be forgiven for thinking that globalization was not part of the picture at all. Where the Left analysis differs from the conservative one is only in causation, because its economism leads it to more or less read off the cultural transformations from the economic ones. Yet ultimately, we get no explanation as to why Ireland has been part of "a Pan-Celtic Revival in the years leading up to the millennium" and has lived "what amounts to little less than another Cultural Renaissance" (Smyth 1997, 175), as a radical cultural critic put it. If we are not to fall back on mystical notions of national culture, we must necessarily begin with the cultural political economy of globalization in seeking an explanation.

I find it helpful to start my alternative reading with a travel story of my own. If you were to visit Ireland, you might wish to travel with "Ireland's cheap fares airline," Ryanair. If you made a telephone booking, you would be politely put on hold and left listening to the rousing theme music from Riverdance, as much flamenco and Broadway as traditional Irish music. From this postmodern pastiche or melange, your thoughts might turn to the company itself. Ryanair is typical of the new hollowed-out company, whose brash manager Michael O'Leary is actually the company and epitomizes the new confident Irish entrepreneurial classes. It contrasts with the bureaucratic, more formal national carrier Aer Lingus that still lingers in the statist era and claims massive compensation for its alleged losses following 11 September. But you travel Ryanair and arrive in Dublin along with thousands of European weekend tourists keen to sample the delights of the fashionable Temple bar area. As you get to passport control, there is a billboard with a leprechaun (a traditional icon of Irish folklore) and a caption that reads, "If you think this is an icon of traditional Ireland you are away with the fairies." A small symbol in the corner of the billboard indicates this is an advertisement for ICON, the marketing company for the traditional global Irish cream liqueur Bailey's. Can we really talk about Irish traditions anymore?

It seems clear to me that globalization has radically redefined what we know as tradition. But then tradition was always invented. It was invented in the Ireland of the 1920s, the 1960s, and the 1990s. In the 1920s, as Declan Kiberd (1995) put it, the country engaged in "the reconstruction of a national identity, beginning from the first principles all over again" (p. 286). De Valera and the founders of the national Irish state were in the business of constructing a modernity based on tradition. To refer to tradition or cultural authenticity today makes little sense when we realize how pragmatic an affair the construction of a national identity is. In the 1960s, there was a reconstruction based on transnational values, first American and later European. Then in the 1990s, there was another reconstruction of Irish identity within global parameters. The dance of Riverdance, the music of the Chieftans, and the new Irish film cannot be understood as national cultural forms. They may be partly constituted locally, but it is with reference to a global cultural market: they are local cultural keys turning global locks.

I can only conclude by rejecting any essentialist notion of Irishness that is fixed from time immemorial. Neither Irish culture nor Irish identity can be seen as self-contained, immutable, or closed. A new state of flux, typical of postcolonialism and globalization, opens up a new era of more fluid and uncertain construction of cultural identity. This is also manifest at the political level—where the future of the island is, as always, uncertain. There is hardly a comfortable situation of cultural diversity being constructed where gender, ethnicity, and religious conflicts become safely defused. Ireland's culture is currently showing a more threatening side. Current racism around the issue of immigration and refugees highlights some of the more worrying sides of the uncertainty we now face. This is hardly the positive scenario of Gemma Hussey (1995), for whom insularity has been replaced by "the confidence of an outward-looking young generation" (p. 484).

MOVING

Cultural critic Terry Eagleton (1997) once wrote that while on one hand, Ireland signifies "roots, belonging, tradition," it also spells at the same time "exile, diffusion, globality, diaspora" (p. 11). We could posit that Ireland was always/already part of the story of globalization, which would mean pushing back its conventional temporal origins. Being Irish was always associated with movement, even while being at home. Irish migration and the substantial Irish diaspora in different parts of the globe meant that Irishness was in a very real sense a globalized identity. That was the case at the last turn of century, but now, in the era of globalization, migration is not so prevalent or economically necessary. It is perhaps ironic, then, that today Irishness is finding confident homegrown roots and that home has a certain stability to it. Irish presidents recently (Robinson and McAleese) have foregrounded the wish to bring the diaspora home, culturally and politically, if not physically. The confidence of Irishness on the island of Ireland today has even led to intense

hostility to today's migrants created by globalization—the asylum seekers and refugees.

Movement in the nineteenth century meant dislocation, rupture, and trauma in Ireland. It was associated with the famine, the British landlord, and unemployment. Emigration was, indeed, the national trauma. Today, movement means travel, working abroad, or coming home. The Irish media portray its citizens as the "Young Europeans": computer literate, confident citizens of the world. Migration, then, cannot have a simple meaning as a symptom of globalization. It can signify expulsion or, as in Ireland today, success. The diaspora was once an integral element of Irish identity. Today there is a move to bring it home, but home is not what it used to be. The Ireland of today has seen the full effect of deterritorialization of culture. Observer Fintan O'Toole (2000) noted that at once "US culture is itself in part an Irish invention" and that "Irish culture is inconceivable without America" (p. 12). Fluidity and hybridity have always been part of the Irish condition, but today, this occurs under the inescapable aegis of the United States, not some fuzzy, indistinct era of globalization.

Ireland was always part of broader flows of people and ideas; it was always globalized, and it was always a floating signifier. National tradition was located as much in the diaspora as at home. And home today, as the accelerated movement of globalization takes effect, is reinstated in the global Irish family our politicians call the diaspora. National identity is translated and appropriated by the new global culture. When U2 refer to the famine, they do so in a way that makes it part of the new global history in the making. What might make an interesting analogy to extend this analysis would be John Urry's (2000) concept of sites of "pure mobility" (p. 63). For Urry, society is today replaced by mobility, with such icons as the airport becoming truly "non-places." What if Ireland were to be conceived as a place of pure mobility, dominated by movement and fluidity? Though only an analogy, and one that cannot be stretched too far, it may help us understand why Ireland is significant for an understanding of globalization, too often read from the perspective of stable, settled, and dominant world powers.

CONCLUSION

It would seem that the cultural political economy of Ireland might take us beyond the stark American and Third World options for placing Ireland. We cannot retreat to an essentialist notion of Irishness existing since time immemorial. The cultural political economy of Ireland has never been self-contained, immutable, or closed. The era of globalization, coinciding in Ireland with that of a postcolonialism, which put the British shadow firmly behind, has created the new context for Irish development. And yet Ireland was always part of a world of flows, never static, never fixed. The elements of uncertainty and undecidability, which many see as pertaining to globalization and/or postmodernity, have always been Ireland's lot. We cannot, in Ireland, produce "a finished image of finished reality" (Smyth 1997, 67) because it has always been in flux. To engage with such a society, a novelist or short story writer is necessarily "constrained to open meaning up rather than close it down," (Smyth 1997, 67) as one cultural critic put it. The social and political scientist can hardly do otherwise.

A recent International Studies Association conference contained presentations that referred to globalization and the "preservation of local identity" in Ireland (White 2001). Ireland is seen as one of those states that have "taken advantage of the new opportunities afforded by contemporary globalization" (White 2001), and the conclusion is that "the Irish have culturally escaped from a parochial sense of nationalism and become a proud member of the international community" (White 2001). While capturing something of what is happening in Ireland today, I think it is clear, in the light of my analysis above, why this approach is insufficient. It seems to buy in totally to the ideology of globalization: if we take advantage of it, we can escape parochial nationalism. It was thus patronizing politics I sought to contest in declaring at the start that this article was neither nationalist nor postnationalist. Many social groups in Ireland, many women especially, have always contested the smug conservative self-serving myths of Irish nationalism. Postnationalist accounts that imply that we have moved into a sea of tranquillity where all conflict will be peacefully resolved in Brussels or Washington are also problematic. Ultimately, what the Irish case study shows us is that the world is a more complex place than a simple binary opposition of "Jihad versus McWorld" (Barber 1995).

References

Anderson, B. 1983. *Imagined communities*. London: Verso.

Barber, B. 1995. *Jihad vs McWorld*. New York: Ballantine.

Caherty, T., A. Storey, M. Gavin, M. Molloy, and C. Ruane. 1992. *Is Ireland a Third World Country?* Belfast, Ireland: Beyond the Pale.

Dunkerley, J. 2000. *Americana*. London: Verso.

Eagleton, T. 1997. The ideology of Irish studies. *Bullan* 1 (1): 5-14.

Featherstone, M. 1995. *Undoing culture: Globalization, postmodernism and identity*. London: Sage.

Gibbons, L. 1988. Coming out of hibernation? The myth of modernity in Irish culture. In *Across the frontiers: Ireland in the 1990's*, edited by R. Kearney. Dublin, Ireland: Wolfhound Press.

Gilroy, P. 1993. *The black Atlantic*. London: Verso.

Gramsci, A. 1971. *Selections from the prison notebooks*. London: Lawrence and Wishart.

Hobsbawn, E., and T. Ranger, eds. 1983. *The invention of tradition*. Cambridge, UK: Cambridge University Press.

Hussey, G. 1995. *Ireland today: Anatomy of a changing state*. London: Penguin.

Kiberd, D. 1995. *Inventing Ireland: The literature of the modern nation*. London: Jonathan Cape.

McVeigh, R. 1998. The British/Irish "peace process" and the colonial legacy. In *Dis/Agreeing Ireland*, edited by J. Anderson and J. Goodman. London: Pluto.

O'Hearn, D. 1998. *Inside the Celtic Tiger: the Irish economy and the Asian model*. London: Pluto.

O'Toole, F. 2000. *The ex-isle of Erin: Images of a global Ireland*. Dublin, Ireland: New Island Books.

Smyth, G. 1997. *The novel and the nation: Studies in the new Irish fiction*. London: Pluto.

Sim, N.-L. 2000. Globalization and its "other(s)": Three "new kinds of Orientalism" and political economy of transborder identity. In *Demystifying globalization*, edited by C. Hay and D. Marsh. New York: Palgrave.

Thrift, N. 2000. State sovereignty, globalization and the rise of soft capitalism. In *Demystifying globalization*, edited by C. Hay and D. Marsh. New York: Palgrave.

Urry, J. 2000. *Sociology without society*. London: Sage.

Waters, M. 1995. *Globalization*. London: Routledge.

———. 2001. *Globalization*. 2d ed. London: Routledge.

Whitaker, T. K. 1973. From protection to free trade—The Irish Case. *Administration* (winter).

White, T. 2001. Globalization and the preservation of local identity: The case of Ireland. Paper presented at the International Studies Association Convention, Hong Kong.

ANNALS, *AAPSS*, **581**, May 2002

Democracy and the
Transnational Capitalist Class

By LESLIE SKLAIR

ABSTRACT: While globalization means many different things to many different people, there is growing consensus that capitalist globalization is its most powerful contemporary form. This article argues that capitalist globalization, and thus effective power in the global system, is increasingly in the hands of a transnational capitalist class (TCC) comprising four fractions: those who own and control the major corporations and their local affiliates, globalizing bureaucrats and politicians, globalizing professionals, and consumerist elites. The TCC engages in a variety of activities that take place at all levels, including community, urban, national, and global politics, and involve many different groups of actors. Two sets of questions are addressed: (1) What forms do these activities take? and (2) Do they enhance or undermine democracy? The role of the TCC is analyzed through brief case studies on Codex Alimentarius and the global tobacco industry.

Leslie Sklair teaches and directs the Ph.D. program in the sociology department at the London School of Economics and Political Science. He has researched transnational corporations all over the world and is author of The Transnational Capitalist Class *(2001),* Assembling for Development: The Maquila Industry in Mexico and the US *(second edition 1993), and* Sociology of the Global System *(1991; second edition 1995), which has been translated into Japanese, Portuguese, Persian, Chinese, and Spanish (forthcoming). A new version of this book, titled* Globalization: Capitalism and Its Alternatives, *will be published by Oxford University Press in 2002.*

NOTE: Parts of this article were previously published in *International Political Science Review*, 23 (2): 159-174 (April 2002).

TRANSNATIONAL corporations (TNCs) and those who support them clearly engage in political activities of various types, but the exact forms of these engagements and the roles of the various actors in them have not been subject to a great deal of systematic research.[1] These activities take place at all levels, including community, urban, national, regional, and global politics, and involve many different groups of actors, including those in government, political parties, and what we might call the service industries of politics. In this article, I shall focus on two sets of questions: (1) What forms do these activities take? and (2) Do they enhance or undermine democracy? It is commonplace to argue that in the age of capitalist globalization, in most countries, political parties rarely make any significant differences because no political party that seriously challenges capitalist globalization stands much chance of being elected (or if elected, much chance of hanging onto office). If we accept this argument, then the focus turns to the global political system as a whole rather than the parts of the system described by national politics.

While TNCs have always been political actors, the demands of economic globalization require them to be political at the global level in a more systematic sense than previously. The political action of TNCs at the global level, like most political action, is a mixture of the haphazard and opportunistic on one hand and well-organized and systemic behavior on the other. One way to capture this theoretically is to conceptualize the systemic organization of politics for global capitalism in terms of a transnational capitalist class (TCC). The material base of this class is in the corporations they own and/or control. In my formulation, the TCC is composed of four main, interlocking groups:

- those who own and control the TNCs (the corporate fraction),
- globalizing bureaucrats and politicians (the state fraction),
- globalizing professionals (the technical fraction), and
- merchants and media (the consumerist fraction).

While each of these groups performs distinct functions, personnel are often interchangeable between them. Key individuals can belong to more than one fraction at the same time, and the transition from membership of one to another group is more or less routinized in many societies.[2]

Historically, the relationship between the economic power and the political power of TNCs has been very controversial. The involvement of ITT in the bloody coup against the government of President Allende in Chile in 1973, for example, was one of a small number of exceptions rather than the rule in the second half of the twentieth century. Research on organizations influential in regional and global politics suggests that major corporations are currently using more subtle methods to achieve political objectives that will serve their economic interests. The European Roundtable of Industrialists (ERT) is a typical example of how this process operates and how the corporate interest can shift the emphasis of policy making even in a rich and powerful coalition of states like the European Union, with substantial implications for global politics (Corporate Europe Observatory [CEO] 1997). ERT was founded in 1983 by a group of visionary captains of industry, notably Agnelli of Fiat, Dekker of Philips, and Gyllenhammer of Volvo, and performs an agenda-setting role in European institutions for global free trade and competitiveness. It comprises the leaders of around forty-five TNCs, prominent among which in the 1990s were BP, Daimler-Benz, Fiat, Shell, and Siemens, all globalizing corporations.

The European Centre for Infrastructure Studies, an offshoot of ERT, is said to have been instrumental in persuading the European Commission to establish the Trans-European Networks (a program of 150 environmentally sensitive infrastructure projects), bypassing the European Parliament. Founded by Umberti Agnelli of Fiat in 1994, it brought together regional and national governments, municipalities, European Union institutions, research institutes, banks, and corporations. In a very familiar pattern for globalizing elites, former European Commissioner vice president Henning Christopherson joined the board of the centre when he left the commission. So it is not too far-fetched to argue that corporate interests are, at least, highly influential in the making of European Union transport policy. One central consequence of the political efficacy of the coordinated power of TNCs is the failure of governments everywhere to shift the

balance from private cars and lorries to public transport and rail freight, despite almost universal rhetoric on the need to do this.[3] CEO (1997) gave two telling examples: (1) German milk is freighted to Greece to be made into feta cheese and then sent back to Germany for sale, and (2) in the 1960s, Unilever had soap factories in most European countries, but now there is one huge factory in England to supply all of Europe. So dairy products companies in Germany and Unilever in Britain contribute to the enormous increase in long-distance transport of goods through Europe because lean production and just-in-time (key concepts for economic globalization) make production much more efficient for the producers and, in a sense, for consumers if the real price of the products actually falls with no decline in quality, but this is inefficient for essential road users, those who lose jobs, and in the long term, our relationships to the environment. Such practices are, of course, not confined to Europe.

In 1995, the European Union and the U.S. government in consultation with more than 1,200 corporations active in the United States and the European Union, established a transatlantic business dialogue (TABD) to pursue globalization-friendly policies. According to its U.S. business coordinator (cited in CEO 1997), "TABD is a private-sector force designed to respond to the new reality of trade; namely that companies are functioning globally and their involvement in the making of international trade policy is a natural outgrowth of such globalization" (p. 28). This is, of course, one small organization among thousands of others, but its leading personnel included one European Commissioner (Sir Leon Brittain), senior executives from major European and U.S. corporations, high officials from the U.S. Treasury and State Department, and the former GATT secretary-general, Peter Sutherland. Organizations such as these can be found in many parts of the world, for example, within the networks of the International Chamber of Commerce and the many overseas branches of national Chambers of Commerce, the World Economic Forum, and now the United Nations system (see Karliner 1999).

This article discusses two spheres of TCC activities. These are the Codex Alimentarius Commission, where corporate power is exercised in the global politics of food, and the ongoing struggles of the global tobacco industry to resist the coalition against it, a vivid illustration of the global politics of regulation (with a strong dose of cultural politics intermingled).

CODEX ALIMENTARIUS

Codex was established in 1963 with the express purpose of facilitating both world trade and consumer protection in foods through the establishment of international standards. Clearly, under some circumstances, this could result in food standards (for hygiene, nutrition, safety and so on) being raised all over the world to those of the strictest regulatory authorities or, conversely,

reduced to some set of lowest common denominators (see Public Citizen 1997, 38-42). One of the key issues that has exercised Codex over the years is the fact that countries that impose the highest standards of food safety and quality and those with the lowest standards are both accused of unfair trade practices. Potential conflicts between the safety and quality regulatory tasks of Codex, on one hand, and the facilitation of global trade tasks, on the other, are endemic to the organization. Thus, it is important to know who, exactly, makes the policies that governments and intergovernmental organizations generally take as their benchmarks for food.

Codex is an intergovernmental body run by the United Nation's Food and Agriculture Organization (FAO) and the World Health Organization (WHO), and they take turns hosting biennial commission meetings in Rome and Geneva. According to the official guide to Codex history and practices,

representation at sessions is on a country basis. National delegations are led by senior officials appointed by their governments. Delegations may, and often do, include representatives of industry, consumers' organizations and academic institutes. . . . A number of international governmental organizations and international NGOs [nongovernmental organizations] also attend in an observer capacity. Although they are "observers", the tradition of the Codex Alimentarius Commission allows such organizations to put forward their points of view at every stage except in the final decision, which is the exclusive prerogative of Member Governments. (FAO/WHO 1999, 13)

Much play is made of the openness of Codex procedures (notably country Codex Contact Points and National Codex Committees), and the overall impression is of commendable transparency, joined-up intergovernmental thinking, and genuine representation in this most vital area of public policy. However, when we probe beneath the surface, a rather different picture emerges.

A first clue that the system is not as evenhanded as it appears comes from Codex USA (located in the Department of Agriculture—a case, some might argue, of poacher turned gamekeeper). While observer status is important, membership of the official government delegations is the key to understanding the decision-making process. Guidelines issued by the U.S. Codex office explain the process of the selection of delegates to Codex meetings in more detail. U.S. delegates to Codex are government officials from the lead agencies involved (U.S. Department of Agriculture, Food and Drug Administration, Environmental Protection Agency, and Commerce).

The delegates develop U.S. positions on issues to be considered. All interested parties are invited to provide information and comments on the issues. As the delegates prepare for the meetings of their committees, they form delegations comprising individuals whose support they think necessary at the meetings. *These individuals participate as members of the official U.S. Delegations, at their own expense* [emphasis added]. (Codex USA n.d.)[4]

The maximum for each delegation is twenty-five persons per committee,

and the criteria that govern selection of nongovernmental members to delegations are (1) obtaining informed views, (2) determining whether opportunities to provide written comments would be an adequate alternative, and (3) providing balanced representations of all interested parties. Individuals and representatives wishing to become members of the U.S. delegation are invited to contact the U.S. delegate or Codex manager, who will consider all requests, may seek volunteers, and "may identify and solicit for membership . . . from labor groups, the academic community, trade associations, specific business firms, public interest groups, and from other sources, including the public at large" (Codex USA n.d.). Nongovernment members of the delegation are expected to attend all Codex committee sessions, be available to assist the U.S. delegate, and attend meetings called by the U.S. delegate. Thus, being a nongovernment member is an expensive and time-consuming responsibility.[5]

In the only systematic study of Codex to date, Avery, Drake, and Drake (1993) documented the affiliations of the 2,578 people who participated in the 1989-1991 session of Codex. In the twelve specialist committees in which the work of this session was conducted, 105 governments and 140 food and agro- chemical companies were represented. In addition to those representing national governments, there were 660 industry representatives, compared with a mere 26 from public interest groups. One of the largest food corporations in the world, Nestle, had 38 representatives, more than most countries. At the two meetings on food additives and contaminants, 41 percent of those present were from TNCs and industry federations; at the meetings on pesticide residue levels, 127 (33 percent) were from TNCs, compared with 80 from all the developing countries.

In the 1989-1991 session, the U.S. policy for selection of delegates produced a total of 243 delegates, of whom 2 came from nongovermental organizations, 10 were consultants, 112 were from the U.S. government, and 119 (49 percent of the total) came from industry. Overall, industry supplied 35 percent of the membership of the ten largest national delegations and 22 percent of all delegates. Only eight nongovermental organizations provided members of delegations, four in the Canadian delegation and two each in the U.S. and Netherlands delegations. Industry supplied 61 percent of the delegation from Switzerland, 44 percent of the Japanese, 40 percent of the French, 34 percent of the German, 31 percent of the British, 23 percent of the Canadian, 22 percent of the Italian, and 21 percent of the Dutch delegations, reflecting the global importance of food industry corporations domiciled in these countries. Most of the major food TNCs (led by Nestle and including Philip Morris/Kraft, Unilever, Pepsico, Coca Cola, Heinz, and CPC International) and agrochemical TNCs (including Ciba Geigy, ICI, Rhone Poulenc, Bayer, Dupont, Dow, Monsanto, Hoechst, Shell, and Sumitomo) were represented on Codex committees, some of them as official delegates (see Avery, Drake, and Drake 1993, Tables 5.1.1, 5.3.1, 5.4.1, 5.5.1, Appendix Tables 5, 6, and 7).

Rather disingenuously, the official Codex guide informs us that "a feature of the committee system is that, with few exceptions, each committee is hosted by a member country, which is chiefly responsible for the cost of the committee's maintenance and administration and for providing its chairperson" (FAO/WHO 1999, 15). This system generally results in most of the meetings' being held in and financed by groups in First World countries in which major food industry corporations are domiciled. Examples of this are clearly to be seen in the commodity committees, for example, at the 1999-2000 meetings. The Fish and Fishery Products Committee was hosted by Norway; Milk and Milk Products, and Meat Hygiene by New Zealand; Cocoa and Chocolate, and Natural Mineral Waters by Switzerland; Processed Meat and Poultry Products by Denmark; Fats and Oils, and Sugars by Britain; and Processed Fruits and Vegetables, and Cereals by the United States. The only exception was Mexico, which hosted Fresh Fruit and Vegetables, of which it is a major exporter to the United States. While Codex gives some prominence to the role of consumers and their organizations in formulating policy on food, it is very wary of encouraging this role at the global level. Indeed, the guide specifically states, "The Commission has continued to involve consumer interests in its work while recognizing that it is at the national level that consumers can make their most valuable and effective input" (FAO/WHO 1999, 22). The Codex strategy is one of ensuring that consumer input is safely channeled through national governments.

The last point to be made about the Codex process as an exemplar of how the TCC works in global politics concerns the role of the globalizing professionals, the food scientists and technologists on whom the whole activity is said to rest. "From the very beginning, the Codex Alimentarius has been a science-based activity" (FAO/WHO 1999, 27). This is, of course, not quite as simple as it sounds. The history of the links between science, big business, public policy, and in particular, the cheap-food policy on which most capitalist industrialized societies are based suggests that science-based corporations are sometimes reluctant to err on the side of caution (the precautionary principle) at the expense of their short-term profits. Governments always have to balance out the interests of consumers in the safety and quality of what they consume, the interests of food industry workers, and the interests of those who own and control the food companies. The scientists (the technical fraction of the TCC in this case) provide the technical basis for decisions, but when the scientists differ (as, e.g., was for many years the case in the debate over the health risks of smoking; see below), governments, industry, and consumers in the main tend to accept the least costly and most reassuring conclusions (at least until it is too late).

Preliminary evidence from the 1999-2001 round of Codex deliberations suggests that despite some very well-publicized and costly failures in the global food system (in terms of both human and animal health and industry profits), nothing much has changed in the past decade. The Food Labelling Committee that met in Ottawa in May 2000, for example, consisted of more than 200 official participants attached to member country delegations and more than sixty observers, five from international governmental organizations and about fifty from nongovernmental organizations (including industry groups). Of the official country participants, 48 were from TNCs and/or industry associations, while only 4 were from nongovernmental organizations (mostly consumer protection organizations). Of the nongovernmental organizations, 13 were from citizens or consumer groups of various types while at least 35 were industry associations. Codex produced a list of observer organizations participating in its activities in June 2000 that shows a similar distribution. In addition to intergovernmental organizations (including United Nations Conference on Trade and Development, the Organization for Economic Cooperation and Development, and the World Trade Organization), almost 150 international nongovernmental organizations were listed. Of these, more than 80 were clearly industry associations. There were perhaps 10 consumer groups, and the rest were technical organizations of various types, some of which may be controlled by corporate interests.[6]

Precisely the types of disasters (BSE, food poisonings, and contamination) and ongoing problems (pesticide residues, inadequate and misleading food labeling) that Codex was established to prevent are still with us (Public Citizen 1997). The next big battle will be over genetically modified organisms, and while Monsanto and other major biotechnology corporations suffered setbacks to their plans in the late 1990s, genetically modified organisms are still very much on the agenda. Despite campaigns by consumer groups and professionals independent of the TNCs for reforms to the Codex process, there are no signs that World Trade Organization procedures will diminish the ability of food and agrochemical TNCs to cut corners with nutritional quality and food safety to increase profitability.

BIG TOBACCO

The tobacco industry presents challenges, at both the theoretical level and the empirical level, to the thesis presented in this article. Real curbs on the freedom of tobacco companies to advertise their wares wherever and however they wish and bans on smoking in public places in some countries, restrictions that apply to very few legal products, suggest that the unity implied by the concept of the TCC and thus the concept itself are flawed. The empirical evidence presented in this brief case study, however, demonstrates that far from challenging the concept of the TCC, the case of the tobacco industry provides telling evidence for the existence of a TCC and shows that its members continue to play an important role in serving the interests of global capitalism through building the economic power of their corporations, the political power of their industry, and the culture-ideology of consumerism.[7] The ongoing struggle of the major tobacco companies all over the world to market their unhealthy products illustrates well how corporate interests affect the global politics of regulation.

The global tobacco industry at the turn of the century was dominated by four firms. Largest by a long way was Philip Morris, which ranked 31 on the *Fortune* Global 500 in 2000, with revenues in excess of $61 billion; Japan Tobacco and British American Tobacco ranked 221 and 226 (with around $20 billion in revenues each). RJ Reynolds Tobacco ranked 436 with revenues of more that $11 billion.[8] Outside the Global 500, American Brands (acquired by British American Tobacco in 1995), Rothmans International, the German firm Reemstma, and several state monopolies, notably the Chinese, made up the strong second tier. Widely publicized events since the mid-1990s have led some to believe that the tobacco industry in the United States, and perhaps the rest of the world, is on its last legs. My analysis predicts that the industry, supported crucially by some state agencies despite attacks from other parts of the state apparatus, and the promotional culture of cigarettes (see below) will continue to sell cigarettes and make good profits while the TCC retains its powers within global capitalism.

Though cigarette sales in First World countries declined in the 1990s, premium price brands, notably Marlboro, increased their market share all over the world, thus making up for some of the lost revenue in volume. The situation in the Third World and the New Second World of eastern Europe and the former USSR is more complex (see INFACT 1998, 76-83). Industry sources (see annual reports of tobacco industry companies) and critics (Frey 1997) alike have documented the targeting of Third World (and increasingly New Second World) consumers as a deliberate strategy to compensate for the decline in revenues anticipated in the First World. Philip Morris, RJ Reynolds, and British American Tobacco brands in 1995 had more than two-thirds (often more than 90%) of the market in Barbados, Ghana, Honduras, Hong Kong, Kenya, Morocco, Nicaragua, Sri Lanka, and Turkey and more than one-third in Pakistan, Slovak Republic, and Zaire (see the October 1996 issue of *Tobacco Reporter*). Marlboro is the top selling imported brand all over the world. Whereas in the mid-1980s the global tobacco companies had legal access to less than half of the potential world market for cigarettes, by the mid-1990s this had risen to around 90 percent. The reasons for this dramatic increase were the trend to deregulation of foreign investment and trade in general, strategic alliances between local and global cigarette companies, and the decline of government monopolies all over the world. Social factors like increasing prosperity of the new middle classes and the drive to upgrade their consumption patterns, which often means preference for expensive imported cigarettes over cheaper local cigarettes, the growing freedom for women to indulge in previously male-dominated pastimes like drinking alcohol and smoking cigarettes, and massive advertising and promotional campaigns by the global corporations (INFACT 1998), have all contributed to the rapid increase in sales of globally branded cigarettes in the Third World and eastern Europe.

The reason the global tobacco companies are increasingly targeting the Third World is that there are, relatively speaking, fewer smokers of cigarettes there, though this pattern is changing. The WHO estimated that in 1995, the average number of cigarettes smoked per day was 22 in industrialized countries and 14 in developing countries, mirroring a decline in the habit of 1.4 percent per annum in the former but an increase of 1.7 percent in the latter. The WHO has documented the rise in cigarette smoking per person per year in key Third World markets from the 1970s to the 1990s. In most of the largest countries (China, Indonesia, South Korea, Bangladesh, India, and Thailand), per capita consumption has increased. Gender, class, age, and ethnic and religious variables would undoubtedly give a sharper picture, but the brute fact remains: the potential for cigarette industry growth lies not in the First World where fewer and fewer people are smoking and restrictions on smoking and marketing tend to be more strictly enforced but in the Third World where groups that previously were outside the market for manufactured and particularly globally branded cigarettes are rapidly being brought into its orbit. Given the health risks of cigarette smoking, which are widely known, and the increasing levels of local campaigning against these risks, for the industry to be surviving, let alone thriving, suggests that it has managed to assemble a powerful coalition of support over a wide range of social groups and institutions.

The global system theory outlined above and its central concept of the TCC suggests how we might fruitfully analyze the promotional culture of cigarettes and the social forces that support it. TNC executives, globalizing bureaucrats, politicians and professionals, and consumerist elites all play their parts individually and in concert to bring this promotional culture of cigarettes and smoking into as many institutional sectors of all societies as they can and to create a dependency on both the drug (nicotine) and the money (financial dependency of many types) that the tobacco industry brings with it.

The global tobacco industry is supported by a corporate elite, drawn from a wide spectrum of prestigious institutions, interlinking the corporate and the noncorporate worlds. Most major corporations have networks of connections from the corporate center through joint ventures, strategic alliances, and other business links to local and national government agencies and the people who run them, to the advertising and media industries, to the retail and entertainment sectors, and to many other social spheres (particularly those who come to rely on their largesse for sponsorship money) wherever they do business in the world, effectively all the inhabited parts of the planet.

Globalizing bureaucrats, politicians, and professionals have long been friendly to the tobacco industry, and very few have taken the real risk of public and militant opposition to it. The reasons are obvious: the tobacco lobby is rich, well organized, and well connected in most countries;[9] there are many more smokers than active antismokers; and those who stand for public office or who depend on the state or the business community for their prosperity generally avoid antagonizing such interests. The major exceptions to this rule in the case of the tobacco industry are those public health officials and medical researchers who have campaigned against the health risks since the 1960s (the major medical associations have mostly come off the fence on the issue), those antismoking politicians whose secure electoral bases have saved them from the revenge of the industry (e.g., President Clinton in 1996, though some tobacco money went to the Democrats too), and those lawyers who have taken on the task of suing the tobacco corporations for destroying the health of their clients (often on a no win–no fee basis). This certainly appears to be a formidable coalition, but in the context of the majority of local and national politicians who stay neutral and the other massed professionals working directly and indirectly for the smoking interests—lawyers, advertisers, business consultants, and industry-funded medical researchers—the sides look less evenly matched.

It is also important to balance out the picture of smokers under continual social pressures to give up or to indulge their habit in private rather than public spaces with the continuing actual and iconic presence of the cigarette in most societies. There are very few countries where nonsmoking regulations are strictly enforced. In the 1990s in the United States, where the antismoking movement has gone furthest, although there were widespread advertising bans in the media, characters still smoked in films, plays, photographs, and other representational forms, and this may be increasing as part of a new hedonistic culture. The sight of small groups of smokers huddled together outside buildings is now common in many countries, no doubt for some people adding to rather than detracting from the attraction of the habit.

Globalizing bureaucrats who promote the interests of the tobacco industry are opposed by those, mostly in the health and education spheres, who are part of the antismoking movement. Indeed, the struggle between protobacco government agents and agencies in revenue and industrial departments and antismoking activists in health and education appears to be an increasingly global phenomenon. The cases of the United States and the United Kingdom are now well documented, and evidence from other places is also building up (see Sklair 1998).

Disagreements at the local and countrywide levels between groups for and against the tobacco industry have been paralleled internationally through the United Nations system by conflicts between the Food and Agriculture Organization—supporting the interests of tobacco growers—and the WHO—in the interests of disease reduction—on the role of tobacco in development.[10] Nevertheless, despite all this practical and ideological mobilization by the antismoking movement during at least the past three decades, more cigarettes are being smoked globally than ever before, the tobacco corporations continue to make substantial profits, most of their shareholders seem content to take their dividends, and the promotional culture of cigarettes shows no sign at all of abating.

CORPORATE POWER AND
GENUINE DEMOCRACY

Much of the research on corporate-state connection is in the form of obscure reports from and about obscure lobby groups. This perfectly illustrates my thesis that the TNCs do work, quite deliberately and sometimes rather covertly, as political actors and often have direct access to those at the highest levels of formal political and administrative power with considerable success. The research of CEO and INFACT could, I am sure, be replicated for most countries and many cities in the world. Everywhere, we find corporate executives, globalizing politicians and professionals, and consumer elites (merchants, marketers, and advertisers) telling us in public and doing their best to ensure in private that the globalizing agenda of contemporary capitalism driven by the TNCs and their allies is inevitable and, eventually, in the best interests of us all. They would see the corporate lobbies working effectively within the European Union and the Organization for Economic Cooperation and Development, within Codex, and for the tobacco industry globally as doing a fine job in paving the way to universal prosperity.[11]

I have argued that the TNCs and their allies are political actors and that they do achieve significant success in getting across their message that there is no alternative to global capitalism. The route to prosperity for all, the corporations argue, is through international competitiveness decided by the "free" market and "free" trade, institutions and processes that they largely control themselves or through their friends and allies in local and national governments and international organizations.

Does this present a problem for democracy? In one sense it does not. TNCs are legal bodies with every right to act legally to further their interests. They are formally owned by millions of individual shareholders whose main interest is in seeing the value of their investments increase, though effective control is usually vested in small groups of owner-executives and institutional shareholders. The other side of the matter is that all major trade and investment treaties are profoundly undemocratic in structure and process. In 1994, just before the U.S. Congress was due to vote on the Uruguay Round of GATT, the Washington-based organization Public Citizen offered to donate $10,000 to the charity of choice of any member of Congress who had read the 500-page agreement and who could answer ten questions about it. Only one member, a "free-trader," eventually accepted the challenge, and as a result he changed his vote from *for* to *against*

the agreement (after having voted for NAFTA, which, presumably, he had not read). Congress approved GATT in December 1994, the inference being that most U.S. legislators voted for an agreement that would fundamentally change the global economy without knowing what was in it in any detail.[12] Neither do most legislators in the member countries of the European Union appear, on the whole, to be better informed than those in the United States on such matters. So apart from the very big issues about whether to join or accede to treaties, which are very occasionally put to the vote in a referendum, our elected representatives appear to nod through, on a regular basis, legislation that affects our daily lives in many different ways. As the evidence from Codex and the tobacco industry suggests, the interests of global capital are generally better represented because the TNCs have the resources and the commercial motivation to see that their interests are fully represented. Even such a relatively well-endowed organization as Greenpeace Germany had only one Brussels-based lobbyist in 1997: "In comparison with the swarms of industry lobbyists to be found in Brussels corridors, environmentalists are an endangered species" (CEO 1997, 57).

The political activities of the TNCs and their allies, therefore, raise serious doubts about how well our democracies are working with respect to everyday economic issues, global trade, foreign investment, the environment, and health and safety of workers and citizens in general. Attempts by bodies like the International Labor Organization and the now-dismantled United Nations Centre on Transnational Corporations to develop universal codes of conduct to encourage the best practices of TNCs and to outlaw their much-documented bad practices all over the world have come to very little, and though the rhetoric of stakeholders and sustainable development is all the rage in TNCs and governmental organizations (see Sklair 2001, chaps. 6-7), capitalist globalization generally promises more freedoms to the TNCs without imposing many compensating responsibilities. This is all in the name of globalization, free trade, international competitiveness, and the hope that somehow it will make poor people better off. As I argue elsewhere (Sklair 2002), the crises of class polarization and ecological unsustainability that are direct consequences of capitalist globalization make the search for alternatives to capitalist globalization urgent.

Notes

1. The major exceptions have been the study of lobbyists. See, for example, Jacobs (1999) on the United States, Pedlar and van Schendelen (1994) on Europe, and Gierzynski (2000) on Political Action Committees in the United States.

2. For an extended analysis of the transnational capitalist class (TCC) based on *Fortune* Global 500 and similar corporations, see Sklair (2001).

3. The wave of protests that swept Europe in 2000 over rising fuel prices is only one serious consequence of the failure of national and Europe-wide governments to work out sensible, environmentally sustainable transport policies. The role of oil, automobile, road-building, supermarket, and other industries in this

quasi-conspiracy against sustainability urgently requires systematic research.

4. I am grateful to Codex officials in Rome and country offices in the United States (U.S. Department of Agriculture), United Kingdom (Food Standards Agency), and Australia (National Offices of Food Safety) for providing the documents on which this section is based and comments on this section.

5. Avery, Drake, and Drake (1993, 38) reported that pressure from the International Organization of Consumers' Unions resulted in Codex's agreeing in July 1991 that "governments should encourage funding for consumer experts and representatives to participate in Codex and other food quality and safety work." So far, only Norway and India (some time ago) appear to have actually done this.

6. The affiliations of some participants were difficult to identify, and time and resources did not permit a finer analysis. Lists of participants can be found on the Codex Web site by clicking on the ALINORM boxes for the dates of meetings.

7. For a more extended discussion of the global tobacco industry and the TCC up to 1997, see Sklair (1998), where copious references will be found.

8. This is the tobacco arm of what had been RJR Nabisco. For a variety of reasons, RJR was demerged from the parent company, and its overseas tobacco business was sold off to Japan Tobacco. Nabisco was later acquired by Philip Morris.

9. See Sklair (1998) for details of and references to these connections.

10. In 1999, the World Health Organization (WHO) began a serious campaign to control the "smoking disease epidemic" globally, details of which are available from the WHO Web site.

11. For a theoretical discussion that attempts to provide a Gramscian basis for the argument that global capitalism needs to be politically active to sustain its project and creates elite social movements based on the transnational corporations (TNCs) for this purpose, see Sklair (2001, chap. 2).

12. For details, see Nader and Wallach (cited in Mander and Goldsmith 1996, chap. 8). The book as a whole, an early manifesto for the International Forum on Globalization, provides many good examples of the political actions of TNCs and the growing opposition to

them. For a systematic analysis of antiglobalization movements, see Starr (2000).

References

Avery, N., M. Drake, and T. Drake. 1993. *Cracking the Codex: An analysis of who sets world food standards.* London: National Food Alliance.

Codex USA. n.d. Guidelines. U.S. Department of Agriculture. Mimeographed.

Corporate Europe Observatory (CEO). 1997. *Europe Inc: Dangerous liaisons between EU institutions and industry.* Amsterdam: Corporate Europe Observatory.

FAO/WHO. 1999. *Understanding the Codex Alimentarius.* Rome: FAO/WHO.

Frey, R. S. 1997. The international traffic in tobacco. *Third World Quarterly* 18:303-19.

Gierzynski, A. 2000. *Money rules: Financing elections in America.* Boulder, CO: Westview.

INFACT. 1998. *Global aggression: The case for world standards and bold US action challenging Philip Morris and RJR Nabisco.* New York: Apex Press.

Jacobs, D. 1999. *Business lobbies and the power structure in America.* Westport, CT: Quorum.

Karliner, J. 1999. Co-opting the UN. *Ecologist* 29:318-21.

Mander, J., and E. Goldsmith. 1996. *The case against the global economy.* San Francisco: Sierra Club.

Pedlar, R. H., and M. van Schendelen. 1994. *Lobbying the European Union.* Aldershot, UK: Dartmouth.

Public Citizen. 1997. *NAFTA's broken promises: Fast track to unsafe food.* Washington, DC: Global Trade Watch.

Sklair, L. 1998. The transnational capitalist class and global capitalism: The case of the tobacco industry. *Political Power and Social Theory* 12:3-43.

Sklair, L. 2001. *The transnational capitalist class.* Oxford, UK: Blackwell.

Sklair, L. 2002. *Globalization: Capitalism and its alternatives.* Oxford, UK: Oxford University Press.

Starr, A. 2000. *Naming the enemy: Anticorporate movements confront globalization.* London: Zed Books.

ANNALS, *AAPSS*, **581**, May 2002

Democratizing Globalization
and Globalizing Democracy

By BARRY K. GILLS

ABSTRACT: The article begins with a critique of the failure of the present world order, based on its exclusivity and reliance on a traditional international relations paradigm, including nationalism and cultural particularism. The post–cold war impetus toward universal liberalism has brought about conditions rendering this paradigm untenable. Globalization requires a new political order if universal economic liberalism is to be stable. However, there remains a clash of paradigms rather than a clash of civilizations, and a new balance is needed between realist, liberal, and Marxist paradigms. An alternative world order will require democratizing globalization and globalizing democracy and will rest on articulating radical new conceptions and practices of citizenship bridging local, national, regional, and global political spaces. New concepts and values such as global justice, global solidarity, global democracy, and global citizenship are taking form and informing the course of the democratic revolution on the global scale.

Barry K. Gills is a reader in international politics at the University of Newcastle upon Tyne in the United Kingdom. He received his Ph.D. in international relations from the London School of Economics and did additional postgraduate research at St. Anthony's College, Oxford. He is the chairperson of the World Historical Systems theory group of the International Studies Association and a faculty affiliate of the Globalization Research Center of the University of Hawaii. He directs the program in international political economy in the Department of Politics, University of Newcastle upon Tyne. His recent works include Globalization and the Politics of Resistance *(2001, Palgrave) and* World System History *(2000, Routledge, coedited). He is currently working on a critical analysis of capital in global history.*

It is only from the nations themselves that reforms can be expected.

—Thomas Paine,
Preface to the French Edition
of *The Rights of Man* (1791)

The present world order is based on very traditional thinking, both politically and economically. There has been much discussion of the so-called nonstate actors and the rise and importance of nongovernmental organizations and other international societal factors in recent years of globalization. Yet we can observe for ourselves how it is still the most powerful governments of the world that determine the primary course of action and define the parameters of mainstream discussion whenever there is a crisis. Thus, the embedded power structure of the world order has been highlighted even in the so-called era of globalization. Nevertheless, if we look deeper, we can see things differently, and we may realize the potential for positive change. Rather than accepting the still reigning paradigm of (past) international relations, with its enduring feature of governance by a few great powers based on their ability to use military force, we must urgently look for ways to turn to a positive alternative. We must search for ways to break out of the iron cage of the old paradigms.

FAILURE OF THE POSTWAR LIBERAL WORLD ORDER

At the end of the last world war and in the aftermath of the Great Depression, it was already obvious that nationalism and empire were concepts that had brought enormous human suffering, conflict, and upheaval. No stable or just world order could any longer be based on either a narrow nationalism or the drive for empire by the Western bourgeois (Carr 1968; Linklater 1997) with which it was historically associated. It was objectively necessary to go beyond the confining limits of nationalism and embrace a new order marked by much higher levels of international peace and cooperation. It was equally necessary to abandon imperialism and enter a period when potentially all peoples had the right to sovereignty and in which all shared in international duties and responsibilities in the common world order. It was also recognized, by realists as well as idealists, that to enable the construction of this new world order, the West would have to abandon a narrow cultural particularism and attempt to adopt more universal and even cosmopolitan bases for the right to lead or govern at the center of world power (Bull 1977).

The reality, however, fell somewhat short of this expectation. Postwar international history was marred by decades of endemic global conflict, which historians call the cold war era. During that period, the great powers often acted brutally and cynically in pursuit of their perceived power interests. The foreign policy of the West, led by the United States, sometimes sacrificed even its central value—liberty—in whose name the conflict was ultimately waged, by making expedient political alliances with reactionary and antidemocratic forces and governments. Rather than constructing a truly inclusive world order, and despite the existence of the United Nations Organization, world order remained based on a clear hierarchy of power among states. This international hierarchy, once established, exacerbated the problem of historically embedded asymmetry of power and wealth between the Western powers and the formerly colonial peoples of the world. The opportunity for inclusion was therefore compromised. The world order was maintained by the traditional means of balance of power, alliances, and diplomacy in a manner that perpetuated the old international relations paradigm. The Westphalian system, being based on the principle of sovereignty for states and their intrinsic right to use military force, produced a system dominated by a few states wielding the greatest military and economic power.

With the end of the cold war came an opportunity for the West to review its policies and to reassess the project of universal liberalism. Suddenly, there was more official support for democracy than during the previous cold war period of ideological and strategic rivalry, during which the West had often supported undemocratic regimes and suppressed popular movements for social, economic, and political change (Cox, Ikenberry, and Inoguchi 2000). Above all, however, there was a renewed and vigorous attempt to construct a liberalized world economy and make this system universally inclusive. Within a short time, this impetus toward universal liberalism based on the social and economic practices of the West became popularly known as globalization. In a previous generation, this impetus had been understood simply as Westernization or modernization.

It is the very extension of this Western project of universal liberalism that has brought about new conditions that now render the old paradigm of international relations and world order historically inadequate. Taking globalization seriously must imply taking its logic to logical conclusions. In other words, to the extent that there is now—in the post–cold war interregnum—already a truly global economic system based on the free movement of capital, then there is also an objective and logical need for new forms of global political order to accompany this global economic system. Simply maintaining the international political status quo will not suffice. Without a correspondingly new global political order, the world (economic) order will be unstable. By remaining too exclusive, the West will guarantee instability and disorder in the future. You cannot sustain a truly international, or global, political and economic system on the basis of the exclusion of the majority from real power or influence over it. If the West fails to measure up to this challenge, it risks undoing the liberal and capitalist order it has sought to construct since the last great world crisis and most recently under the slogan of globalization.

To put it differently, having largely already succeeded in bringing about a global liberal and capitalist economic order, the West, in partnership with all the world, must now realize that this economic order requires an accompanying global political system. This new political order is necessary to stabilize the world economy and make it function properly. However, if we have learned anything from the past century of the expansion of capitalism to a global system, it must be that the market alone cannot maintain a stable social, political, or economic order over the long term. The classic nineteenth century liberal world order ended in a historic cataclysm (Polanyi 1944) and revealed itself to be unstable and unsustainable. The real character of that world order was not, however, truly liberal but rather a condition of the coexistence of antagonistic principles: liberal and imperial, competitive and monopoly capitalism, freedom and slavery (including the colonial enslavement of whole populations to imperial rule). These contending antagonistic principles coexisted not in a stable harmony but rather in a very high state of historical tension. In the aftermath of the debacle of that world order, it was widely recognized and accepted that the market economy needed stabilizing through new types of state regulation and intervention and new social compacts. The state, popular political processes, and domestic and international institutions have all been crucial in maintaining the conditions for both the stability and expanded reproduction of the capitalist economic system (Habermas 1988). In fact, it is legitimate to argue that the lesson of the failure of the previous liberal-imperial world order was that capitalism itself could not exist without an appropriate role for the state or an inclusive social contract that gave labor essential rights and legitimate political participation. The post–World War II world order was based, therefore, on the pragmatic need to establish a balance that avoided the extremes represented by the Scylla of market-oriented savage capitalism and the Charybdis of state-dominated and imperial or monopoly capitalism.

A CLASH OF PARADIGMS, NOT A CLASH OF CIVILIZATIONS

Speaking as an international political economist, it may be worth saying that we are still witnessing a historical clash of paradigms rather than a clash of civilizations as the defining dynamic of world order. In the present impetus toward (neo)liberal economic globalization, we are seeing the continued playing out of the attempt to realize the liberal utopia first fully explicated by Adam Smith more than two hundred years ago. In the liberal paradigm's vision of the future, the traditional international relations paradigm—with its basis in state sovereignty exercised over a national economy and the states' intrinsic right and ability to use military force—is overthrown. Rather than warfare and survival as key concerns, liberalism promises peace and prosperity to all humanity. The idea that we can eliminate all distortions introduced into the world economy by the interventions and other actions of governments has been a constant in the whole history of liberalism and in its recent reincarnation as neoliberalism. One central liberal idea is the harmonization of interests, despite the inequalities generated by private property, commodity production and exchange, and capital-wage relations, as well as the uneven development in space and time that is a feature of world economic history. In the liberal utopia, all production will be maximized as market actors are free to allocate resources most efficiently, and all consumption will be optimized as all consumers are free to choose the best products at the best prices. In this vision, the prosperity of humanity is maximized due to the optimum economic efficiency of the entire system, which then comes to operate as a self-regulating mechanism, finding its own equilibrium and having a tendency to allow prices, profits, and wages to equalize over time and space in the system as a whole. This too is the utopian promise of neoliberal economic globalization as espoused today.

Once again, the reality is very different, and it has been for more than two hundred years of liberalism's history. The liberal paradigm has not entirely replaced the realist or driven it out. The realist international relations paradigm, with the survival and the power of states as its central interests, refuses to disappear, and it constantly reasserts its prerogatives, thus distorting the presumed pure natural order of the liberal economy. Moreover, as Marx's critique of the political economy of capitalist social relations tried to argue, there is an ingrained exploitative feature in the unceasing quest for greater profits, in the expansion of capital-wage relations, and in the process of commodification of more and more spheres of life. This exploitation is not easily

amenable to any natural harmonization of interests; rather, it generates a continued source of social conflict, displacement, and antagonism, which Marx referred to as the "class struggle" though others may simply call it politics and now the politics of globalization.

The Marxist critique rejected both the realist and the liberal paradigms and argued that both were fatally flawed. The Marxist alternative vision of the future of the world economy was, however, every bit as utopian as was the liberal. Marx predicted a world without states, without classes, without money, without poverty, without exploitation, in which production would be maximized and all human needs would be met, all "uneven development" would be resolved, and a great harmony of interests would prevail over permanent social peace. This was to be achieved through means opposite those of the liberal paradigm, that is, via the abolition of private property and the market and their substitution by common property and a planned economy, which in the medium term would require a major direct role for the state in the economic system.

We can easily recognize elements of truth in all three paradigms, which is to say that while none of the three is really an accurate or perfect paradigm, there is something in each that we can recognize, even on the grounds of common sense. In reality, all three paradigms are in historical tension with one another, and they continue to contend with one another in the world today. It is naive in both analytical and historical terms to believe that one of the three is likely to, or indeed ought to, entirely succeed and completely displace the other two. This being the case, the real question is how to shape the process of economic globalization, which is already so powerful, in ways that can reduce the levels of social disruption and human suffering involved and that do not repress the popular will but rather empower it. In short, the emergence of a new paradigm of world order suited to the material conditions of economic globalization today is not a technical, technological, or purely economic matter but a thoroughly and profoundly political matter to be resolved through political processes alone. This is therefore not a matter of calibrating only states and markets but rather states, markets, and social forces (or classes if you prefer) and their mutual relations. In short, it is not a question of the ultimate victory of one paradigm over the others but of constructing a sustainable and just world order that brings some new balance among all three contending paradigms of world order: realist, liberal, and Marxist.

BUILDING AN ALTERNATIVE WORLD ORDER

While a few years ago, many people could still believe that a liberal global capitalist economy would look after itself and constitute a natural order, it is now all too apparent that no such natural economic order exists. The advocates of global economic liberalization as the only way forward, the single best practice for all economies, have learned that the process is far from being apolitical.

However, they have apparently still not accepted the full political consequences of the liberal economic order they espouse. The "politics of resistance" to globalization (Gills 2000c; 2001) and the rise of the myriad so-called anticapitalist movements around the world during the past few years should be understood as being representative of the popularly perceived need to construct a universal, just, and inclusive form of world order. This new conception of world order is based on radically new conceptions and practices of citizenship bridging local, national, and global political spaces. It clearly brings into focus, in terms of political discourse, the need felt by ordinary people to be fully included in the major decisions that determine their life chances. Most important, therefore, it is not only elites and governments that must be directly included in the reconfigured world order of globalization but ordinary people, from all walks of life, all genders, all religions, and all regions of the globe. This constituency is in fact the global citizenry.

What was once posed as a national question (i.e., political order) now becomes a truly global question, perhaps for the first time in human history. This debate is no longer a matter of Whether globalization but rather of Which globalization. This is essentially a political matter, not a narrow technical or economic issue. Thus, it is not very useful to understand the new (global) social movements arising to protest the present direction of globalization processes as simply being antiglobalization (or even anticapitalist for that matter, since this invokes an all-encompassing but inherently vague notion of capitalism itself). Nor is it fruitful or right to merely reject the legitimacy of such growing popular protest to economic globalization and its social and environmental effects as being merely wrongheaded. Ignoring the problem or resorting to repressive tactics will only further exacerbate the underlying reasons for these global protests, which in fact represent only the tip of an iceberg of popular responses to the myriad impacts of globalization on our lives (Bourdieu et al. 1999).

So we should view today's global protest movements as being symptomatic of something far greater than a mere reaction to globalization. They represent a popular response to the question of Which globalization and as such, they are an expression of the popular desire for meaningful political participation in its governing processes. As John Kenneth Galbraith (2000, 2001) has argued, the governing elites of the past decade have tended to talk too much about free trade and not enough about social justice and stability. Moreover, the new resistance movements instinctively represent the view that whatever globalization may be, it should not come at the expense of the social gains of the past century. Nor should the imperative of further economic globalization via liberalization and free trade constitute an obstacle to improving social, political, economic, and human rights in the future, particularly of labor and in regard to women, agriculture, and the environment. In other words, perhaps the people of

the world would like globalization to represent a continuation of social and political progress rather than a sacrifice of this progress on the high altar of the free market.

When I recently asked a group of my students, studying the political economy of development, to discuss the differences between national development and global development, their responses were somewhat surprising, and enlightening. They strongly tended to associate the national not only with welfarist goals but also with selfish, zero-sum, and conflict-oriented goals and behavior. They associate global development, however, with an aspiration for or potential of transcending the barriers that governments erect between peoples and with finding common solutions to common problems through increasing cooperation. That is, their instincts are searchingly positive when it comes to the global dimension of world order, as opposed to their suspicions of the traditional national framework of action and understanding, which they seem to think has too many negative aspects.

Given that the popular movements of this era, as in the past, should be assumed to represent an expression of the popular will rather than an irrelevant minority, we should heed the words of that great democratic revolutionary Thomas Paine, that it is from the popular will that real reforms can be expected. The recent financial and economic crises in east Asia illustrated the potential negative side of globalization, that is, that as neoliberal economic globalization proceeds, it generates increased risk of macro-economic destabilization. But it also creates popular demands for democratization and greater opposition to existing oligarchic-authoritarian power structures (Gills 2000a). Globalization, therefore, cannot be left to elites alone or to governments only to sort out, which would only reinforce the reigning paradigm of international relations and reproduce the embedded global inequality over which the states system presides. What we need is a very strong, healthy dose of globalization from below. Only this can create a necessary balance between governmental and popular political will and adequately redress the question of who controls the direction of globalization.

Only by democratizing globalization, which means enacting an inclusiveness in the political sphere in ways that incorporate the expression of the popular will not only of citizens of the rich countries but of all peoples, can we establish such a balance. That is, only by global democratic revolution will economic globalization find its appropriate political counterpart. The alternative to this is further exclusiveness and a narrowing of political power to a small elite. Such an elitist alternative in fact represents the antithesis of the globalization of democracy. We should remember that Adam Smith himself, the founder of the liberal tradition in international political economy, was reacting against a mercantilist order that was dominated by and favored a small collusive elite of financiers, manufacturers, merchants, and state rulers. He saw both

political freedom and economic freedom as the necessary revolutionary counterpoint to the oligarchic-authoritarian capitalism that he so abhorred and that he intellectually denounced as parasitic on the nation, indeed all nations, and their common wealth. If in the end, the project of universal economic liberalism is understood in the popular imagination to mean only that real power has been taken from the people or the nation and concentrated in an elite, even if this is a global or transnational class, then increasing resistance to this world order will be historically inevitable. Again, this very real political problem will not go away simply by ignoring it or by repressing it. In fact, the extent to which repression is used against the popular movements is a measure of the extent to which globalization actually undermines democracy. This tension, which we have all recently witnessed in the official and police responses to a series of major global protest events staged at economic summits, indicates the possibility of a serious contradiction or even open antagonism between popular democracy and neoliberal economic globalization.

CONCEPTS AND VALUES OF
A GLOBAL DEMOCRATIC THEORY

If there is global capitalism, then the system gives rise to and in fact requires fundamental counterparts, including global justice, global solidarity, global democracy, and global citizenship, the last of these perhaps being especially significant. We need a credible political theory of global democracy based on the new concept of global citizenship rather than merely a pragmatic problem-solving approach. If democracy is a process of building countervailing powers, then the democratic theory we have at present, which is based on countries and their domestic political order, must be transposed to the global level. To do so, we must also elevate or transpose the classic enlightenment democratic ideals of equality, justice, solidarity (fraternity), and liberty to the global level. Defining "global equality," "global justice," "global solidarity," and "global liberty" will be the prerequisites to formulating a theory of global democracy and global citizenship. In my own view, these definitions and this global democratic theory does not necessarily require a global or "world polity" (Ruggie 1998) or a theory of a "global state" as such (Shaw 2000).

The tenor of this new period, which is above all given to a diversity of social movements from across the globe, does not provide grounds for easy acceptance of a centralization of power and authority, but actually the opposite. As in the history of many other world orders, states, and civilizations of the human past, there may come a point when whatever the elite at the apex of the social system have designed or intended, they can no longer hope to control the direction of change. Rather, it is the social forces from below, often representing the lowest social orders, that do at such times make the real difference. Christianity, for example, began as a tiny movement within a great and powerful empire, and its membership was drawn from the lowest social strata, such as slaves, political outcasts, women, and downtrodden and oppressed peoples such as the Jews of Palestine. In the end, however, it was not the mighty empire of the Romans that prevailed, but rather the strikingly antipodal communal and compassionate ideology represented by the Christian religion that transformed Rome itself into a holy city and remade the whole of Western civilization. The search for human liberty does not usually find its true expression in the construction of huge edifices of centralized and bureaucratic state power, however welfarist the claims within which their attempts at legitimation may be couched.

Rather, liberty, when popularized and captured by the popular will and imagination, immediately tends to become a truly revolutionary idea and brings in its train the challenging of the status quo. As the great student of American democracy, Alexis de Tocqueville (1840), remarked on the process of the democratic revolution,

a people that has existed for centuries under a system of castes and classes can arrive at a democratic state of society only by passing through a long series of more or less critical transformations, accomplished by violent efforts, and after numerous vicissitudes, in the course of which property, opinions, and power are rapidly transferred from one to another. (P. 320)

It is clear that we can expect the democratic revolution on a global scale not to be a smooth and easy political process but rather one of conflict, tumult, and upheaval, indeed even one in which the world turns upside down.

There is therefore a particular importance in addressing the emphasis given to the idea of freedom in the past twenty years of discourse on economic liberalization and globalization. This neoliberal discourse has emphasized a Hayekian understanding of freedom as freedom above all for capital, for the movement of commodities, and for markets, that is, a freedom for the holders of property to pursue maximum flexibility and profit. In contrast, freedom as a popular concept is aligned with the protection of popular rights and the extension of popular participation, and thus with democracy. Freedom for the common man and woman is only possible when equality, justice, solidarity, citizenship, and finally democracy itself, are all fully integrated aspects of both theory and practice. Indeed, "the price of freedom is redistribution" is one way of formulating democratic theory (Sartori 1987). As Galbraith has pointed out, nothing so constrains the freedom of the individual as a complete absence of money.

It bears repeating that economic globalization, and indeed the entire range of processes we are currently referring to as globalization, does not bring convergence to one narrowly constructed set of choices. Globalization actually opens up a wider range of choices to a wider range of social actors than any previous social system in world history. That is, globalization adds immense complexity to our global social order, not simplicity. This provides social forces today with an unprecedented scope for action, within which they may define new sites of action and new forms of social power, form new coalitions and solidarities (including transnational), find new institutional forms, and explore new ways of practicing governance in world order. By linking together directly the many diverse forms being experimented with in so many manifestations of social action, the potential resistance to globalization becomes the locus and medium of the transformation of globalization into global democracy. Therefore, analytically speaking, we should not understand resistance as being something external to globalization but rather as intrinsic or internal to the process of opening and to the greater complexity that globalization brings about. Globalization is characterized not by a uniformity but rather by a historical dialectic between homogenization and heterogenization, both processes occurring simultaneously and throughout the globe.

Thus, there is likewise a historical dialectic between globalization and democratization, a process that is unavoidable. I firmly believe, on both historical and moral grounds, that this historical dialectic leads strongly, even inexorably, toward the practices and theory of global democracy, that is, to the globalization of democracy and the democratization of globalization. Insofar as neoliberal economic globalization has succeeded, it creates the conditions for further critical social responses that lead to renewed struggles for democratic freedoms and participation by the ordinary people affected by these changes. In these processes of renewed democratic struggles, we may expect to see continued efforts at self-government by many peoples and also expanded representation. Globalization allows the transcending of old established and fixed territorial units and borders of political representation, thus allowing a more territorially diffuse pattern of political community to emerge, and to do so globally. This process deepens democracy by extending it to the global arena but moreover by also devolving power to self-constituting communities seeking self-government and representation in the political order, whether this be on a local, national, regional, or global level.

A nascent and informal global peoples' assembly is therefore one aspect of these efforts to redefine and extend political representation beyond the confines of the present territorially bounded entities, that is, the states of the present international order and the United Nations system. Such processes are beginning to formulate global popular initiatives based on common concerns and to communicate these concerns to a whole panoply of political entities, above and beyond the national or state framework. Thus, a new tier of popular—and I would argue, legitimate—governance is gradually emerging alongside the existing global political order constituted of states and governments (Kiely 2000; Kumar 2000; Markoff 1999). We are witnessing ever-increasing popular will for initiatives on global environmental preservation, global peace and conflict resolution, global emergency relief, global rights or common

standards, and the global alleviation of poverty, debt, illiteracy, and injustice. Thus, in my view, we are witnessing the birth of a common set of values that will define and animate the practice and the theory of global democracy. The emergence of a global civil society is indeed linked to the emergence of an alternative world order (Cox 1999) and to the prospects for a more cosmopolitan form of democracy (Held 1997).

THE END OF THE WORLD
AS WE KNOW IT?
THE IMPERATIVE OF
MULTICIVILIZATIONAL DIALOGUE

In this sense, we may conclude that we are living through the (gradual or sudden?) demise of the old world order and the (slow or sudden?) birth of a new one. Economically, this new order is based on an increased level of global economic integration and unison. Politically, however, it is premised on the need to translate grassroots participatory political action into increasingly popular democratic forms of governance at local, national, regional, and global levels (Gills 2000c; 2001). Moreover, it is also based on a real need to combine the peoples and social forces of North and South in new ways, bringing together new coalitions drawn from movements around the world. The governments and the corporations of the world must now listen to and accommodate the demands of the peoples of the whole world, who represent the voice of the governed. This new reality, which in my view is an objective one and not mere idealism, therefore requires a new paradigm. This new paradigm of world order must be based profoundly on multicivilizational dialogue and universal inclusion. Rather than a political order based on one nation, we are moving toward the need for a political order based on one humanity, and only democratic norms can accommodate such a form of governance.

Dialogue requires a dialogic approach. This means not simply sharing ideas derived from different cultures and religious traditions, or ideologies, and not simply toleration in the sense of listening and accepting a difference but something much more than that. The dialogic process that we need among civilizations must contain a process of progression to something different from where we started. That is, it is not enough simply to be content with understanding one another and all of our many differences, though tolerance is certainly preferable to intolerance and certainly necessary. But tolerance must now be seen as an absolute minimum for our world order, not as its highest achievement. A dialogic approach to multicivilizational world order implies and requires that all the participants be willing to engage openly and willingly in a true dialogue in the spirit of mutual learning and progressing toward something new, something that is the product of dialogic communication itself. This something would therefore be a multicivilizational product, not the product of one dominant civilization presiding over the rest. It would consist of a set of common values, around which a new sense of genuine world community could be based. It is

therefore not the mere repetition of established values or civilizational perspectives and their mutual toleration. Toleration is a necessary condition for the new paradigmatic order but not a sufficient one. What is sufficient will have to be the product of multicivilizational dialogue.

The criteria for genuine multicivilizational dialogue must begin with the desire to arrive at a common set of core values that will lead to new democratic and popular forms of global governance, which go beyond the confines of the existing power structure. After the tragic events of 11 September 2001 in the United States, many there have been consoled by peoples all over the earth, who share with them one of the most fundamental values of all—the recognition of the value and sanctity of human life. It did not matter whether the people were Muslim, Buddhist, Hindu, Christian, Jewish, Confucian, or any other cultural and religious heritage—all agreed that these were terrible acts of mass murder.

This crisis therefore shows us that humanity can unite around explicitly shared values, setting aside our differences in the realization of a higher unity. Other common values can be discovered through dialogue. We need to identify common values that allow a new sense of global citizenship to take real shape and to form our new political consciousness, underpinning the gradual emergence of global democracy. We must explore what global justice may mean in a multicivilizational dialogue. Likewise, global solidarity may be a central value or key concept by which we can strive to achieve a new sense of humanity's oneness, its unity, and its common interests, which will animate the popular politics of the coming world order. Global history, moreover, is the idea of a humanocentric account and appreciation of the common heritage of all humankind, based on the mutual and cumulative contributions and influences of all peoples and cultures to the common progress of humanity. We must reconstruct knowledge of the human past so that we can escape from the narrow confines of national history and teach new generations a global vision of humanity's past and its future. On this basis, we can establish a more common basis for both civilization and democracy, which unites all humanity in one common heritage and future.

This is the United Nations year of civilizational dialogue, and that, in my view, is symbolic of the call to an alternative world order. We cannot tolerate the old order any longer, where a few ultrarich and militarily powerful states rule via a universalism that is in fact neither truly universal nor even cosmopolitan. Nor can we allow the world order to drift into a nightmare scenario of a clash of civilizations where intolerance and hatred begin to tear our world apart and leave us all spiritually and materially impoverished. We have only one choice, and it is in fact based on realism, not utopian idealism. The old world order is unstable, and only a leap into multicivilizational dialogue can provide a real solution. We have the historic choice of either bringing about this new world order based on the fruits of dialogic

communication or suffering the consequences of failing to do so. It is the end of the world as we know it, but this should be a cause not for despair but rather for renewed hope and vigorous effort. There is a whole new world to be gained and so much in it to be shared. Despite anger and hurt, we must turn from vengeance and by our nobler reason find our virtue in that rarer action that leads us to justice and peace, for all humanity, now and to come.

The terrible events of 11 September 2001 have changed the world. Apart from the horror and revulsion that so many people have felt at witnessing such atrocities, there has also emerged a widespread sense of unease and foreboding about the future. This malaise of the spirit is fueled by fears that even worse acts of terrorism and perhaps widening warfare and conflict are to come and by a pervasive sense that we do not know what the future will bring. One thing seems apparent, however: we stand at a crossroads of modern and human history, facing a choice between world orders based on very different principles. Will we enter an age of chaos and conflict, in which the claims of security override those of liberty and in which the rich and powerful protect themselves at the continued expense of the poor and powerless? Or will we once and for always rise above and go beyond the old paradigms of international relations and economics and invent a new form of world order in which all peoples share in both its governance and its benefits? This, to my mind, is the real significance of the present crisis and will remain its central problem until we find a genuine and common solution that will be, in effect, part of the global democratic revolution.

References

Bourdieu, Pierre, ed. 1999. *The weight of the world: Social suffering in contemporary society.* Oxford, UK: Polity.

Bull, Hedley. 1977. *The anarchical society.* London: Macmillan.

Carr, Edward Hallett. 1968. *Nationalism and after.* London: Macmillan.

Cox, Michael, G. John Ikenberry, and Takashi Inoguchi, eds. 2000. *American democracy promotion: Impulses, strategies, and impacts.* Oxford, UK: Oxford University Press.

Cox, Robert W. 1999. Civil society at the turn of the millennium: Prospects for an alternative world order. *Review of International Studies* 25 (1): 3-28.

de Tocqueville, Alexis. 1840. *Democracy in America.* Vol. II. Hertfordshire, UK: Wordsworth Editions Ltd.

Galbraith, John Kenneth. 2000. Foreword: The social Left and the market system. In *Globalization and the politics of resistance*, edited by Barry K. Gills, ix-xiv. London: Macmillan.

Gills, Barry K. 2000a. The crisis of postwar east Asian capitalism: American power, democracy and the vicissitudes of globalization. *Review of International Studies* 26:381-403.

———. 2000b. Overturning globalization: Rethinking the politics of resistance. In *Globalization and social change*, edited by Johannes Dragsbaek Schmidt and Jacques Hersh, 227-49. London: Routledge.

———, ed. 2000c. *Globalization and the politics of resistance.* London: Macmillan.

———, ed. 2001. *Globalization and the politics of resistance.* Foreword by John Kenneth Gailbraith. Palgrave.

Habermas, Jurgen. 1988. *Legitimation crisis.* Cambridge, UK: Polity.

Held, David. 1997. Democracy and globalization. *Global Governance* 3 (3): 251-67.

Kiely, Ray. 2000. Globalization: From domination to resistance. *Third World Quarterly* 21 (6): 1059-70.

Kumar, Krishnan. 2000. Democracy again. *Review of International Political Economy* 7 (3): 505-13.

Linklater, Andrew. 1997. The transformation of political community: E. H. Carr, critical theory and international relations. *Review of International Studies* 23:321-38.

Markoff, John. 1999. Globalization and the future of democracy. *Journal of World-Systems Research* 5 (2): 277-309.

Paine, Thomas. 1791. Preface to the French edition. *The rights of man.* London: Meridian Books (Penguin).

Polanyi, Karl. 1944. *The great transformation.* New York: Farrar and Rinehart.

Ruggie, John Gerard. 1998. *Constructing the world polity: Essays on international institutionalization.* London: Routledge.

Sartori, Giovanni. 1987. *The theory of democracy revisited.* Chatham, NJ: Chatham House.

Shaw, Martin. 2000. *Theory of the global state: Globality as an unfinished revolution.* Cambridge, UK: Cambridge University Press.

Review Article

Beyond the Deluge?
Politics of Globalization

WATERS, M. 2001. *Globalization*. 2d ed. Pp. 247. London: Routledge.

SCHOLTE, A. 2000. *Globalization. A Critical Introduction*. Pp. 361. Basingstoke, UK: Macmillan.

BECK, U. 2000. *What Is Globalization?* Pp. 180. Cambridge, UK: Polity.

MITTELMAN, J. 2000. *The Globalization Syndrome*. Pp. 180. Princeton, NJ: Princeton University Press.

***

YEATES, N. 2001. *Globalization and Social Policy*. Pp. 195. London: Sage.

COHEN, R., and S. RAI, eds. 2000. *Global Social Movements*. Pp. 231. London: Athlone Press.

PRAKASH, A., and J. HART, eds. 2000. *Globalization and Governance*. Pp. 352. London: Routledge.

FAUNDEZ, J., M. FOOTER, and J. NORTON, eds. 2000. *Governance, Development and Globalization*. Pp. 457. London: Blackstone Press.

***

ROSENBERG, J. 2000. *The Follies of Globalization Theory.* Pp. 205. London: Verso.

HAY, C., and D. MARSH, eds. 2000. *Demystifying Globalization*. Pp. 197. Basingstoke, UK: Macmillan.

PETRAS, J., and H. VELTMEYER. 2001. *Globalization Unmasked: Imperialism in the 21st Century*. Pp. 183. Nova Scotia, Canada: Fernwood.

BRECHER, J., T. COSTELLO, and B. SMITH. 2000. *Globalization from Below: The Power of Solidarity*. Pp. 164. Cambridge, MA: South End Press.

After the deluge of books and articles, conferences and seminars, Web sites and discussion lists on globalization and its discontents, where should the discerning reader at the start of the twenty-first century begin to understand these debates? Not at random, but certainly exercising a good degree of choice, I will examine a dozen texts that have appeared since the year 2000. Some are introductions, some are critiques, and others deal with specific aspects of globalization, but all are examined here for what they say about the politics of globalization. In that sense, we do not take the usual more economic (not to say economistic) reading of globalization, and hence some elements of these texts are ignored. The other way of reading after the deluge is in relation to world events. The fall of the Berlin Wall in 1989 led to one series of global events including the accelerated internationalization of the world economy. The other as yet unfolding set of events after New York 2001 can, arguably, allow us to focus now on the politics of globalization. If they did nothing else, these events and their complex ramifications across the world brought home the integration of politics across the globe and the importance of movement toward a global democracy.

It was Malcolm Waters, writing perhaps appropriately from Tasmania, who published the first proper globalization textbook in 1995. Now a second edition, updated and with a trenchant response to the critics, will again make its mark. This is a little book with a big remit. It traces reliably the genealogy of the term "globalization" and explores its economic, political, and cultural aspects. For Waters, it is the cultural domain that "leads" as it were, within his view, the economy and the polity continuing to be globalized to the extent that they are culturalized. Waters considers whether this is "the end of the world as we know it" but does it in a way that says neither that we have seen it all before, as some of the critics of the globalization thesis argue, nor that this is something completely new and unknown (and unknowable) we are witnessing. A new final chapter constitutes a robust defense of the globalization perspective or paradigm against the critics who wanted business as usual to carry on. The "myth of the powerless state," for example, which many debated fiercely, was never actually something that globalization theory proposed. Ultimately, Waters believes that globalization dilutes power and opens up a (new) path for progressive alternatives.

If Waters is a good basic text for students[1] and laypersons alike, it is Jan Aart Scholte who has provided us with the full workshop manual for the globalization vehicle. Following a broad historical and conceptual overview of globalization as an era and field of study, Scholte dives into globalization and production, governance, community, knowledge, security, justice, and democracy. Far richer than a simple economic/ political/cultural division of the field, it is also presented in an extremely accessible way. Scholte succeeds admirably in his objective to develop a distinctive concept of globalization and to provide us with a multidimensional understanding of it. He is particularly strong on causation mechanisms in contrast to some globalists who simply marvel at how the world is "stretched" or at the "time-space compression" effects. There is considerable historical depth to his analysis and abundant empirical material. There is nothing sketchy, hyped-up, or overly politically driven about Scholte's analysis. It is direct in its analysis and clear in its presentation.

For Scholte, globalization is taken to be mainly the rise of supra-territoriality or deterritorialization, that is to say, the emergence and strengthening of transborder or transworld spaces. Thus, Scholte examines the overlapping networks of production, political practices, civil society, and knowledge across national borders. Our understanding of global politics is undoubtedly enriched, and the multiple determinations of the seemingly facile term "globalism" are made explicit. Scholte seems to miss out a bit on uneven development in today's world, and the essentially Dutch social-democratic perspective he provides is somewhat bland given the dramatic crises that may loom ahead of us. For Scholte, the bottom line is that while "Internationality is embedded in territorial space; globality transcends that geography" (p. 49). Has territorial geography really been transcended? Have the old issues of nationalism, territory, community, identity, and religion really been superseded? Scholte's book at least gives us the tools to examine critically what is (or was) new in the world as we enter the twenty-first century.

As globalization studies kicked in during the 1990s, the academic disciplines began to have their say. Ulrich Beck, the well-known German theorist of the "risk society," provides an elegant sociological essay on the globalization thesis. For Beck, "globality is an unavoidable condition of human intercourse at the close of the twentieth century" (p. 15). While inescapable, Beck believes we must explore the ambivalences and paradoxes of globality, which he sees as a broad, new, second modernity. As we move from a national-national to a global-local focus, so Beck argues, we enter not the era of the end of politics but a new beginning. Beck is always acute—as when he dubs neoliberal globalism "the rebirth of Marxism as a management ideology" (p. 122)—but this book is basically a political essay and lacks a solid research foundation.[2] There are certainly interesting research leads, such as an extension of the "risk society" concept to a global level, but little in the way of empirical foundations for any of the ideas advanced. When Beck advances the fear that globalization may result in the "Brazilianization" of the West, he sails close to the Eurocentrism of his predecessor Habermas.

James Mittelman is writing as a reflexive veteran of globalization studies, from what can be broadly called a critical political economy stance. Refreshingly non-Western-centric in its approach, this volume ranges widely from southern Africa to southeast Asia, from gender studies to the study of global crime. Focusing closely on the new international divisions of labor and the often-neglected (within global studies) issue of regionalism, Mittelman adds much-needed substance to the sometimes flimsy buildings erected by the globalization theorists. It is a holistic and multilevel understanding of globalization we are provided by Mittelman, far removed from the one-sided polemics and visionings of the early writers. Where Mittelman is most radical is in fully integrating the element of resistance into his theory of globalization. Building on Gramsci, Polanyi, and James C. Scott, Mittelman shows us how resistance to globalization should be seen as an integral element of its unfolding. This is a good guide to "globalization and its discontents" from a grounded critical perspective.

Do these four introductory or overview texts provide us with a sound understanding of what globalization is? We certainly can conclude that on balance, globalization does provide "value-added" compared to the concept of internationalization, let alone those of Westernization or Americanization. Our world is more complex, and chaos or complexity theory is increasingly influential in its analysis. To some extent, all the texts must reduce this complexity even if only for presentational reasons. However, they are keenly aware of the diverse logics of the economic, political, social, and cultural processes at play. Very few now reify globalization as something "out there" and instead understand how at the same time it is "down here," affecting and fed by what is happening in any locality. The development of globalization is inevitably uneven, but it is combined, that is to say, its diverse logics are intertwined. There is an emphasis on connectivity between regions but also between and within social and political processes. If I still had a lingering doubt about the globalization problematic, it would be its Northern focus and its seeming inability to understand the different positionality of the Southern perspective(s).

When a new term, problematic, field of study, or paradigm emerges, it is often best pursued and tested in specific or applied subareas. Nicola Yeates provides us with an intelligent overview of how globalization affects social policy and, just as important, the reverse process. Social policy is a key terrain on which the politics of globalization are fought over and defined. Moving beyond a simple political economy approach, we learn how the welfare state is being transformed and the impact this is having on communities, families, households, and individuals. The simplistic image of globalization's undermining the welfare state gives way to a complex, interactive picture where agency is given a genuine role. We are witnessing here the emergence perhaps of a new field of study, a global social policy (Deacon, Hulse, and Stubbs 1997) concerned with global social redistribution and the role of supranational organizations in shaping national social policy. While Yeates recognizes the clear dangers globalization poses

for social standards worldwide, she also shows that there is a continued role for political institutions in regulating the global economy in the social interest. A socially progressive politics of globalization would do well in pondering the lessons of this book.

If social policy is being transformed by globalization, so are the social movements that characterized, while challenging, the era of national, industrial modernity. Robin Cohen and Shirin Rai have put together an interesting collection on the global social movements of human rights, place, indigenous people, women, workers, environmentalism, and religion, which were dubbed in the 1970s the "new" social movements.[3] The development of these social movements at a global level seem to reflect the processes of globalization while at the same time challenging the dominant form. The editors argue that "a global age needs global responses" (p. 8) and show how opportunities have emerged for new transnational social mobilization, with social action becoming more participatory and direct than in the past. The politics of globalization, if we take the diverse findings of this book to heart, will not be determined only in the corridors of power but through the politics of an emerging civil society. This book provides a comparative academic perspective on the issues raised by the sometimes rushed and heated post-Seattle antiglobalization texts.

An area where advances are also being made is in relation to how globalization is affecting governance and the state. Prakash and Hart provide us with a lucid overview of some of the main debates within international political economy on this vital issue. Over and beyond the dispute between neoinstitutionalists and constructivists, however, is a sustained engagement with one of the most critical issues of the day (especially in light of the post–11 September world crisis), namely, how to achieve sustainable global governance. Globalization has not only forced analysts in various fields to rethink their terms of analysis and their paradigms but has also made them focus on the new boundaries between domestic and international governance. Some chapters argue that the state today still has sufficient policy instruments at its disposal to deal with the pressures created by globalization, but most see at least a serious rearticulation of the state to make it fit for the new global era we are entering. The most radical perspective (from my point of view) is articulated by Ian Douglas, for whom globalization is itself the new dominant form of governance so that the "disappearance" of the state is, like the replacement of the scaffold by the prisons, a way to punish better, not less.

What Julio Faundez and coeditors add in their collection *Governance, Development and Globalization* is a much-needed perspective from the South. Too much of the globalization literature seems to be written for the North by the North. It is time to realize that the majority of the world's population has a different take on the issues at stake. This particular volume is focused specifically on how the governance agenda will be facilitated at the legal level. It explores

the neglected links that exist between the institutional structures of domestic governance in particular countries and regions and the international legal regimes covering investment, trade, and technology in particular. In this new borderland—both epistemologically and politically—of development, governance, and globalization, we find new issues being debated and new perspectives emerging. In its apparent specialist niche, this volume has also identified some general issues that will have considerable impact, I believe, as the various interlocking processes of globalization unfold in the years to come.

As Joseph Thome puts it in *Governance, Development and Globalization*, "perceptions of an interdependent and complex global economy and democratization relationship[s?] with legal systems . . . has led the World Bank and other global players . . . to demand changes in the administration of justice, leading to complex legal reform processes" (p. 63). A working assumption lying behind this process of transformation is that a robust and predictable legal environment is essential to market-friendly development. Especially post–Washington Consensus, globalization cannot rely on the likes of General Pinochet to carry out its mandate. Yet while the rule of law is a necessary building block for democracy, it would also seem to be a necessary prerequisite for neoliberal governance, which now seems to have a more technical and less political flavor than it might have had. This volume provides insights into a cluster of topics often neglected (or relegated to footnotes) in the mainstream literature, from intellectual property rights to climate change, from trade law reform to anti–money laundering legislation, from privatization issues to good governance as political conditionality.

If in the early 1990s the hegemony of neoliberal globalization was largely uncontested (at least from above), that was no longer the case by the end of the decade. What Richard Higgott (2000) called the post–Washington Consensus is driven as much by ethical considerations as by the need to contest those contesting its effects. Governance is not only necessary to ensure a stable politics of globalization but also to reinforce the values of equity and justice the West claims to uphold. The concept of global governance is now coming to the fore (see, e.g., O'Brien et al. 2000) in a way that extends our interest from political institutions to the global social movements created by and contesting globalization. When the free market is seen to be insufficient, as Karl Polanyi (1957) recognized a long time ago, the issue of governance assumes center stage but so does the old problem of development as we saw above. Likewise, the debate around the need for a welfare safety net, which Polanyi and others since have debated in terms of the nation-state, is now extended to the global level. While global governance and global welfare rights are an important new area of globalization debates, it is important for them, and us, to recognize that politics is still in command, as they used to say.

Having considered, in broad outline, the overviews and applications of the globalization concept, we must turn to the critiques. Many of the above texts are, of course, reflexive and self-critical, but the language of the critique camp points to a divide. Here globalization is unmasked; it is demystified and its follies are exposed. This is hardly the language of staid academic debates, but it reflects well the high stakes around the credibility or otherwise of the globalization paradigm.

A theory can be said to have arrived when it receives its first serious critique. Justin Rosenberg does justice to what he calls "globalization theory" in a careful but passionate critique that needs to be taken seriously by the more glib advocates of it in academia and beyond. Jan Aart Scholte (2000) is carefully picked over with a philosopher's tools as is Rob Walker's work, but the main recipient of Rosenberg's critique is the British sociologist and Third Way guru Anthony Giddens. What Rosenberg is justifiably concerned with is how globalization, which is at first sight a simple descriptive category, has been elevated to a central theme within social theory in the new millennium, a new overarching theoretical framework for everything under the sun. For Rosenberg, the main problem is that "globalization as an outcome cannot be explained simply by evoking globalization as a process tending towards this outcome" (p. 2). This would be the methodology implicit in Giddens's enterprise that rests on an undertheorized and underspecified notion of "time-space compression," basically the notion that the world is smaller and is moving faster today than it was.

What Rosenberg argues is that the whole idea of a spatio-temporal problematic is incoherent from the point of view of social theory. To view it as the essential tendency of modernity, as Giddens does, is certainly putting too much weight on it. While as a descriptive geographical category, globalization makes some sense, it is only a series of conceptual illusions that allow Giddens to make it seem that it rests on secure foundations in terms of social theory. The critique of Scholte is not so total, and Rosenberg acknowledges the care and attempted precision of his construction that he dubs rather unkindly "Scholte's folly" in an analogy with architectural follies of old. Yet Scholte is chastised for his very caution, his "buts" and "althoughs," his attention to the "intricate interplay" of different aspects of globalization. As in the Giddens critique, Rosenberg is drawn back to how Karl Marx analyzed globalization in his day. We are left with the distinct impression that for Rosenberg, the Marxist tradition is sufficient to understand the complexity of the world we live in.

The collection put together by Hay and Marsh seeks to demystify globalization but in a way that distances itself from the self-appointed debunkers of "globaloney." If the first wave of globalization studies suffered from starry-eyed enthusiasm, the second wave tended to carry out a critique that vainly tried to put the genie back in the bottle as it were. Now, the third wave of globalization studies profiled here sees itself as postdisciplinary and "seeks to develop a multi-dimensional approach to the various processes that interact—often in highly complex and contingent ways—to produce the phenomena variously referred to as economic, political, social and cultural globalization" (p. 3). Taking us beyond global mythology, this approach is more nuanced and differentiated from what usually passes as critique. The collection contains an innovative contribution by Peter J. Taylor that examines all the "izations" ("Americanization," "modernization," etc.) associated with globalization that have done so much for the cause of obfuscation. Nigel Thrift invites us to build a cultural political economy of globalization that might be a useful way to bridge the gap between economistic and culturalistic studies of globalization.

For Petras and Veltmeyer, globalization is little more than imperialism in a new guise. They effectively puncture some of the intellectual pretensions and expose some of the inconsistencies of the globalization literature and introduce the term "globaloney" to highlight the contrast between globalist rhetoric and contemporary realities. We can see how terms such as "global village" or "global interdependence" of nations are vacuous and may mask inequalities. We may also be persuaded that "contingency, not inevitability, marks the origins and unfolding of the globalist project" (p. 43). The critique becomes less convincing when the authors argue that while contemporary globalization may be quantitatively different from that of the past, in qualitative terms, the fundamental structures remain the same. This would seem to fall into the "height of obtuseness" (p. 46) they rightly accuse the globalists of for refusing to recognize its differential impact of globalization on different classes, races, generations, and genders. And while globalization may, indeed, operate as an ideology, it is hard to see how imperialism can suddenly become a self-sufficient, precise, and scientific way of describing the new realities we face.

It is perhaps ironic that the more politically engaged book by Brecher, Costello, and Smith is less fundamentalist than that by Petras and Veltmeyer. Springing from the activities and thinking that have gone on since the "Battle of Seattle" in 1999, this book makes an effective case for globalization from below and thus is appropriate to close this review article. They recognize clearly and early on that "globalization in all its facets presents new problems that the old [social] movements failed to address" (p. 17). They even recognize that globalization presents new opportunities to a movement for social transformation and democratization. This is a welcome change from bleak prognoses of unrestrained capitalist expansion, unchecked social exclusion, and an unrelieved cultural homogenization as our inescapable future. The politics of globalization may be more open than a binary opposition of "from below" versus "from above," but this text, while openly activist in orientation, is also reflexive and self-critical. Perhaps it has been read in the corridors of economic and political power?

Can we conclude that the critics have unmasked globalization and exposed its follies for all to see?

"Critique" can mean many things, I suppose. We can expose logical contradictions in an opponent's argument, flaws in his or her empirical evidence, or doubts about its relevance. We can say that we know better, that it is really imperialism that the globalization theories are talking about. Or we can be self-critical and reflexive, taking on board what new theories, arguments, and politics advance in an open, if necessarily skeptical, manner. It would seem, for example, that Brecher, Costello, and Smith have learned from the globalization debates while arguing for a globalization from below to counter that from above. In that sense, these critical debates can perhaps move on toward the new post–Washington Consensus terrain that the architects of globalization are now exploring to better meet the requirements of effective governance in the era of globalization. There is little mileage, from a genuinely critical perspective, in simply repeating that globalization does not represent an epochal or historical shift and that it is still capitalism that we are dealing with. Even if it were true, it is hardly an original call to action.

In conclusion, then, we could argue that globalization is beginning to move beyond the intellectual confusions of a decade ago. While conceptual inflation is still a problem— it can be made to mean too much— some clarity is emerging, especially through studies of its relevance in particular fields (see, e.g., the plethora of titles on the specific subfield of globalization: Tomlinson 1999; Buelens 1999; Rajput and Swarup 1998; Singh and Thandi 1996;

Rothstein 2001; Roller 1997; Wahab and Cooper 2001; Edwards and Usher 2000; Organization for Economic Cooperation and Development 1997; Ballard and Couture 1998; Singh 1999; Twining 2000; Findlay 1999). The definitional deficit, which had also been alluded to, is also being overcome, especially if we take the best from the best of the dozen texts reviewed above. The first blush of enthusiasm has passed, as has the righteous indignation of early critics (bar an exception or two). While less likely to be seen as a panacea for all our ills or their unique culprit, globalization is increasingly viewed as the inescapable horizon for our diverse possibilities. I am personally still persuaded by the slightly less than deadly serious verdict of Daniel Drache (1999) that the study of globalization is one-third oversold, one-third a process we cannot yet understand because it is still unfolding, and one-third something radically new. Today the proportions may have changed somewhat, but it is a prescription for the study of the politics of globalization that avoids the starry-eyed and the jaded view alike.

Notes

1. Another would be the sophisticated yet accessible text by Cohen and Kennedy (2000).

2. This is in contrast to the massive research foundations (if less verve or politics) to be found in Held et al. (1999).

3. I declare an interest here insofar as I contributed one of the chapters on global labor in this collection.

RONALDO MUNCK

References

Ballard, P., and P. Couture, eds. 1998. *Globalization and difference.* Cardiff, Wales: Cardiff Academic Press.

Buelens, F., ed. 1999. *Globalization and the nation-state.* Cheltenham, UK: Edward Elgar.

Cohen, R., and P. Kennedy. 2000. *Global sociology.* New York: New York University Press.

Deacon, B., M. Hulse, and P. Stubbs. 1997. *Global social policy: International organizations and the future of welfare.* London: Sage.

Drache, D. 1999. Globalization: Is there anything to fear? Working paper no. 23, Centre for the Study of Globalization and Regionalization, University of Warwick, UK.

Edwards, R., and R. Usher. 2000. *Globalization and pedagogy.* London: Routledge.

Findlay, M. 1999. *The globalization of crime.* Cambridge, UK: Cambridge University Press.

Held, D., A. McGrew, D. Goldblatt, and J. Perraton. 1999. *Global transformations: Politics, economics and culture.* Cambridge, UK: Polity.

Higgott, R. 2000. Contested globalization: The changing context and normative challenges. *Review of International Studies* 26:131-53.

O'Brien, R., A. M. Goetz, J. A. Scholte, and M. Williams. 2000 *Contesting global governance: Multilateral economic institutions and global social movements.* Cambridge, UK: Cambridge University Press.

Organization for Economic Cooperation and Development. 1997. *Economic globalization and the environment.* Geneva: Organization for Economic Cooperation and Development.

Polanyi, K. 1957. *The great transformation.* Boston: Beacon.

Rajput, P., and H. L. Swarup, eds. 1998. *Women and globalization*. New Delhi, India: Ashish.

Roller, D., ed. 1997. *Globalization of the automotive industry*. Croydon, UK: Automotive Association.

Rothstein, M., ed. 2001. *New age religion and globalization*. Aarhus, Denmark: Aarhus University Press.

Singh, Kavaljit. 1999. *The globalization of finance*. London: Zed Books.

Singh, P., and S. Thandi, eds. 1996. *Globalization and the region*. Coventry, UK: Association for Punjab Studies.

Tomlinson, J. 1999. *Globalization and culture*. Cambridge, UK: Polity.

Twining, W. 2000. *Globalization and legal theory*. London: Butterworths Law.

Wahab, S., and C. Cooper, eds. 2001. *Tourism in the age of globalization*. London: Taylor & Francis.

You aren't looking at
a future pilot.

You're looking at YOUR
future pilot.

Higher academic standards are good for everyone.
What a child learns today could have a major effect tomorrow. Not just on him or her, but on the rest of
the world. Your world. Since 1992, we've worked to raise academic standards. Because quite simply,
smarter kids make smarter adults. For more information, call 1-800-38-BE-SMART or visit www.edex.org.

The Business Roundtable • U.S. Department of Education • Achieve
American Federation of Teachers • National Alliance of Business
National Education Association • National Governors Association

Education Excellence Partnership

BUY RECYCLED.

AND SAVE.℠

Thanks to you, all sorts of everyday products are being made
from materials you've recycled. But to keep recycling working
to help the environment, you need to buy those products.

So look for products made from recycled materials, and buy
them. It would mean the world to all of us. For a free brochure,
please write *Buy Recycled*, Environmental Defense Fund, 257
Park Ave. South, New York, NY 10010, or call 1-800-CALL-EDF.

Ad Council — A Public Service of This Publication

♻EPA

ENVIRONMENTAL DEFENSE FUND EDF